PERGAMON INTERNATIONAL LIBRARY
of Science, Technology, Engineering and Social Studies
The 1000-volume original paperback library in aid of education,
industrial training and the enjoyment of leisure
Publisher: Robert Maxwell, M.C.

EDUCATION IN THE USSR

INTERNATIONAL STUDIES IN EDUCATION AND
SOCIAL CHANGE
General Editor: Professor Edmund J. King

Other titles in the series

MALLINSON
The Western European Idea in Education

Other forthcoming titles

BARON
The Politics of School Government

BOUCHER
Tradition and Change in Swedish Education

TOWNSEND COLES
Non-Formal Education

A related Pergamon journal

EVALUATION IN EDUCATION
Editors: B. H. Choppin and T. N. Postlethwaite

The aim of this series is to inform those involved in educational evaluation in both developing and developed countries of progress in the various aspects of the theory and practice in educational evaluation.

Free specimen copies available upon request

EDUCATION IN THE USSR

by

JOSEPH I. ZAJDA, M.A., Ph.D.
Bendigo College of Advanced Education, Australia

PERGAMON PRESS

OXFORD · NEW YORK · TORONTO · SYDNEY · PARIS · FRANKFURT

UK	Pergamon Press Ltd., Headington Hill Hall, Oxford OX3 0BW, England
USA	Pergamon Press Inc., Maxwell House, Fairview Park, Elmsford, New York 10523, USA
CANADA	Pergamon of Canada, Suite 104, 150 Consumers Road, Willowdale, Ontario M2J 1P9, Canada
AUSTRALIA	Pergamon Press (Aust.) Pty. Ltd., P.O. Box 544, Potts Point, NSW 2011, Australia
FRANCE	Pergamon Press SARL, 24 rue des Ecoles, 75240 Paris, Cedex 05, France
FEDERAL REPUBLIC OF GERMANY	Pergamon Press GmbH, 6242 Kronberg/Taunus, Hammerweg 6, Federal Republic of Germany

First edition 1980

British Library Cataloguing in Publication Data

Zajda, Joseph I
Education in the USSR.—(International studies in education and social change).
1. Education—Russia
I. Title   II. Series
370'.947   LA832   80-40363

ISBN 0-08-025807-7 (Hard cover)
ISBN 0-08-025806-9 (Flexi-cover)

Printed in Great Britain by A. Wheaton and Co. Ltd., Exeter

TO REA AND NIKOLAI

Preface

In the Soviet Union many teachers read eductional newspapers and periodicals. They range from *The Teachers Newspaper* (Uchitelskaya Gazeta) to *Preschool Upbringing* (Doshkolnoe Vocpitanie). They are not academic or research oriented. For instance, the thrice weekly *Uchitelskaya Gazeta* is full of news, reports, photos, articles, book reviews, international news and letters to the editor. Such periodicals provide the Western reader with the great insight into the actual day-to-day operation of the Soviet eductional system. New developments and achievements in curriculum, problem areas, future projections and also strains in the system are all found here. Most of the articles are constructive, full of praise for the achievements, yet a surprising degree of frankness is tolerated where problems exist in Soviet schools. From time to time, high-ranking educational administrators (including the Minister of Education of the USSR) in their major speeches and articles air these problems. The letters to the editor are particularly revealing for the outsider.

Much of the research for this book was based on these widely read educational periodicals. The reader will find occasional references to my own experiences as a school boy in the Soviet Union, where I received part of my schooling prior to my family's emigration to Poland and subsequently to Australia.

I have used Russian terms as I believe these will give the reader an authentic feeling for the Soviet educational system and its philosophy, which translated seems to diminish. I hope the reader will consult the glossary provided, where I have accentuated the Russian words to help the reader with the correct pronunciation.

June 1980

JOSEPH I. ZAJDA
Bendigo, Australia

Contents

4. Education for Labour, Patriotism, and Defence   181

5. Education of Teachers   225

CHAPTER 1

The Origins of Soviet Educational
Philosophy

1. Introduction

It has been suggested that the roots of Soviet educational philosophy may well be found in the era of Peter the Great (1662–1725).[1] Peter I, otherwise known as Peter the Great, was the first Russian monarch to accept the immense value of scientific education on his return to Russia after having visited England. Peter founded a School of Mathematical and Naval Sciences in 1701. The first Russian newspaper, *Vedomosti* (*News*), which appeared on 2 January, 1703, indicated that 300 students studied mathematics.[2] By 1724 Peter had decreed that the first Russian Academy of Sciences was to be established in St. Petersburg, Russia's new cultural centre and an 'abiding symbol of westernization'.[3] He had imported German professors who, short of students, attended each other's lectures.

Peter's reforms, which marked the modernization and westernization of Russia during the first quarter of the eighteenth century, were scientific and military in essence. In his efforts to promote knowledge and education, which was modelled on the Baltic German provinces, Peter stressed scientific, military, and technical skills of use to the State. It is in 1703 that we first observe such a concentrated effort on the part of any Russian monarch to increase and expand the State control over 'traditional ecclesiastical and feudal interests'.[4] Peter's *Vedomosti* and the first secular book in Russian history (1703, the

---

[1]Hans, N., *The Russian Tradition in Education*, London, 1963, p. 155.
[2]Hamlyn, P., *The Life and Times of Peter the Great*, Feltham, 1968, p. 36.
[3]Billington, J., *The Icon and the Axe*, New York, 1970, p. 181.
[4]Ibid., p. 183.

year of the founding of St. Petersburg) showed, clearly, that to him education is virtually synonymous with vocational training.

By the time Russia had entered into the nineteenth century, religious thought, being dominant for the past nine or so centuries, was becoming more or less dormant. By 1850 religion in Russia received its first serious challenge from positivism, materialism, and empiricism, and Turgenev's nihilism acknowledged the seriousness of the perennial debate between conservative religious factions and radical materialists. One of the offshoots of this debate was the emergence of Marxism in the 1890s.

A close examination of the works of A. Hertsen (1812–70), N. Pirogov (1810–81), K. Ushinsky (1824–70), N. Chernyshevsky (1828–89), D. Pisarev (1840–68), and other Russian progressive thinkers reveals that Soviet educational philosophy owes a great deal to the social thought and revolutionary radicalism and populism of the 1850s and 1860s. For instance, imbuing schoolchildren with socially useful labour, which is one of the main tenets of Soviet pedagogy today, could be traced to Pisarev's *The Thinking Proletariat* and Chernyshevsky's novel *What is to be done?* (1863). The proponents of labour colonies of the twenties, notably S. Shatsky, P. Blonsky, and A. Makarenko, in their acceptance of children's collectives as autonomous, self-governing institutions, bear remarkable similarity to Tolstoy's ideas on progressive education between 1859 and 1869.

Recently formulated Soviet dialectical materialism is not entirely new, for its precursor was the Marxist Georgy Plekhanov (1856–1918), the man who was responsible for the first major demonstration of the revolutionary populists in St. Petersburg in 1878 and who was destined to become the father of Russian Marxism. The Russians by that time were already familiar with Engel's *Condition of the Working Class in England* and Marx's *Critique of Political Economy* and *Capital*. In his controversial manifesto *Socialism and the Political Struggle* (1883), Plenkhanov had defined his Marxism in terms of scientific communism of the 1970s. In short, the principles of militant nationalism, socially useful labour, polytechnical and scientific training, and dialectical materialism, which permeated Russian intellectual thought during the last turbulent quarter of the nineteenth century, are still characteristic and, unmistakably, fundamental features of Soviet educational philosophy in the 1970s. However, it would be a mistake to conclude that the 1870s through to the 1890s were alone responsible for great educational reforms. One has to consider the nineteenth-century heritage as a whole in order to arrive at a valid and reliable conclusion as to the origins of Soviet educational philosophy.

2. The nineteenth-century heritage

Among the main political and social philosophers who contributed substantially towards the radical, new, and progressive western-oriented philosophy of education were V. Belinsky (1811–48), A. Hertsen (1812–70), N. Pirogov (1810–81), N. Chernyshevsky (1828–89), N. Dobrolyubov (1836–61), and K. Ushinsky (1824–70).

Vissarion Belinsky, considered to be one of the greatest revolutionary democrats, the forerunner of Russian Social Democrats (who became known as Bolsheviks and Mensheviks after the split in 1903), was Russia's leading thinker who, more than any other single man, had changed the course of Russian intellectual history during the 1840s, yet was destined to see the failure of the revolutions of 1848 in the West.

Following A. N. Radishchev, Belinsky had accepted the maxim that man is a social animal and that nature creates man but society develops and educates him. In his famous letter to Gogol he expressed his atheistic views: 'Russia sees its salvation not in mysticism, not in asceticism, not in pietism but in the successes of civilization, education, and humanism'.[5] Being influenced by Robert Owen and his socialist Utopia, Belinsky believed that environment rather than heredity affected man's upbringing and education. By the 1840s he came to believe that only socialism would make it possible to educate a universally developed, harmonious identity. To him the main task of education is moral—education for life and society. To become a human, thinking being, to win the right to be called man, was the fundamental task of Belinsky's Utopian dream of equal opportunity for all. He rejected religion for the sake of materialism. He developed the idea of narodnost in political education. He wanted

[5] Konstantinov, N., *Istoriya pedagogiki*, Moscow, 1974, p. 197.

to abolish sex discrimination in education and to imbue children with patriotism, love of labour, and civic involvement. He divided education into the physical, moral, and academic. The rearing of children in the spirit of communal awareness and moral responsibility is the most important task of education. In moral education, feeling is superior to reason in the early stages of human development. Belinsky held that children had to accept the concept of good, emotionally rather than intellectually. 'Feelings precede knowledge. He who has not experienced morality does not understand it.'[6] Children were to be encouraged but not forced to accept positive values. 'The younger the child, the more direct', wrote Belinsky, 'ought to be his moral education'.[6]

Belinsky suggested that formal and systematic education was to begin after the age of 7 and that it should incorporate both the humanities and sciences. The former, he believed, aided moral education and the socialization of the child and what he called ochelovechivanie (humanizing the individual). He was critical of the utility and empiricism in textbooks and stated that the child was to master human knowledge as well as develop a philosophy of life. He noticed a marked discrepancy between the school and society, between knowledge and experience, and urged that education and life be brought closer together.

The idea that the main task of education should be the formation of a humane, free individual who would live in the interests of his society and who would aspire to change his society, was the fundamental thesis of Alexander Hertsen, the contemporary of Belinsky. Hertsen was a radical revolutionary democrat, a talented writer, and a political philosopher. He was one of the most outstanding philosophers of dialectical materialism during the pre-Marxian era in Russia. According to Lenin he came 'face to face with dialectical materialism'.[7] Hertsen rejected the tenets of enlightened rationalism of Rousseau and Pestalozzi, which, he thought, were idealistic.[8] He was also critical of Rousseau's theory of educational freedom, and insisted that

[6]Konstantinov, N., *Istoriya pedagogiki*, Moscow, 1974, p. 200.
[7]Lenin, V. L., *Collected works*, Vol. 18, p. 10.
[8]Dupuis claims that Rousseau's theory of educational freedom was 'quite idealistic' in his book *Philosophy of Education in Historical Perspective*, Chicago, 1966, p. 112.

the child had to be taught responsibility, obligation, and self-discipline. Discipline is the key factor which determines success or failure of moral education: 'without discipline there is neither tranquil confidence nor obedience.'[9] This, clearly, in contrast to Rousseau, who rejected the conservative notion of discipline, makes Hertsen a kind of disciplinarian. Hertsen upheld materialistic upbringing, and his two educational works *Opyt besed s molodymi lyudmi* and *Razgovory s det'mi* explain the crucial role of nature study in upbringing. In his novel *Byloe i dumy* he appears to have accepted the scientific views of the Utopian socialism of Robert Owen, for he, too, shared the belief in the power of environment to shape the individual's intellect, the mind, and the psyche.

If Belinsky and Hertsen dominated socio-educational theory during the 1830s and 1840s, Pirogov, Chernyshevsky, Dobrolyubov, and Ushinsky were the main representatives of revolutionary and democratic tendencies in educational philosophy between the 1850s and 1870s. Other important pedagogues included P. Kapterev (1849–1922) who developed the idea of autonomy in the school; Ventsel (1857–1947) who upheld freedom in education; Ostrogorsky (1840–1902) who stressed the value of the aesthetic indoctrination of literature and language; and P. Lesfaft (1837–1909) who was a strong supporter of physical training in kindergartens and schools.

Nikolai Pirogov, a surgeon by training, became interested in educational reforms during the Crimean War, and in 1856 published his article 'Voprosy zhizni'. This article, which examined the nature and the role of upbringing, made Pirogov famous throughout Russia. Later, Ushinsky said that it had awakened in Russia educational thought that, until then, was dead. For Pirogov education meant humanism and the creation of a true man and a citizen. He could not agree with the emphasis on utility, vocational training, and early specialization in the school. He was convinced that the utility, which required early specialization, was harmful, for it narrowed the pupil's attitude towards life, restricted his creative powers, and retarded his moral development. He attacked the so-called turn towards applied sciences and the one-sided specialization. 'Do not hurry with your reality of applied sciences. Let the inner man mature and

[9]Konstantinov, op. cit., p. 207.

strengthen.'[10] 'How to become a man—this is what moral education should lead to,' wrote Pirogov. His proposed school curriculum consisted of two years for elementary and nine years for secondary education. Major disciplines to be studied were a foreign language, Russian language and literature, mathematics, and history. He advocated the abolition of examinations in favour of progressive assessment. In his article 'Must we thrash the children..?' (1858) he attacked corporal punishment. Pirogov's career as an educationalist–reformer was short-lived, for in 1861 he was sacked from his post of the Governor of the Odessa Educational Region—no doubt for his radical ideas.

The materialism of Feuerbach and the rationalism of Rousseau and the English utilitarians, which were sweeping Russia during the sixties, had influenced Chernyshevsky and Dobrolyubov, two ex-seminarians, now on the editorial staff of an influential journal *The Contemporary*.

Chernyshevsky developed a new ethics based on rational egoism. He preached the equality of sexes, the primacy of the applied sciences, and attempted to live and work communally. In his pre-Marxist manifesto, 'Anthropological principles in philosophy' (1860), which was an exposition of Utopian socialism, a forerunner, no doubt, of a communist ideal to come, he stated that environment was a major determining factor in shaping man's moral, psychological, and social qualities. He also stressed patriotic upbringing in the school. 'The historical role of every man', wrote Chernyshevsky, 'may be measured by his service to his country, his human dignity by the intensity of his patriotism.'[11]

Chernyshevsky's close friend and associate was Nikolai Dobrolyubov (1836–61). He was a revolutionary democrat, a prolific writer, and literary critic. His contribution to education is to be found in many articles published in the *Journal of Upbringing* between 1857 and 1859. A materialist by conviction, Dobrolyubov was against religious upbringing, which had dominated all public education in Russia for centuries. But he was equally against any form of authoritarianism in education, which he openly condemned in the article 'On

[10]Konstantinov, op. cit., p. 212.
[11]Ibid., p. 221.

the meaning of authority and upbringing' (1857). He believed that educators paid little or no attention to the development and needs of the child's identity. True education, as envisaged by Dobrolyubov, meant a deep respect of the child's personality, and understanding and consideration of his nature and abilities. The main task of the school should be, therefore, to give the pupil an all-round education in both humanities and sciences, to teach him to think independently and to educate him with solid and correct convictions, to develop in him will-power, to make him morally stable and physically fit. The article 'Organic development of man...' (1858) put forward the idea that physical fitness enabled man to reach great heights in his intellectual and spiritual development.

Dobrolyubov was particularly keen on moral upbringing. His moral training encompassed patriotism, humanism, the love of labour, and social involvement. His new criteria of discipline had no place for punishment, and the article 'All Russia's illusions destroyed by the cane' (1860) showed the destructive influence of corporal punishment on the pupil's identity.

Konstantin Ushinsky (1824–70), regarded today as one of Russia's greatest educationalists during the 1850s, was a Darwinist by training.

He graduated from the Faculty of Law at the University of Moscow, and at the age of 22 (1846) he was the youngest appointed law professor at the Law College in Yaroslav. Because of his progressive views he was soon dismissed and became a civil servant. Five years later (1854) he was hired as a teacher and very soon became a local school inspector.

Between 1857 and 1858 he published the following major articles: 'On the usefulness of educational literature', 'On the civic element in societal upbringing,' and 'The three elements of the school,' which immediately brought him fame.

He became famous for his monumental sociological study *Man as the Subject of Upbringing*... (2 vols., 1867–9). He put forward a claim that educational theory, in order to be effective and valid, has to be based on the laws of human anatomy, physiology, psychology, philosophy, history, and related disciplines. His educational theory was to open and clarify the whole process of upbringing. Ushinsky argued against useless pedagogical jargon and the so-called pure pedagogy, which was becoming far too abstract and theoretical, departing further and further away from practical teaching and experiences dictated by life situation rather than speculations: 'If pedagogy aims at educating man in all interactions then it must, above all, accept man with all of his interactions.'[12] In his article 'On the rational consciousness in social upbringing', Ushinsky stipulated development of rational identity in the child: 'There is one, common to all, natural tendency, which could always be used in upbringing. It is, what we would call, a rational consciousness, upbringing created by the people themselves. . . .'[13]

Development of patriotism and a deep love for one's country became the fundamental concept of Ushinsky's theory of upbringing. The child was to become a perfection of physical, intellectual, and moral upbringing. Moral development, in particular, was to be the main task of enlightened education, being more important than intellectual development. Moral education was designed to develop in the child the feeling of humanism, honesty, truthfulness, integrity, discipline, responsibility, and diligence. A strong character, will, duty, and fortitude were some of the main features of Ushinsky's civic upbringing. In 'Work and its psychological and instructional significance' Ushinsky asserted that work was an essential factor in the physical, mental, and moral perfection of man. 'Upbringing,' wrote Ushinsky, 'if it desires happiness for man, must train him not for happiness but prepare him for the labour of life.' Although Ushinsky regarded the textbook as the necessary 'foundation of good teaching', the role of the teacher was equally important. He believed that the teacher's influence was so important that it could not be substituted by anything else, for the 'teacher's identity meant everything in the upbringing process'.[14] Ushinsky's educational theory, based on empirical sensualism, concerning moral upbringing, patriotism, work training, and self-discipline, lends itself to an interpretation that is readily acceptable for communist upbringing.

Ushinsky, as an educationalist, had made a profound impact on

[12]Konstantinov, op. cit., p. 231.
[13]Ibid., p. 232.
[14]Ibid., p. 242.

education in Russia for the ensuing fifty years. Medynsky, a Soviet authority on Ushinsky, finds Ushinsky's idea concerning the unity between school and life as being particularly important.[15] Ushinsky claimed that life very easily destroys the school that stands in its path. True education ought to be an 'intermediary' between school, life, and knowledge. This very concept was used almost a hundred years later by Khrushchev (1956) in his criticism of schools for being 'divorced from life', which in 1958 culminated in his controversial decree 'Strengthening the ties of the school with life, and further developing the system of public education'. The retreat from the overwhelmingly academic character of the school and the stress on socially useful labour and work training for all was, no doubt, what Ushinsky would have wished.

3. Soviet education between 1917–78

3.1. CURRICULUM REFORMS BETWEEN 1917–29

After 1917, following the October Revolution, education had entered into its second and completely new phase of development. The pre-revolutionary educational system, with its century-long traditions officially, at least, had ceased to exist, and the new, people-oriented, Marxist-inspired Soviet education was born. In practice, however, the vestiges of pre-revolutionary education remained until the 1930s.

Education was completely reorganized after the October Revolution. On 9 November 1917 the People's Commissariat of Education (Narkompros) was formed and a prominent Marxist philosopher and literary critic, Anatoly Lunacharsky (1987–1933), was appointed as the first People's Commissar of Education. The Tsarist administrative division of education into regional directorates was abolished. The Narkompros swiftly nationalized all educational institutions and issued a famous and controversial decree (20 January 1918) 'On freedom of conscience, the church and religious orders' (on separation of the Church from the State and school from the Church). The

[15]Medynsky, E. N., Velikii russkii pedagog K. O. Ushinsky, *Istoriya pedagogiki*, Moscow, 1974, p. 244.

administrative dualism of the school between the State and the Church had been abolished by 1918, and the Church lost all its influence on education. A series of decrees was issued to consolidate the power of the Narkompros. The decree of 23 February 1918 had placed all educational establishments, including parish schools, in the hands of the Narkompros, and the decree of 30 May 1918, 'On unification of all types of educational and teaching establishments...' was responsible for creating the monolithic nature of Soviet education. For the first time, pre-school, primary, secondary, and higher education became one, organic, secular whole administered by a single ministry. At the first Russian Congress of teacher–internationalists (25 August to 4 September 1918), Lenin suggested a uniform school system throughout the Republic consisting of two levels—five years for the primary school and four years for the secondary school. Together, these two stages would constitute a secondary general educational labour polytechnical school, or, more briefly, a secondary polytechnical school. This monolithic school structure considerably simplified the previous complex hierarchy of schools, which included primary schools (3–5 years), upper elementary schools, trade schools, agricultural schools, commerce schools, boys' grammar schools, comprehensive secondary schools, girls' grammar schools, and so on. 'The fundamental principles of a single labour school', published on 16 October 1918, announced new political and pedagogic principles of the Soviet school. It stressed the unity between the school and politics as the most significant principle of Soviet pedagogy. The teaching of religion in schools was forbidden.

Emphasis was placed on physical and aesthetic upbringing. Education was to cater for individual differences. Teachers were to respect, love, and inspire the pupils. Developing the pupil's self-respect, dignity, independence, initiative, and moral fibre was far more significant than the actual learning itself. Corporal punishment was strictly forbidden. The 1918 'Declaration' was extremely radical. Examinations, assignments, and homework were abolished and the pupil was encouraged to study labour and manual skills, often at the expense of his formal schooling.

At the Seventh Congress of the Russian Communist Party of the Bolshevik [RCP (b)] in 1919 the Party agreed on a policy statement on education, which was worked out by Lenin. The document read:

> In the field of education the RCP aims to complete the task that began after the October Revolution of 1917, transforming the school from the weapon of the ruling class of bourgeosie into the weapon of total obliteration of the class division within the society, into the weapon of a communist metamorphosis of the society. During the period of dictatorship of the proletariat, i.e. the period providing conditions, which make it possible for a complete realization of communism, the school not only must be a leader of communist principles in general but also a guide of ideological, organizational and educational influence of the proletariat on semi-proletarian and non-proletarian strata of the working class, aiming at training the generation capable of establishing communism completely.[16]

The resolution decreed, among other things, free and compulsory education for all between the ages of 8 and 17, creation of pre-school establishments, co-education, and so on. Illiteracy (66% in 1916) was a serious problem in the newly created Republic, and to add to the problem over 2.5 million neglected children roamed the country.[17] The decree 'On the liquidation of illiteracy among the population of the RSFSR' of 26 December 1919 compelled the individuals between the ages of 8 and 50 to learn to read and write in Russian or the native tongue. In 1930 illiteracy amounted to 38% being approximately half of that in 1916. The All-Union drive on illiteracy between 1919 and 1939 was, by all indications, very successful.[18]

During the 1920s and the so-called new economic policy period, Russia experienced a new wave of cultural renaissance. Modernism, notably futurism and acmeism, dominated poetry and prose. Suprematism and constructivism were the two *avant-garde* movements in art. The former was, according to Malevich, man's desperate attempt to free art from the 'ballast of the objective world.' On the other hand, constructivism was concerned with a practical bridge between art and industry. Education, too, was influenced by this Silver Age of Russian culture, the age of experiment.

The idea that permeates Soviet education today is that work training and socially useful labour are the very essence of secondary education. This particular view was already developed by Pavel Blonsky (1884–1941) in the twenties, an influential Soviet educational psycho-

[16]*KPSS v rezolyutsiyakh* ..., Vol. 2, Moscow, 1970, p. 48.
[17]Konstantinov, op. cit., p. 346.
[18]Ibid., p. 355.

logist. He completed his degree at the University of Kiev (1907) and taught education and psychology in Moscow girls' secondary schools. In 1913 he was awarded an MA and began lecturing in psychology and philosophy at the University of Moscow. From 1915 he began to publish his works on education. He wrote that the school is not only an educational organization but the school of the child's whole future, that the cursed dichotomy between the school and life should be immediately abolished, that upbringing was to be social and political in nature.[19] In his articles 'Shkola i rabochii klass' (1917) and 'Shkola i obshchestvennyi stroi' (1917), Blonsky attempted to formulate a class character of upbringing, for the school was necessarily linked with the social order. He developed the tenets of the labour socialist school, which laid the foundations of the Soviet secondary (general educational) labour polytechnic school. He believed that the labour school was unthinkable without active and creative participation of children. His theory of the polytechnical school was described in his book *Trudovaya Shkola*. (1919). In 1921 Blonsky, as a member of the People's Commissariat for Education, participated in curriculum reforms, which were to bring the school closer to society and life. His educational theory is expressed in 'Pedagogika' (1922) and the 'Foundations of pedagogy' (1925). Moral education, in particular, interested Blonsky, and his credo was 'only a living soul can animate other souls', which meant that the teacher had to be the 'rational autonomous man', to use Hirst's concept (1974). During the twenties and early thirties, Blonsky was one of the key figures of the new philosophy of education which combined both pedagogy and psychology. It was called pedology, and his book *Pedologiya* (1925) discussed the main principles. He criticized the idealist psychology of G. I. Chelpanov and, together with another Marxist educationalist, K. N. Kornilov, took part in the debate that was on between Marxism and idealism in educational psychology. Later he became one of the founders of the Krupskaya Academy of Communist Upbringing. However, Blonsky did ignore the two-way process of upbringing affecting the teacher and the pupil.[20] Notwithstanding his immense

[19]Novikov, L., Blonsky, Pavel Petrovich, *Pedagogicheskaya entsiklopediya*, Vol. 1, Moscow, 1964, p. 259.

[20]Shabaeva, M., *Istoriya pedagogiki*, Moscow, 1974, pp. 365–6.

contribution to Marxist theory of education, Blonsky is also remembered in the USSR as a militant opponent of autonomy in education and de-schooling (svobodnoe vospitanie).

The concept of labour school and trudovoe vospitanie (work training) within a pupil's collective was advanced further by Stanislav Shatsky (1878–1934), the founder of the 'First experimental station on public education', which was an academic establishment concerned with solving theoretical and practical aspects of Soviet education. Educated at the University of Moscow, Shatsky began his teaching career in 1905, working with the slum children of Moscow. Shatsky was very interested in extra-curricular activities, which he tried to put to good use in his upbringing work. He established clubs for children, which were closed down by the government, allegedly for an attempt to indoctrinate children with socialism. Shatsky organized yet another society for children 'Children's Work and Recreation', which attempted to give the children a collective upbringing.

He and his wife organized one of the first summer labour schools (bodraya zhizn), where children were encouraged to participate in all forms of manual labour.

Vospitanie for Shatsky was a fusion of physical labour, games, artistic activity, intellectual work, and social and communal living. He believed that work training is most valuable when it is appreciated by the pupil as being necessary for his collective, as being an integral part of communal labour. Believing in the educational function of work training, Shatsky developed guidelines on the methodology of organization of socially useful labour for the pupil. Such work, would, he claimed, become the most effective measure of socialist upbringing.

The Russian prophet of de-schooling during the 1920s was Victor Shulgin, considered to be the most radical of his contemporaries. He hoped to see the ultimate 'withering away of the school; when the artificial division between the school and society would be abolished, giving way to a new "school of life".'[21]

Among the theories that were current at the time were the method (metod) and the universality (universalizm) theories. The former advocated a mastery of methods of perception rather than the acqui-

[21]Shulgin, V. N., O Shkole, *Na Putiakh*, No. 3, Moscow, 1931, p. 37.

sition of knowledge for its own sake, and the latter stipulated the existence of the discovery method.

Owing to the various factions bidding for power, political structure in Russia during the twenties was not very stable, which allowed the cultural life to take its natural course. The followers of the proletarian school of thought and socialist realism were not sufficiently influential to enforce their doctrine on education, literature, and the arts in particular. As the intellectual life in Russia was relatively free and educational thought was yet to be consolidated, many educationalists, particularly those who were not staunch supporters of Marxist pedagogy, took this opportunity to adopt educational theories from the West, particularly the Dalton plan schooling, the method of projects, and the thoughts of John Dewey. By 1934 they had little, if any, influence on Soviet pedagogy. Following the Seventeenth Party Congress (1934) the system was consolidated and everything was put under tight control. The Party began to claim omniscience in all matters. The principle of socialist realism was adopted by the First Congress of the Union of Soviet Writers. Education was to be the engineer of the human soul and serve the Party's needs. The experimental era is glossed over rather quickly in *Istoriya pedagogiki* (Moscow, 1974). Deyneko, in his survey article on the history of Soviet education in *Pedagogicheskaya entsiklopediya* (Vol. 4, Moscow, 1967) mentions the mistakes made during the twenties and the thirties. These mistakes are very serious digressions of some educationalists from a Marxist philosophy of education. The ultimate withering away of the school held by Shulgin and others was faulty and anti-Leninist.[22] The key role in educational thought is attributed to Lenin, his wife Nadezhda Krupskaya, the first Soviet pedagogue–Marxist, and Makarenko.[23]

The aim of communist upbringing, according to Lenin, was a struggle to depose bourgeoisie. The school 'outside life and politics was a lie and hypocrisy'.[24] The new role of the school, adopted at the

[22]Deyneko, M. M., *Pedagogicheskaya entsiklopediya*, Vol. 4, Moscow, 1967, pp. 58–64.
[23]Vul'fson, B. L., Pedagogika, *Pedagogicheskaya entsiklopediya*, Vol. 3, Moscow, p. 64.
[24]Lenin, V. I., *Polnoe Sobranie Sochinenii*, Vol. 37, p. 77.

Party's Seventh Congress in 1919, was to overcome a class division and become a 'tool of communist transformation of society'.[25] The school was to become a leader of the principles of communism, and it was to further the influence of the proletariat on the working class, aiming at bringing up a generation, which would be capable of establishing communism.[25] Youth that was to build communism had to be well educated. Lenin developed a dialectical and materialistic theory of perception: 'From a living perception towards abstract and from it towards practice, such is a dialectical path of perceiving the truth, perceiving objective reality.'[26]

Communist morality was to be based on conscientious discipline (soznatelnaya distsiplina). The foundation of communist morality was defined as 'a struggle for consolidation and realization of communism'.[27] Lenin equated vospitanie with discipline that was politically conscientious. He regarded it as necessary to educate children from their early teens in a 'conscientious and disciplined labour'.[28] Lenin's favourite educational innovation was the polytechnical school. Between 1920 and 1921 he was, according to N. Krupskaya, very much preoccupied with it.[29] In 1920 Lenin, in his public address, said that the fundamental difference between socialist education and its bourgeois antecedent was that the latter was estranged and cut off from life and labour. The link between true tasks of public (people's) labour and education in a bourgeois society 'did not exist'.[30] For Lenin, the problem of realization of polytechnical education was closely linked with a new approach towards labour and discipline. He discussed the essence of communist labour in his article 'Ot razrusheniya vekovogo uklada k tvorchestvu novogo' (April 1920) as the kind of labour that served the common needs; for the benefit of society.[31] An example of such labour became communist Saturdays (subbotniki) voluntary and unpaid public work for the good of the people.

[25] *KPSS v rezolyutsiyakh* . . . , Moscow, 1970, Vol. 2, p. 48.
[26] Lenin, op. cit., Vol. 29, pp. 152–3.
[27] Ibid., Vol. 41, p. 312.
[28] Ibid., Vol. 41, p. 318.
[29] Krupskaya, N. K. *Pedagogicheskie sochineniya*, Vol. 4, Moscow–Leningrad, 1959, p. 421.
[30] Lenin, op. cit., Vol. 40, Moscow, p. 162.
[31] Ibid., p. 315.

What then, did, the first educational reforms of the Lenin government achieve? The decree 'On the transfer of upbringing and education from religious institutions to the People's Commissariat of Education' (11 December 1917) and the decree 'On freedom of conscience, the Church and religious orders' (20 January 1918) established secular education as being the only alternative and forever separated the Church from the State. In May 1918 the Narkompros issued a direction on co-education. Earlier, in December 1917, the difficult Russian spelling was substantially reformed to facilitate more rapid learning. 1918 was the year of numerous teacher conferences and seminars. At the First All-Russian Congress in Education (25 August to 4 September 1918) the uniform system of a monolithic school, consisting of the five-year primary and the four-year secondary education, was put into practice. This, clearly, put an end to a complicated diverse educational system in the pre-revolutionary Russia. The decree 'Regulations concerning the monolithic labour school' of August 1918 marked the beginning of polytechnical education. The Congress also discussed pre-school education and comprehensive and adult education. The August decree on labour schools is, clearly, the most significant educational reform in Russia immediately after the Revolution. Commonly known as the 'Declaration on the single labour school' (Deklaratsiya o edinoi trudovoi shkole), this document announced new ideal political and educational principles of the Soviet school. The declaration emphasized the political nature of the school as being the most vital tenet of Soviet pedagogy.[32] It could, therefore, be said that the roots of the Soviet educational system go back to 1918, when the famous Declaration was issued.

Further details of public education were worked out by Lenin and accepted at the Eighth Congress of the Communist Party [RCP (b)] in 1919. Among accepted resolutions on education were free and compulsory general and polytechnical education for all children of both sexes between the ages of 8 and 17, the establishment of pre-school institutions, realization of the principles of the monolithic labour school, providing the students with food, clothing, footwear, and educational equipment from State funds, training the new cadres of educationalists—who were communists, attracting the working

[32]Konstantinov, op. cit., p. 343.

class towards active participation in education, the many-faceted State help towards self-education and self-development of the workers and peasants, an extensive development of professional education for the 17-plus age group, and so on.[33] The December decree 'On elimination of illiteracy...' (1919), initiated by Lenin and approved by the Narkompros, came into force. People up to the age of 50 were required by law to attend educational centres to learn to read and write. By 1921, or in less than two years, nearly five million people had been taught literacy. Table 1 shows the significant growth of education between 1918 and 1920.

TABLE 1. *The Soviet school in 1920*

Years	No. of schools	Percentage increase	No. of students	Percentage increase
1914/15	105,524	—	7,896,000	—
1920/21	118,398	12	9,781,000	24

Source: *Istoriya pedagogiki*, Moscow, 1974, p. 345.

The number of secondary schools had almost doubled by 1920, the greatest growth being in rural areas. The number of secondary schools in villages grew from 72 in 1914 to 2144 in 1920.[34] For those who missed secondary education the four-year workers secondary faculties (rabfak) were established in 1919. These enabled many workers and peasants to enter higher institutions of learning, which, by 1919 resolutions, were declared open to all.

Pre-school education, to which Nadezhda Krupskaya had a great deal to contribute, became a reality in 1919. The four all-Russian congresses on pre-school education, which were held in the post-revolutionary decade, contributed immensely towards educating children in a spirit of communist morality. The Declaration on pre-school education of November 1917 stated that all public education of children must start in the first few months of life. It also stated that pre-school education was to be organically linked with the entire network of educational structure. Pre-school education achieved

[33]*KPSS v rezolyutsiyakh...*, Vol. 2, Moscow, 1970, pp. 48–49.
[34]Konstantinov, op. cit., p. 345.

many things. It educated children in communist morality. It raised educational standards of the first grades and, among other things, it emancipated women and made it possible for them to continue with their education and join the ranks of the workforce.[34]

Another notable achievement of educational reforms under Lenin was the creation of children's homes to take care of the $2\frac{1}{2}$ million neglected children who roamed the countryside after the October

TABLE 2. *The eight-year school curriculum (the tsarist grammar school, 1914)*

Subjects	Grade level 1	Class hours per week							
		2	3	4	5	6	7	8	Total
Religious studies	2	2	2	2	2	2	2	2	16
Russian language	5	5	4	4	3	5	4	4	34
Mathematics	4	4	4	4	5	4	3	4	32
Latin	—	—	5	5	5	5	5	5	30
French	—	5	3	4	3	3	3	3	24
German	4	3	3	3	3	2	3	2	23
History	2	3	2	4	4	3	2	2	22
Geography	3	2	2	2	2	1	1	1	14
Philosophy	—	—	—	—	—	—	2	1	3
Legal studies	—	—	—	—	—	—	—	2	2
Physics	—	—	—	—	—	3	4	5	12
Nature studies	2	2	2	—	—	—	—	—	6
Art	4	3	1	—	—	—	—	—	8

Source: *Istoriya pedagogiki*, Moscow, 1974, p. 308.

Revolution. 260,000 homeless children were cared for and educated in 5000 homes in 1921. By 1922 this figure had soared to 415,000 children in 8000 homes.[35]

The basic principle of the Soviet educational system was laid down in 1918, but the first curriculum changes commenced in 1920, when a new nine-year school curriculum was published by the Narkompros. Curriculum reforms were of a major nature, for sciences received an increased emphasis and the new disciplines included in the school curriculum were chemistry, biology, astronomy, meteorology, and social studies. Physical culture and art also received a closer attention. Tables 2 and 3 represent curricula of the pre-revolutionary

[35]Konstantinov, op. cit., p. 346.

TABLE 3. *The nine-year curriculum for primary and secondary schools*
(RSFSR, 1920)

Subjects	Primary school (level I)					Secondary school (level II)			
	1*	2	3	4	5	6	7	8	9
Physics	—	—	—	—	—	3	4	4	4
Chemistry	—	—	—	—	—	—	3	3	—
Biology	—	2	3	5	6	3	2	2	4
Geography	—	—	—	—	—	3	2	2	4
Astronomy	—	—	—	—	—	—	—	—	2
Language and literature	—	5	5	5	5	5	5	5	3
Mathematics	—	5	5	5	5	5	4	4	3
Social and historical sciences (politics and history)	—	2	3	2	4	4	4	6	6
Art (music, drawing and painting)	—	3	3	3	3	3	2	2	2
Physical education	—	2	2	2	2	2	2	2	2
Foreign language	—	—	—	—	—	2	2	2	2
Class hours per week	15*	19	21	22	25	30	30	32	32

* Lessons in grade 1 consisted of general and integrated studies which included reading, writing, arithmetic, and science.

Source: *Istoriya pedagogiki*, Moscow, 1974, p. 347.

eight-year grammar school and the newly created nine-year Soviet polytechnical school.

At a glance it can be seen that the Tsarist grammar school emphasized classical education. Three languages, namely Latin, German, and French, were taught. The 1920 curriculum shows that only one modern language, with two (quite inadequate) class sessions weekly, was taught. The grammar school also offered philosophy, law, and biblical studies, which were omitted from the Soviet curriculum. Both philosophy and biblical studies were dropped from the new curriculum as they constituted a potential threat to the new ideology, and the latter, in particular, conflicted with scientific atheism. Legal studies, however, was absorbed into an elaborate social studies programme (taught in all grades and progressively increasing to 6 hours weekly in the last two years of schooling), which also included a detailed study of Marxism, dialectical materialism, and the history of the Communist Party.

By the end of 1920 the civil war was over and the young, starved, ruined Republic was threatened with a complete economic collapse. Lenin was forced to abandon his militant socialism for a petty-bourgeois new economic policy (NEP). The NEP was a drastic compromise. Private trade and ownership were again permitted. Small-scale private manufacturers, petty craftsmen, and with them petty-bourgeois tastes were being tolerated. The peasants were allowed to sell their produce. An independent peasantry and private trade which were given the go-ahead between 1920 and 1927, illustrate how different Bolshevik rule under Lenin must have been. The NEP did help to quickly restore the ruined economy. However, economic, social and cultural liberalization was not accompanied by political liberalization. On the contrary, the NEP induced a thaw of autonomy which necessitated, as Lenin saw, the tightening and consolidation of political power.

Cultural and social freedom during the NEP period was reflected clearly in education. Even experimental Dalton-plan schooling was tolerated. Many educational theories competed with one another. Academic life was still largely controlled by professors who had made their reputations in pre-revolutionary Russia.[36]

Educationalists often refer to the twenties as the era of experimentation. The moderate degree of freedom experienced by educationalists, for censorship did exist, can, no doubt, be attributed to economic and political factors. The NEP was a necessity, and the Party was far from monolithic, being torn by internal feuds between the so-called left opposition, headed by Trotsky and Zinoview, and the Stalinists. Stalin, before 1924, was a minor political figure with little influence. His meteoric rise was due to Lenin, who in 1922 appointed him to the Party's Secretariat, which at that time was a minor post. Following the death of Lenin in January 1924, Stalin began to consolidate his power, which grew significantly after 1927, following his successful smear campaign against Trotsky, who was eventually exiled to Turkey. Stalin's control in 1924 was not yet absolute, for he had Bukharin and other intellectually dominated Marxist groups to reckon with. As the NEP was beginning to break up in the winter of 1927–8 and moderate economic and political leaders were being

[36]Nove, A., *Stalinism and After*, London, 1975, p. 49.

gradually removed, Stalin managed to gain control of the Party Secretariat which, under him, became the most important political control in practice. In April 1929 the Sixteenth Party Congress adopted the first five-year plan. Bukharin had lost his political influence in 1928 and from then on neither he nor any other non-Stalinist Party leader would be published. Stalin's 'revolution from above was already beginning'.[37] The above brief summary of the political climate in the NEP Russia explains, at least partially, why experimental education was not being suppressed even though it must have displeased the hard-liners. Educational reforms in Russia during the twenties represented the final phase of modernism that dominated all spheres of intellectual thought and culture. The contrast with the thirties is very striking. If one were to compare educational thought of 1924, say, with 1934, it becomes clear that by then education, like everything else, had been regimented and remodelled on traditional lines, which included the reintroduction of the pre-revolutionary system with its familiar grading procedures, school uniforms, and formal teaching methods.[38]

What, then, were the main educational reforms during the NEP? Most of them were concerned with curriculum. New school syllabuses were introduced between 1923 and 1925 under the auspices of the State Academic Council (Gosudarstvenny Uchyony Sovet—GUS). They were commonly known as kompleksnye programmes of the GUS. These programmes were topic-oriented rather than discipline-dictated. The aim was to abolish the old system of school disciplines, which, as it was argued, isolated the school from life. The GUS programmes advocated the following interdisciplinary curriculum:

1. Man and nature (biology, physics, chemistry, etc.).
2. Work.
3. Society (history, geography, literature, politics, etc.).

These radical reforms, aimed at breaching the gap between school and society and, clearly, were to inspire Khrushchev in his, equally controversial, educational manifesto 'On strengthening the ties of the

[37] Ibid., p. 37.
[38] Ibid., p. 67.

school with life, and further developing the system of public education' (1958). Now it is argued that the GUS programme was paradoxical in nature and did not provide the pupil with a systematic and deep-rooted knowledge.[39] Since educational standards varied from school to school, Narkompros introduced in 1927 a universal and compulsory school curriculum, which included a wide range of core disciplines that embraced science, humanities, work training, physical culture, and aesthetic upbringing. By this time the following educational structure had emerged:

1. The primary school (level 1—four years).
2. The seven-year school.
3. The secondary school (level 2—nine years).
4. The seven-year factory school.
5. The school of rural youth (until 1934).
6. The trade school (the four-year vocational–technical schools).

Both the seven-year factory school and the four-year trade school prepared semi-skilled and skilled workers for all branches of industry. In 1929 the Narkompros introduced the ten-year school, which was to become the fundamental unit of Soviet education. It is not too difficult to see that the Soviet educational system between the thirties and the fifties was, in fact, based on the school structure adopted in the twenties, namely the seven-year incomplete primary/secondary school and the ten-year school.

Another major educational reform was the introduction of polytechnical work training in schools in 1929. Schools were being equipped with woodwork and metalwork shops.

Political indoctrination in schools was helped by the formation of the Pioneers in 1922 at the Fifth Congress of the Komsomol. By 1925 $1\frac{1}{2}$ million children became Pioneers.[40]

Tight control of education by the Party and a high degree of uniformity of the curriculum, teaching methods, and assessment were already in evidence in the twenties. What then of experimentation in education in the twenties? John Dewey's activity and projects methods, the Dalton assignment plan, and Western progressive tech-

---

[39]Korolev, F., *Istoriya pedagogiki*, Moscow, 1974, chap. 30, p. 357.
[40]Ibid., p. 360.

niques of all kinds had been tried out in the Soviet school. But by 1934, when the Seventeenth Party Congress had met and the doctrine of Socialist realism and partiinost was adopted, the twenties were described as the era of irresponsible experiments in the school.[41] Education under Stalin from 1934 onwards became regimented. The following features were reintroduced: formal examinations (in the twenties examinations were abolished and progressive assessment based on projects and essays was used), formal teaching methods (as prescribed by the Narkompros), standardized textbooks for core disciplines, uniform and compulsory primary/secondary curriculum, uniform assessment, school uniforms (the boys were often dressed like pupils of a military academy, reminiscent of Tsarist times), gold medals for the best pupils who obtained the grade 'excellent' in all final, external examinations), and strict classroom discipline. Soviet education during the thirties witnessed the reintroduction of many features of pre-revolutionary schooling. In short, it was a step backwards—from John Dewey to Nadezhda Krupskaya.

3.2. CURRICULUM REFORMS DURING THE 1930s

The tightening of political controls by Stalin during the first five-year plan (1929–33), the removal of moderate educationalists like Bubnov from office in 1936, arrests of many prominent intellectuals accused of deviating from socialism, all signalled the end of experimentation and freedom in thought and cultural life and the beginning of the omniscience of Stalin's Party in all matters.

Educational reforms during the thirties were designed to consolidate the school curriculum adopted after 1927, to raise academic standards, for in 1931 Stalin had said: 'We are fifty or a hundred years behind the advanced countries. We must make good this distance in ten years or we shall go under; to eliminate the vestiges of educational innovations of the twenties and to intensify moral upbringing in schools.'

In August 1930, following the recommendations made at the Six-

[41]Grant, N., *Soviet Education*, Penguin, 1968, p. 21.

teenth Party Congress, the decree 'On universal and compulsory primary education' was issued. The first three articles stated:

1. 'Introduce from 1930 to 1931 in the Union of SSR universal and compulsory education of children (boys and girls) aged 8, 9, and 10 for a period of at least four years of the primary school....'
2. 'Introduce from 1930 to 1931 compulsory education of children (boys and girls) aged 11 and 15, who did not complete the first four years of the labour school....'
3. 'Introduce from 1930 to 1931 universal and compulsory elementary education of children (boys and girls) of the order of the seven-year school....'[42]

The August decree, in short, announced universal, compulsory primary education up to the age of 15 for, at this stage, more than one-third of the total population was illiterate.

In 1931 the Central Committee of the Party in the decree 'On the primary and secondary schooling' rejected the 1930 curriculum based on the open classroom, interdisciplinary approach, group teaching, and progressive assessment, and introduced radical changes in the school curriculum. The decree stated that the school did not fulfil the new requirements of socialism in that it failed to give a satisfactory range of systematic and comprehensive education. The curriculum was to be restructured according to principles of scientific Marxism. This resulted in reintroduction of discipline-oriented teaching, according to a strict time-table. Polytechnic education, according to Lenin's principles, was stressed at all levels. The new 1931/2 school curriculum not only emphasized teaching of basic disciplines but allocated the greatest number of teaching hours to mathematics and Russian (or a native tongue). It seems that the three basic Rs became the guiding criteria of educational reforms during the early thirties.

Curriculum reforms between 1932 and 1936 could be summarized by the following decrees:

1. 'On school curricula and regime in the primary school' (August 1932).

[42]Konstantinov, op. cit., p. 356.

2. 'On textbooks for primary and secondary schools' (February 1933).
3. 'On the structure of primary and secondary schools in the USSR' (May 1934).
4. 'On the teaching of civic history in the schools of the USSR' (May 1934).
5. 'On the teaching of geography in primary and secondary schools of the USSR' (May 1934).
6. 'On pedological distortions within the system of Narkompros' (July 1936).

The August 1932 decree followed a detailed examination of the subject-oriented curriculum of 1931. The following defects were noted: excessive overloading in learning, which resulted in superficial learning of knowledge; lack of coordination between, say, physics, chemistry, and mathematics; methodological and educational 'errors'; simplification; and so on. The next problem was to reassert the significance of carefully prepared lessons, which replaced the workshop and team method in learning.[43] Another defect was the absence of stable, permanent textbooks. All kinds of teaching material were used in the twenties, which were changed from year to year. The Central Committee of the Party rejected the idea of dynamic and evolving textbooks, which were continuously adapted to the changing society, in favour of a standardized textbook.

Uniformity in the curricula, teaching methods, and textbooks was also followed by a blue-print like uniformity of the entire educational system in the USSR. The decree 'On the structure of primary and secondary schools in the USSR' (May 1934) declared the existence of the elementary school (grades 1–4), the seven-year school (incomplete secondary), and the ten-year school (complete secondary). This type of educational structure had remained in practice until the early sixties.

During the thirties the Party began to claim omniscience on all matters pertaining to education. The Central Committee repeatedly stressed Marxist–Leninist moral upbringing in schools. To celebrate the tenth anniversary of the formation of the Pioneer organization,

[43]Ibid., p. 372.

the authorities issued a decree on improving upbringing. The April 1932 decree 'On the work of the Pioneer organization' stated that the main task of the Pioneers was to develop in children a socialist attitude towards learning, labour, and communal and practical work. In educational thought Marxist–Leninist pedagogy became the sole guiding principle. By 1936 all non-Marxist schools of thought were silenced. Pedology, being a combination of psychology and pedagogy, was refuted and condemned as anti-Marxist. The decree 'On pedological distortions within the system of Narkompros' (July 1936) strongly attacked the entire theory of pedology, in particular the notion that the child's future was predetermined by biological and social factors. Heredity and environment suggested that there was a limit to socialization in school. This reactionary theory contradicted, apparently, the Marxist–Leninist theory of upbringing, which, unlike pedology, asserted that availability of equal opportunity for all would yield the right kind of Soviet people. The 1936 decree put an end to all kinds of reactionary, formalist, and bourgeois educational theories.

Two Soviet educationalists Nadezhda Krupskaya (1869–1939) and Anton Makarenko (1888–1939) are regarded as the pioneers of communist upbringing. Their work during the thirties was of great importance. Nadezhda Krupskaya, the daughter of a Tsarist army officer who was to become Lenin's wife, was, among other things, the author of the first Marxist monograph on education. In her book *People's Education and Democracy* (Narodnoe obrazovanie i demokratiya) of 1915, Krupskaya interpreted Marx and Engels on education and described, in terms of Marxism, basic features of the new school and pedagogy in a socialist society of the future. In her article 'On the problem of the school aim' (1928) she attempted to distinguish between socialist and capitalist education. The aims of capitalist education resulted in repression of the identity and blocking out the conscience. Socialist education, however, aimed at the blossoming of the identity of every child, widening his horizons, deepening his conscience, and enriching his perception.[44] The article 'Mine and ours' (1932) examines a communist attitude towards communal property and communal work. Krupskaya was interested in communist

[44]Konstantinov, op. cit., p. 387.

morality, and her article 'To develop communist morality in children' (1931) examines the problem: 'In our youth organizations we must develop communal opinions and communal discussions of the problems of behaviour as it is important to forge communist and Pioneer morality.... In our life a great deal still remains of the "petty-possessive" and "philistine" vestiges of the past.'[45] As a Marxist, Krupskaya gave the following definition of the aim of vospitanie:

> Society is interested in the common aim of the primary, secondary, and higher education—the upbringing of multi-dimensional people who possess conscientious and organized communal instincts, who possess a purposeful and well-thought-out world view, who clearly understand everything that occurs around them, in nature and communal life; people who are prepared in theory and in practice for any kind of labour—be it physical or mental and who are capable of building a rational, full of meaning, beautiful, and happy communal life. These are the people that are needed for socialist society. Socialism, without them cannot be fully realized.

Like Lenin, Krupskaya was an ardent follower of polytechnic education and in that area alone she has written more than 150 articles. Krupskaya believed that work training was the essence of polytechnic education and hence it had socio-economic and political implications. 'In the country,' wrote Krupskaya, 'where socialism was being built, polytechnism should be the integral part of general education.'[46]

The foremost educationalist of the thirties, the founder of the children's labour communities, Anton Makarenko (1888–1939), was born in the Ukraine of a working-class family. He began teaching before the Revolution, read widely (Gorky, Lenin, Darwin, Timiryazev, Klyuchevsky, and others), was a principal of a college in Poltava (1919), and in September 1920 established the first labour colony (a kind of boys' town) for juvenile delinquents, which served as an experiment for the formation of children's labour collectives. The Gorky labour colony, as it was called, eventually accommodated 120 children and was the first of its kind in Russia. When Gorky visited the colony in 1928 he was impressed by what he saw, particularly with Makarenko's insight into the child's identity: 'He sees everything and he knows every child. He is able to describe him in five words and in such a way as if he has taken an instant photograph of his nature.' In 1927 Makarenko helped to organize another boys' town,

[45]Polianski, S. N. (ed.), *Khrestomatiya po pedagogike*, Moscow, 1967, p. 423.
[46]Krupskaya, N., *Pedagogicheskie sochineniya*, Moscow, 1958, Vol. 2, p. 11.

the Dzerzhynsky children's labour commune near Kharkov in the Ukraine. Encouraged by the authorities, particularly Maxim Gorky who, at that time, was the most prominent literary figure, a man of great political influence, Makarenko published a number of didactic novels. Among the ones with educational flavour are *Pedagogicheskaya poema* (1933), *Kniga dlya roditelei* (1937), and *Flagi na bashnyakh* (1938).* From 1935 Makarenko directed methods of upbringing in labour colonies in the Ukraine.

Makarenko's educational thought was a compromise between formal (authoritarian) and informal (autonomous) education. He rejected authoritarian educationalists who drilled rather than taught the pupil, and he was equally against total de-schooling. The latter, he claimed, often resulted in poor discipline, insufficient learning, and semi-anarchy. He also criticized a sentimental attitude towards the child which regarded him as the flower of life. He saw children essentially as a means to an end. Too much affection, sentimentality, love, and care could, according to Makarenko, produce the opposite—egotism, laziness, or other negative attributes. He advised, instead, a degree of moderation in love and affection, in austerity and sternness. The most remarkable feature of Makarenko's social psychology was the so-called socialist humanism, based on his unsentimental yet dogmatic optimism, for in each child he saw positive features.

The most fundamental feature of upbringing for Makarenko was to educate the individual in a spirit of collectivism. The collectivist was to be the end product of successful Socialist upbringing in the Soviet school.[47] Makarenko's most important law of the collective is the law of dynamics of the collective (zakon dvizheniya kollektiva), which stated that the collective must aspire towards new ideals and not be satisfied with its immediate gains. Gains and successes, according to Makarenko, were to consolidate new tasks and new, long-range objectives. He was one of the first Soviet educationalists to introduce the principle of the system of perspective lines (sistema perspektivnykh linii), which was based on man's insatiable desire for ideals and perfection. Happiness of tomorrow, beauty of the future

[47]Konstantinov, op. cit., p. 401.
*See Glossary.

society, became the main source of man's desire, which compelled and inspired him to live, create, and love.

Makarenko's main task was to infuse his pupils with moral judgements and values. In his article 'Lectures on the upbringing of children' he wrote: 'We demand, from our citizen, that he should fulfil his obligations throughout his entire life, without waiting for directions or orders. He should possess the will of initiative and creativity.'[48] Makarenko's preoccupation with communist ethics is illustrated by such articles as 'Volya, muzhestvo i tseleustremlyonnost', 'O kommunisticheskoi etike', and 'Kommunisticheskoe povedenie i vospitanie' published shortly before his death in 1939.* He defined a communist ethic as that kind of ethic which would 'absolutely leave far behind all moral codes that had ever existed in history'.[49] 'Our ethic', wrote Makarenko, 'should be a prosaic business-like ethic of our today's and tomorrow's normal behaviour.'[50]

3.3. CURRICULUM REFORMS UNDER STALIN (1939–54)

The Seventeenth Party Congress in January and February of 1939 symbolized, so to speak, the end of excessive repressions in educational thought. From 1939 the Soviet school entered into the last phase of education under Stalin. Between 1939 and 1945 (Stalin had died on 5 March 1953) education, interrupted by the Great Patriotic War (1941–5), developed very little. The changes were mainly administrative in nature. The compulsory education of children aged 7, instead of 8, was introduced in the 1944/5 school year. The numerical (1–5) system of assessment was introduced in January 1944. For some inexplicable reason co-education was abolished in 1943 only to be reinstated in 1954. The authorities were increasingly concerned with the quality of education, and the decree 'On measures to improve the quality of learning in the school' (June 1944) introduced:

1. Compulsory exit examinations in the primary, seven-year, and ten-year schools and examinations for the certificate of maturity.

[48]Ibid., p. 404.
[49]Makarenko, A., *Sochineniya*, Moscow, 1958, Vol. 5, p. 427.
[50]Ibid., p. 450.
*See Glossary.

2. Awarding the gold and silver medals to the top pupils completing the secondary school.

This decree marked the beginning of an academic and formal phase in Soviet post-war education. The Academy of Pedagogical Sciences of the RSFSR, the highest educational research institute in the country, was established in October 1943. Educational research received top priority from the forties onwards. The Academy was chiefly concerned with problems of history of education, general and special pedagogy, educational psychology, and methods of teaching discipline in the school.

Maintaining discipline in schools became so important that in August 1943 'Rules for Pupils' were adopted and, with minor modifications, have been in force ever since. Discipline, clearly, was essentially a means towards the moral education of the new man of Soviet society. The pupil was to observe the twenty standard rules which defined the socially approved standard of behaviour, values, and attitudes. These rules convey the essence of moral and political education in the USSR. It was the duty of every pupil:

1. To acquire knowledge persistently in order to become an educated and cultured citizen and to be of the greatest possible service to his country.
2. To study diligently, to be punctual in attendance, and not arrive late for classes.
3. To obey the instructions of the school director and the teachers without question.
4. To arrive at school with all the necessary textbooks and writing materials; to have everything ready for the lesson before the teacher arrives.
5. To come to school clean, well groomed, and neatly dressed.
6. To keep his place in the classroom neat and tidy.
7. To enter the classroom and take his place immediately after the bell rings; to enter and leave the classroom during the lesson only with the teacher's permission.
8. To sit upright during the lesson, not leaning on the elbows or slouching; to listen attentively to the teacher's explanation and

the other pupils' answers, and not to talk or let his attention wander to other things.

9. To rise when the teacher or director enters or leaves the room.

10. To stand to attention when answering the teacher; to sit down only with the teacher's permission; to raise his hand if he wishes to answer or ask a question. . . .

In many ways this strict adherence to prescribed patterns of social behaviour that defined discipline was reminiscent of the thirties, when the authorities were also emphasizing the necessity for a strict discipline.

The war, of course, could have been blamed for many things, including the lowering of academic standards, the slackening of discipline, upbringing, and morality. The war also had revealed that the end product of secondary education did not fulfil the Party's expectations. Rote learning, superficial knowledge of basic disciplines, formalism, and the discrepancy between the theory and practice necessitated urgent reexamination of the curriculum process.

Once again the Party took the necessary steps: between 1949 compulsory seven-year schooling was introduced and 1961 universal secondary education envisaged. A number of educational reforms had taken place. Bearing in mind that Stalin had died in 1953, educational thought, as in the twenties, was more liberal and less dogmatic.

The seven-year compulsory universal education was introduced in 1949, following the decree which stated that all pupils in grade 4 (the final year of elementary school) were to be promoted to grade 5. They were to continue their schooling up to the age of 14. Almost twenty years later a more ambitious task was put into practice—universal, compulsory secondary education between the ages of 7 and 18.

As early as 1952 the Nineteenth Congress of the Party approved in principle a gradual transition from the seven-year to ten-year secondary education for all. Polytechnic training was reintroduced in schools, which culminated in the November 1958 decree 'On strengthening the ties . . .'. It became apparent by 1956 that schools did not prepare youth for work and life. Vocational training was inadequate to meet the needs of rapidly developing industry and agriculture. Meanwhile, in order to cope with a huge influx of matriculants in the fifties, the authorities brought in what seemed to be an ingenious plan of vocational (mainly blue-collar) training for school-leavers. They were advised to enrol in technical colleges and schools which trained students for careers, ranging from fitter and turner to postman.

3.4. CURRICULUM REFORMS DURING DE-STALINIZATION (1954–61)

Educational reforms during de-Stalinization (1954–61) were mainly concerned with improving academic standards and the reintroduction of the polytechnical principle of Blonsky, Krupskaya, and Maka-renko. Khrushchev's reforms in 1958 restructured the Soviet educational system that lasted for nearly four decades. The seven-year schools were hastily converted into eight-year schools, and ten-year schools into eleven-year schools. The latter were reorganized back to ten-year schools in 1964. Khrushchev, with his populist–egalitarian ideas, was convinced that school and study should be successfully combined with work training and industrial experience. The poly-technic principle, was, clearly, one of the principal as well as contro-versial features of Soviet education. Khrushchev claimed that the renunciation of the polytechnic principle of the twenties in education under Stalin, and with it the return to old methods of formal and bookish education, led after two decades to the separation of educa-tion from society and school from life. At the Twentieth Congress in 1956 Khrushchev attacked the schools for being divorced from life, and pointed out that pupils who finished school were insufficiently prepared for practical life. In his memorandum of September 1958 he wrote, indignantly:

> A number of pupils passing out of ten-year schools show unwillingness to go to work at factories, mills, collective farms, and State farms and some of them even consider this to be below their dignity. This lordly and scornful and wrong attitude towards physical work is to be found also in some families.... Physical work becomes something to scare children with, let alone the fact that such views are an insult to the working people of socialist society. Such an incorrect situation, when in our society people are brought up with no respect for physical work and are divorced from life, can no longer be tolerated.[51]

[51]Quoted from Tomiak, J. J., Fifty-five years of Soviet Education, in *The History of Education in Europe* (Cook, T. G., ed), London, 1974, p. 44.

Subsequently, in December 1958 the much-debated decree 'On strengthening the ties of school with life...' was introduced. However, it proved to be no solution to the problem of bridging the gap between education and labour, between mental and physical work. The decree proved to be very unpopular with educationalists, factory management, teachers, parents, and, clearly, the students themselves. The idea to admit into tertiary institutions those with at least two years of work experience in factories and collective farms was extremely unpopular with educationalists and, especially, the upper strata of society.[52] The experiment had met with disastrous social consequences, and the decree was revoked in 1964. The fact that the polytechnic principle and, in particular, work experience was successfully challenged, illustrates how far the present, allegedly, classless Soviet society had departed from Marxism. A substantial stratum of Soviet society was no longer in favour of an egalitarian fusion of study and work that would bring about greater equality among different social strata, of even the classless society itself. A distinct social strata had come into being under Stalin.

Since post-secondary work experience was a failure it could be argued that the single, most significant educational reform under Khrushchev was the increase of compulsory schooling from seven to eight years with a wider range of electives in the curriculum after the eight-year polytechnic school. Students were able to enter secondary specialized schools, technical schools and colleges, and part-time vocational schools—all designed to train them and thus meeting the needs of industry. It seemed as if the retreat from the overwhelmingly academic character of the ten-year school under Stalin and the egalitarian emphasis on work training for all, was the keynote of the 1958 reforms.

Political upbringing became once more the key issue in education for citizenship. Methodological guides, programmes, and syllabuses, which described, step by step, the development of moral training in schools, were being published since the sixties.

Curriculum changes during the fifties included a gradual introduction of a new programme in the 1950s school year in the RSFSR Work training was time-tabled in grades 1–4. In grades 5–7 work

[52]Nove, op. cit., p. 143.

training was treated more seriously, and consisted of woodwork, metalwork, etc. Work training in the upper grades (grades 8–10) consisted of formal training for such professions as mechanic, electrician, agronomist, etc. Humanities, in particular, history, literature, and the constitution of the USSR, were substantially revised and rewritten and new programmes were designed in grades. 5–10 and 8–10.

3.5. CURRICULUM REFORMS UNDER BREZHNEV (1964–78)

During the sixties education was under a strong criticism for its excessive overloading of the pupils with classwork and homework. It was argued that excessive overloading exerted a negative influence on the pupils in that, among other things, it resulted in shallow and superficial study of disciplines. In 1964 the Academy of Sciences and the Academy of Pedagogical Sciences of the USSR set up a 500-man committee to inquire into schooling. As a result of this inquiry, the school curriculum now placed a far greater emphasis on political, moral, and physical training. In that year Brezhnev (58) came to power. The internal policy of Brezhnev was and still is somewhat more repressive than that of Khrushchev. There were, according to the Brezhnev group, manifestations of a penetration of bourgeois ideology and ideological deviations.[53] Political liberalization had reached its apogee with the publication of Solzhenitsyn's spectacular novel *One Day in the Life of Ivan Denisovich* in the leading literary journal *Novy Mir* in 1962. The Brezhnev group began to tighten up (not unlike the twenties) political controls. Education, in particular, received a powerful antidote of moral and political upbringing relevant to the social, political, and cultural metamorphoses in the USSR after the death of Stalin or, more specifically, between 1954 and 1964. Politically, the Soviet school showed signs of slacking off in the area of political indoctrination, which Lenin believed to be the noblest of the aims of education for citizenship and partiinost. To counter this unprecedented relaxation in moral education being, clearly, attributed to upward social mobility, a rising snobbishness of the intelligentsia toward the rest of the population and the Western-imitated

[53]Nove, op. cit., p. 160.

socialization of Soviet youth, the authorities demanded a more effective political socialization of youth. From now on, moral and political education became the most fundamental and the most compelling ideological issue in educational reforms between 1964 and 1978. Another socio-economic enigma, which the Party had to face, was a demographic change when, between 1970 and 1975, over six million peasants moved to towns. Thus by 1975 only 39% of the total population lived in rural areas (55% in 1956). Agriculture and rural industry had experienced a drastic shortage of semi-skilled and skilled workers. Work training and vocational training in schools was meant to restore, no doubt, an appreciation (social, moral, and aesthetic) of physical labour as that type of social involvement that contributes to the greatest happiness of the greatest number. Vocational training is gaining in popularity as more and more students, having failed to be admitted into tertiary institutions, turn to industry. In order to attract urban youth to rural areas, literature developed a new genre of the rural theme (derevenskaya tema) in the late sixties. The Russian countryside, very reminiscent of Turgenev's love for countryside, was described as virginal, spacious, free, primitive, uncorrupted, and eternally beautiful.

Apart from social, political, and economic factors, which spelled out major changes in the Soviet school curricula, academic standards were also taken into consideration. There is a common misconception that Soviet schools set far more rigorous academic standards than we do. One writer wrote that the 15-year-old Soviet student who has completed eight-year school has had '249 hours of physics, 142 hours of chemistry, 465 hours of a foreign language, 286 hours of geography, 79 hours of drafting, and 1663 hours of mathematics, plus Russian literature, history, nature study, politics, physical education, music, singing, work training, and 180 hours of practice on a real job'.[54] These figures represent, more or less, the 1965 eight-year school curriculum. However, the impressive number of contact hours that each Soviet pupil receives does not necessarily guarantee the quality of knowledge and the skills needed by Soviet society in the eighties. The 1964–5 top-level inquiry into education unearthed the fact that teaching in ordinary Soviet schools had 'little relationship to

[54]Pennar, J., *Modernization and Diversity in Soviet Education*, New York, 1971, p. 65.

the first-rate science which produced the sputniks; the latter was the result of concentrated research supported by the Government'.[55]

Qualitative changes in the schools after 1970 represent the most definite proof that education, in general, has fallen short of Soviet goals. In particular, the curriculum reforms in science and mathematics in elementary and secondary schools suggest that these two disciplines are still being regarded as the most important in the school programme. Soviet educators have, apparently, borrowed and adapted, according to Jacoby, the American secondary school curriculum, which encourages creativity rather than rote learning, catering for individual differences and induction before deduction. The article in the newspaper *Literaturnaya Ukraina* in 1970, which was highly critical of low academic standards in the teaching of sciences in secondary schools, was typical of a growing wave of dissatisfaction among educationalists with obsolete teaching methods and textbooks. Curriculum reforms in primary and secondary schools resulted in a total reexamination of syllabuses, teaching methods, and textbooks. The November 1966 decree 'On methods of furthering the improvement of educational process in secondary school' and the decree of universal education up to the age of 17 (June 1972), embodying Lenin's dream in the 1919 law on the fundamental aims and principles of the Soviet educational system, underline the country's insatiable desire to perfect its educational process.

The most remarkable educational reforms have taken place after 1970. As a result of the legislation on shortening the primary phase of education from four to three years in 1969 the 1970/1 school year began with the new three-year primary curriculum. Formal learning of core disciplines began after grade 3. In August 1968, to aid the decree of universal military service, compulsory pre-conscription military training was introduced in all schools for boys aged 15 or more.

From the above it is clear that the fundamental aims and principles of the Soviet educational system, as laid down by the Eighth Congress of the Party (March 1919), have now been almost fulfilled. After 1970 Soviet education has been characterized by an impressive numerical expansion. In 1978, 4.7 million children completed grade 8 (or 95.3% compared with 87.4% in 1970) and 5.1 million completed grade

[55]Jacoby, S., *Inside Soviet Schools*, New York, 1974, p. 18.

10. The number of students who continued their secondary education beyond grade 8 had grown from 80% (1970) to 97.8% in 1978.[56] The teacher–pupil ratio had improved from 1:29 in 1940 to 1:18 in 1976.[57] These figures show that almost all children aged between 7 and 17 were in school and, hence, universal compulsory secondary education was possible. Qualitative changes were equally impressive. Kashin summarizes these in his latest article 'Ob itogakh perekhoda sovetskoi shkoly na novoe soderzhanie obshchego obrazovaniya'.[58] The greatest changes have taken place in grade 4, which has become the first year of secondary schooling. Curriculum reforms in the humanities (which consist of two basic strands: (1) the native tongue, Russian, foreign languages, and literature, (2) history, politics, and economic geography) were designed to improve communist indoctrination and moral education in schools. History courses are more politically oriented. M. Nechkina, who co-ordinated curriculum changes in history in the sixties, has introduced a systematic and sequential study of history in grades 7, 8, 9, and 10 instead of elementary history in grades 7 and 8 and history of the USSR in grades 9 and 10. Here, particular innovations are the works of Lenin, documents of the Party, and Brezhnev's speeches. Marxist–Leninist principles have been incorporated in history courses. Literature was also reexamined on ideological, political, and moral grounds. The potential political and moral role of literature in upbringing was reiterated. The new textbooks include a whole series of Marxist articles such as 'Tolstoy and contemporary working movements', 'On proletarian culture', and others. Soviet literature is studied against the background of the programme of the CPSU, and seminars are held in senior grades. The author, however, is critical of dryness and lack of clarity in teaching methods that need to be changed. The Russian-language curriculum in grades 4–8 was modified to include the culture of speech, stylistics, and lexicology in order to raise the level of instruction.

The most extreme changes have taken place in mathematics and basic sciences. The teaching of mathematics in secondary schools,

[56] *Uchitelskaya gazeta*, 20 Feb., 1979, p. 2.
[57] Panachin, F., O podgotovke i povyshenii kvalifikatsii...', Ibid., p. 8.
[58] Kashin, M., *Sovetskaya Pedagogika*, No. 3, 1976, pp. 26–30.

according to Soviet educationalists, required immediate attention. The immediate problem was that of transferring advanced mathematics into junior grades, and the most successful curriculum reform was in mathematics in grades 4 and 5, which now organically links the teaching of arithmetic, algebra, and geometry. The programme in grades 9 and 10 was expanded to include mathematical induction, linear equation, logarithmic and trigonometric functions, analytic geometry, algebraic analysis. In physics in grades 6–7 the pupil had to study molecular kinetic, electronic, and atomic theory. The programme in grades 8–10 included the theory of relativity, Maxwell's electromagnetic field, and so on. New textbooks were written for chemistry and biology. Many new electives (additional courses to the ones that are prescribed) have been introduced, among them cybernetics, geology, and logic. The Ministry of Education of the USSR has approved seventy new electives in 1975, and the number of pupils taking these electives has increased by almost one-third from 5,804,000 in 1971 to 8,501,000 in 1973.[59]

The above curriculum reforms in Soviet education reflect the Party's concern with the quality of education (high academic standards are being achieved) as well as political socialization in the school. The twenty-fifth Congress of the Party (1976) has emphasized the unity between political, labour, and moral upbringing. The first important task of teachers, as envisaged in the editorial of *Sovetskaya Pedagogika* (June 1976) is to educate 'ideologically convinced and highly moral young citizens of the land of the Soviet; to impart to children the love of labour and respect towards manual professions and active striving to participate in the creation of material and spiritual values of communist society'.[60] Brezhnev had this to say about moral upbringing at the Congress: 'Nothing elevates the identity as much as an active position in life, conscientious attitude towards civic duty, when the unity of word and deed becomes the everyday norm of behaviour.'[60] Addressing school delegates of the Third All-Union Congress, 'The study of life, activity, and works of V. I. Lenin in secondary schools', Brezhnev summarized the primary Party organizations tasks thus: 'The honorary duty of Party organiz-

[59]Kashin, M., *Sovetskaya Pedagogika*, No. 3, 1976, p. 30.
[60]Editorial, *Sovetskaya Pedagogika*, No. 6, 1976, p. 7.

ations, pedagogical collectives, and the Komsomol is to maintain, at any cost, the aspiration of youth for the Leninist work, to perceive the leaders' contribution to life, and the historical experience of the CPSU. It is very important that fulfilling the Leninist behest to study communism should become a deep, inner requirement of every young person.'[61]

4. Conclusion

We may, therefore, conclude that in one respect, one aspect of Soviet education remained undeviating and stereotyped during the past sixty years, namely the key role of the Party in formulation and implementation of educational policy. Lenin's idea that education is a decisive component of the cultural revolution and political socialization has been 'constantly borne in mind and scrupulously observed'.[62]

Soviet education has made great strides since the 1919 Declaration on the principles of communist education, which were so high that it took nearly sixty years and ten five-year plans to accomplish, but not completely, what has been envisaged.

How much has the Soviet educational system changed, in retrospect, between 1917 and 1978 and how does it differ from the Tsarist education?

In the 1920s Soviet education had to solve the following two problems: to educate 100 million illiterate people and to create a Soviet intelligentsia. As these two tasks were fulfilled by 1939, the authorities were able to concentrate on curriculum reforms, which were to improve the overall quality of education and upbringing (political socialization) and to raise the minimum compulsory schooling from the seven-year (1949) to the ten-year (1975) programme.

There were, of course, deviations from the 1918 decree concerning the single labour school in the RSFSR. During the 1920s, Soviet educational thought was under the influence of pragmatism and the theory of education for its own sake (education not bound by the

[61]Navstrechu XXV syezdu KPSS, *Sovetskaya Pedagogika*, No. 2, 1976, p. 6.
[62]Tomiak, op. cit., p. 49.

demands of utility) during which it departed considerably from Marxist pedagogy. For instance, the proponents of de-schooling defended, we are told, anti-Leninist views regarding upbringing. Some had put in the first place biological factors and heredity in upbringing (pedology). The Marxist position was reasserted in the June 1936 decree, which ended, once and for all, anti-Marxist, i.e. other than Marxist, schools of educational thought.

At the beginning of the 1950s, the end of the Stalinist period in education, educationalists became increasingly aware of the gap between school and life.

It was an excuse to increase compulsory schooling from seven to eight years and to reintroduce the forgotten feature, namely production or work training in the upper grades. However, secondary general educational labour polytechnical schools (secondary polytechnics for short) being, despite its name, highly formal and academic, which we are now told was a form of élitism under Stalin (not more than 10% of the 18-year-olds completed the ten-year school in the 1950s), were unable to provide adequate and effective production training. In short, the attempt to de-formalize schooling by introducing work training was a dismal failure for reasons that were not entirely educational but socio-political, economic, and practical. It became clear that the ten-year school should give a general comprehensive schooling for Soviet youth instead of ill-advised early vocational training for blue-collar professions.

There is little doubt now that the Stalinist educational system was élitist. This resulted in a growth of the Soviet intelligentsia, some of whom became the ruling stratum, the Establishment or a State bourgeoisie. To offset the qualitative distinction between the intelligentsia, especially the ruling stratum and workers, the ten-year compulsory schooling was achieved in 1975. This means two things. Every new worker would have completed secondary education after 1975 and hence, in terms of education, would be superior to his semi-educated predecessor. This, hopefully, would bridge the gap between the intelligentsia and the workers. Perhaps it aims to diminish the prestige of the university-educated class by extending the general education of the worker–technicians and in many cases paying them higher wages than tertiary educated professionals. For example, a bus driver gets the same salary as a holder of an MSc employed in scientific research.[63]

The official view or theory subscribed to in the USSR is that Soviet society of today consists of two classes, workers (including kolkhoz workers) and a 'prosloika' (stratum), i.e. intelligentsia. This intelligentsia, as pointed out by Nove (1975), can include everyone who is not a worker. The intelligentsia consists of a great many badly paid professionals ranging from shop assistants to teachers, who really are the lower intelligentsia. As higher education is a necessary (though not sufficient) condition of upward social mobility (senior posts, especially for almost all of the ruling élite are tertiary trained), it is obvious that access to tertiary education is vital for upward social mobility.[64] It would be interesting to compare social groups that made up the Soviet intelligentsia during the late thirties, when the children of the former exploiting and ruling classes were discriminated against with that of the seventies. It would not be unreasonable to suggest that the original people's intelligentsia, drawn, in the main from workers and peasants, is no longer feasible in the eighties. This may be attributed to at least two major factors. Demographic changes between 1939 and 1975 with respect to a dramatic shift between rural and urban population from 67:33 (1939) to 27:73 in 1975 more than reversed the former dominance of the rural population in favour of the urban class. Matthews (1975) shows that the 1966/7 sample of first-year students at Rostov University consisted of children from the kolkhoz workers (2.5%).[65] The table in *Narodnoe khozyaistvo SSSR v 1970 godu** (Moscow, 1971) illustrates the following social structure of the VUZ (vysshee uchebnoe zavedenie—higher education institution) student body employees (53.1%), workers (36.2%), and peasants (10.7%). Thus the Soviet pattern for social groups in higher education is similar to the pattern in bourgeois countries.

Another interesting sociological development is a manifested horizontal rather than vertical mobility among the eighteen-year-olds in

[63]*Novy Mir*, Vol. 6, 1976, p. 215.
[64]Nove, A., Is there a ruling class in the USSR?, *Soviet Studies*, Oct., 1975, p. 617.
[65]Matthews, M., Soviet students..., *Soviet Studies*, Jan., 1975, p. 88.
*See Glossary.

1975. In 1965 between 96% and 98% of all eighteen-year-olds who completed the ten-year school wished to enter university. Now only half of them wish to complete higher education. The differences between the 1975 and 1976 career expectancy of the eighteen-year-olds are tabulated below.

Type of career	1976 (%)	1975 (%)
Tertiary student (VUZ)	15	50
Technical student (tekhnikum) }	21	20
PTU*		2.5
Work	64	27

*Vocational/technical schools.

It is estimated that of all school-leavers less than 15% may want to continue with their tertiary education after 1976 and were accepted in the 1975/6 academic year. The vast majority would have entered technical colleges (PTUs) or joined the workforce. In other words, the USSR has experienced an influx of university-trained professionals but what the country really needed in the late seventies and early eighties is a vast army of secondary-educated technicians (tekhniki) because the PTUs have failed to attract sufficient numbers of school-leavers.

The statistics concerning higher education in *Narodnoe khozyaistvo SSSR v 1974 g.* (Moscow, 1975) show that Soviet universities have reached their saturation point and the rate of intake of new students is tapering off. If the intake rate was approximately 30% between 1965 and 1970 it has decreased to 10% between 1971 and 1975. There has also been a decrease of graduates in engineering, communication, agriculture, health, and education. In most cases the 1975 figures are as low as those of 1970 or earlier. For example, mechanical engineering has decreased from 75,000 graduates in 1971 to 72,000 in 1974, a loss of 4%. In agricultural science and forestry the number has decreased from 58,000 in 1970 to 51,000 in 1977, a loss of 12%.[66] 'We have tens of thousands of holders of DSc (doktor

[66] *Narodnoe khozyaistvo SSSR v 1974 g.*, Moscow, 1975, pp. 693–5.

nauk) and hundreds of thousands of MSc (kandidat nauk),' writes a Soviet sociologist, 'but what is the degree holder able to do?'[67] The author is suggesting that higher education is no longer a means for upward social mobility as it was in the case of the 1950s.

The problem of the schools being divorced from life, which was debated by Pisarev, Tolstoy, Plekhanov, Ushinsky, and others in the second half of the nineteenth century, and later continued by Krupskaya, Lenin, and others in the 1917 educational reforms, is just as relevant today as in the past. It seems that the gap between school and life is being gradually solved by Soviet educators and the party. Khrushchev's battle-cry 'prepare for practical work' (1958) did not stir workers and peasants, and it upset the intelligentsia. Today's secondary school is not comprehensive enough in its approach to education. The upper grades act as introductory faculties to university. But the matriculants have a vague notion of contemporary technology, literature, and art; they know neither technology nor foreign languages. 'It's time', writes Bestuzhev-Lada, 'to consider a truly comprehensive education, inseparably linked with vocational training.'[68] This critical comment suggests that the ten-year school is still academically oriented and that its matriculants still regard themselves as one in twenty (true of the 1950s) and that they have failed to understand that the era of one in twenty is over. The structure of the secondary school is still geared to university entrance. So the first choice of its pupils is higher education followed by technical college. Professional–technical school is the third choice. Ideologically, Soviet education (which includes vospitanie or moral education) has remained conditioned and restrained in that it has been an instrument of the Party since the October Revolution. The Party plays the key role in formulation and implementation of educational policy. Political socialization and moral education in a secular state, which will be examined later, has been intensified under the Brezhnev regime. Collective upbringing, in which the children's collective becomes the agent of adult society, has been perfected. The process of collective socialization will be thoroughly discussed later.

[67]Bestuzhev-Lada, I., Sotsialnye problemy sovetskogo obraza zhizni, *Novy Mir*, No. 7, 1976, p. 219.

[68]Ibid., p. 218.

The process of collective (socio-political) socialization is, clearly, the main difference between Soviet and Tsarist education. Dialectic materialism, which permeates the Soviet educational system, had little in common with materialism and idealism in Russia before the Revolution. The one thing the two systems had in common was that education lacked autonomy and was directly controlled by the State and politics.

Finally, contrasting the ten-year curriculum of Soviet schools in 1980 with the eight-year Tsarist grammar school in 1914, we see certain remarkable similarities. In both schools the emphasis in the upper grades was on Russian language, mathematics, and physics. The study of history, geography, and nature (junior science) is similar. The marked departure of the Soviet secondary school was away from foreign languages towards science. The Tsarist grammar school emphasized Latin, French, and German, which represented one-third of the curriculum in the final year. In the Soviet school the study of languages has been cut back by 400%, from 77 lessons per week in all grades (1914) to 16 (1975).[69] In place of biblical studies, philosophy, and legal studies, Soviet educationalists introduced military training, social studies, chemistry and biology, and work training. The Tsarist grammar school maintained a delicate balance between the humanities and sciences, which, until now, has not been the case of the Soviet ten-year school. Further similarities could be observed in the curriculum reforms of 1914 and 1980. Both introduced legal studies to aid, no doubt, the would-be civil servants. The grammar schools began to adopt the uchebnye kabinety (departments) in history, geography, mathematics, etc., before 1914.[70] Now we learn from Soviet educational periodicals that schools are organized into various departments and that kabinetnaya sistema is, indeed, the latest innovation (1975) in Soviet education. In short, the Soviet ten-year school in 1980 has much in common with the academically oriented Tsarist grammar school of 1914.

[69]*Istoriya pedagogiki*, Moscow, 1974, p. 308.
[70]Ibid., p. 309.

CHAPTER 2

The Soviet School as an Organization

1. Introduction

1.1. SOCIAL AND POLITICAL STRUCTURE OF THE USSR

The official statistics show that the social structure in the USSR is changing with a steady growth of the working class and the intelligentsia, and a gradual decline of the collective farmers. The percentage of urban population against rural population was 48:52 in 1959 but 62:38 in 1978. However, the ratio of the working class and the intelligentsia against the collective farmers has changed dramatically since 1939 from 50:50 to 85:15 in 1978.[1] In 1978 the collective farmers (kolkhoznoe krestyanstvo) constituted only 15.1% of Soviet society and 84.9% were workers and professionals (rabochie i sluzhashchie). The white-collar workers numbered 38 million against 16 million of the kolkhozniki.[2]

Rural population and the collective farmers are now in a minority in the Soviet Union. The growing urban population suggests that fewer educational opportunities would be available in the rural areas and that the opportunities for workers may well exceed those for collective farmers. The social structure of the USSR can be seen from Table 4.

Demographic changes have influenced education planning. The country's population has increased by 66 million between 1956 and 1978, but the rate of growth is slowing down. For instance, the overall birth rate in the USSR has declined from 47 per 1,000 of population in 1913 to 18.2 in 1978. In 1969 it went as low as 17 per 1000.

---

[1] *Narodnoe khozyaistvo za 60 let*, Moscow, 1977, p. 8.
[2] *Narodnoe khozyaistvo SSSR v 1978 g.*, Moscow, 1979, pp. 7–9.

TABLE 4. *The social structure of the USSR* (*millions*)

	1913	1924	1928	1939	1959	1970	1975	1977
1. Intelligentsia	2.4	4.4	5.2	16.7	18.8	22.7	22.0	22.7
2. Workers	14.6	10.4	12.4	33.5	49.5	56.8	60.9	61.6
3. Collective farmers co-operative handicraftsmen	—	1.2	2.9	47.2	31.4	20.5	17.1	15.7
4. Peasants and handicraftsmen	66.7	75.4	74.9	2.6	0.3	0.0	0.0	0.0
5. Bourgeoisie	16.3	8.5	4.6					

Source: *Narodnoe khozyaistvo SSSR v 1974 g.*, Moscow, 1975, p. 38. *Narodnoe khozyaistvo za 60 let*, Moscow, 1977, p. 8.

The proportion of children in the population has decreased from 12% in 1959 to 8.5% in 1970, but it has improved to 9% in 1974.

The general rate of population growth in the USSR in 1974 was 9% compared with 18% in 1960. The rate of growth of the different republics varies greatly (Table 5). Soviet Asia reports the highest general rate of growth of population and the Baltic states the lowest.

TABLE 5. *The rate of growth of population in the USSR* (*1978*) (*per 1000 of population*)

USSR	8.5	(9.2 in 1969)
Tadzhikistan	29.2	(28.6 in 1969)
Uzbekistan	27.0	(26.8 in 1969)
Turkmenistan	26.4	(27.3 in 1969)
Kirghizstan	22.3	(22.6 in 1969)
Azerbaidzhan	18.2	(22.3 in 1969)
Kazakhstan	17.0	(17.3 in 1969)
Armenia	16.7	(17.6 in 1969)
Moldavia	10.3	(11.5 in 1969)
Georgia	9.7	(11.2 in 1969)
Byelorussia	6.8	(8.5 in 1969)
Lithuania	5.3	(8.7 in 1969)
RSFSR	5.6	(5.7 in 1969)
Ukraine	4.0	(6.0 in 1969)
Estonia	2.7	(4.2 in 1969)
Latvia	1.2	(2.9 in 1969)

Source: *Narodnoe khozyaistvo SSSR v 1978 g.*, Moscow, 1979, p. 27.

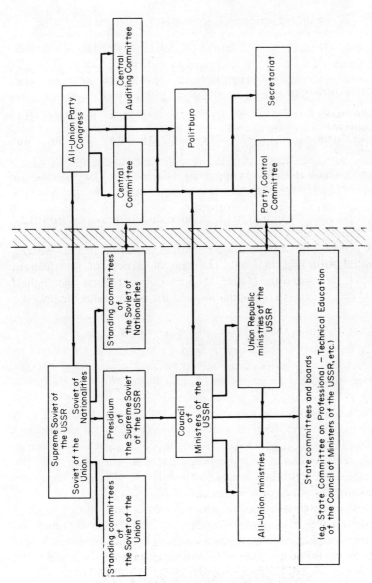

FIG. 1. *Structure of the Soviet Government and the Communist Party*

The political structure of the Soviet Union

In theory (Fig. 1) the structure of the Soviet Government resembles the pattern of a Western European democracy. According to the constitution, the highest organ of power in the USSR is the Supreme Soviet of the USSR (Verkhovny Sovet SSSR), which is elected every four years. In practice, much of the work of the Supreme Soviet is performed by the two main subordinate bodies—the Presidium of the Supreme Soviet and the Council of Ministers.

The Supreme Soviet consists of two chambers resembling the Upper and Lower House in the British Parliament, the Soviet of the Union (1 deputy for every 300,000 of population), and the Soviet of Nationalities, the latter representing union republics, autonomous republics, and autonomous regions. The membership of the Soviet of Nationalities would be elected on the following formula: 25 deputies for every union republic, 11 deputies for every autonomous republic, 5 deputies for every autonomous region, and 1 deputy for every national area. The total number of deputies in 1970 was 1517.

The Supreme Soviet is said to exercise exclusive legislative power. It elects the Presidium, appoints the Council of Ministers, and, if required, amends the constitution by a two-thirds' vote.

The Presidium of the Supreme Soviet convenes the sessions of the Supreme Soviet, issues decrees, interprets laws, releases and appoints (subject to the recommendation of the Chairman of the Council of Ministers) ministers of the USSR, appoints and removes high military and diplomatic officials, ratifies treaties and confers decorations and honours. The Presidium consists of 33 members: a chairman (a nominal Head of State), 15 deputy chairmen (1 for each union republic), 1 secretary, and 16 other deputies. The Presidium, like the Supreme Soviet and the Council of Ministers, is subordinate (in practice) to the Politburo and Secretariat.

The Council of Ministers of the USSR (formerly the Council of People's Commissars) consists of 7 deputy chairmen, the premiers of the 15 Union Republics, the head of the Central Statistical Department, the chairmen of 18 other State committees, the chairman of the State Bank (Narodny Bank), 15 ministers, the chairman of the Capital Investment Bank, 5 members of the State Planning Commission

(Gosplan), the chairman of the Commission of Soviet Control, and 7 others of ministerial rank. Normally, the Presidium of the Council of Ministers, which is the executive, consists of the chairman of the Council, and 3 first deputy chairmen. The Soviet Union is ruled by the Council of Ministers and the Presidium. Their membership is drawn from the highest ranks of the CPSU. The Chairman of the Council of Ministers is referred to, outside of the Soviet Union, as the Soviet Premier, who is the chief executive of the Soviet Union. In the past this post was occupied by Lenin, Stalin, and Kosygin. The Council of Ministers co-ordinates and directs the administration of the ministries, ensures execution of the national economic plan, ensures the maintenance of public order, directs and conducts foreign policy, co-ordinates the armed forces, maintains the stability of monetary and credit systems, issues decrees and directives ensuring enforcement of laws throughout the Soviet Union, and so on. In theory it is responsible and accountable only to the Supreme Soviet. In practice, however, there is an interlocking directorate between the Politburo (the top executive body of the CPSU) and the council of Ministers, which is the centre of power and control. Since the Council of Ministers and the Supreme Soviet are too large for effective decision-making and implementation process (e.g. the Council of Ministers includes nearly 100 members), the Presidium of the Council of Ministers (Kosygin—chairman and 2 first deputy chairmen, and 9 deputy chairmen) assumes the overall responsibility for the governing of the Soviet people.

The Communist Party

It is suggested that the interlocking directorate of the CPSU and Government characterizes the dual control of the Soviet system. The Party–State duality (the Politburo versus the Presidium of the Council of Ministers and the Presidium of the Supreme Soviet) distinguishes the Brezhnev leadership. Theoretically, the supreme organ of power is the Party Congress, which is required to meet not less often than once every four years. The CPSU rules require the Party Congress to elect the Central Committee, which, in turn elects the Politburo and the CPSU Secretariat. In practice, however, the Politburo and the Secretariat recruit their own members. The Politburo appears to be some kind of closed oligarchy. It is also a self-perpetuating body. Its members are sponsored or chosen, the entire process being virtually predetermined by the CPSU pyramid-like hierarchy.

The three most important loci of power and control are the Politburo, the Secretariat, and the Central Committee of the CPSU. The Central Committee directs party policies between meetings of the All-Union congresses and it meets at least twice a year. Membership (although very unstable) in the Central Committee provides prestige, status, access to information, and power. Membership has risen from 225 in 1956 to 360 in 1966. The Secretariat of the Central Committee is the most powerful political organ in the Soviet Union. It ranks (unofficially, of course) only second to the Politburo in power and control. The six secretaries (1971), Brezhnev, Ustinov, Suslov, Demichev, Kulakov, and Kirilenko, who are members of the Politburo, represent the dual relationship between the two executive organs. The number of secretaries in the Secretariat varied from three (February to July 1955) to ten (December 1957 to 1960). In 1971 there were still only ten secretaries responsible for the administration of the Secretariat and implementation of the CPSU policies on all matters affecting the Soviet society.

The Politburo, regarded by many as the apex of power within the CPSU and the locus of power and control in the Soviet Union, is the nerve centre of the Party and the Government. Its membership is very small. In April 1971 the Twenty-fourth Party Congress increased the Politburo membership to fifteen. The Politburo includes both permanent and probationary (kandidat v chleny) members. There is a powerful inner circle within the Politburo itself. It would normally include up to six very senior and very influential leaders of the Party. In the past, the five most powerful men within the Politburo were Brezhnev, Suslov, Kirilenko, Kosygin, and Podgorny.

1.2. ADMINISTRATIVE STRUCTURE OF SOVIET EDUCATION

The entire system of public education in the Soviet Union is administered by a pyramid-like structure of the highly centralized government bureaucracy. The Party, in particular the Politburo and the Central Committee of the CPSU, together with the USSR Supreme Soviet and Council of Ministers, is responsible for policy making in education. Each republic and there are fifteen of them, has its own Ministry of Education which, in theory, may enact legislation

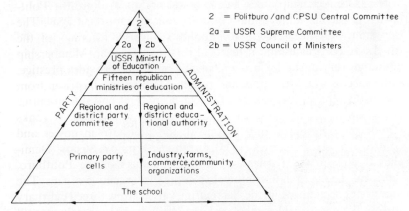

FIG. 2. *Administration of Soviet education.*

on education. In practice, however, the USSR Ministry of Education and the Ministry of Education of the RSFSR (the Russian Republic) seem to set a pattern for other ministries to follow. At the regional and local level, educational policy is implemented by the regional and local educational authority (Oblono and the Rayono). Neither of these institutions has the power or the means to formulate legislation on education. The main task of the Oblono and the Rayono in this educational hierarchy is to estimate projected enrolments, staffing, and budgeting.

Two administrative characteristics (Fig. 2) are peculiar to the Soviet educational system, namely the Party's rigid control of all levels of education and the highly centralized bureaucracy.

There are three separate All-Union ministries of education responsible for education. Pre-school, primary, and secondary education is controlled by the USSR Ministry of Education (since 1966). Secondary specialized (colleges) and tertiary education are under the jurisdiction of the USSR. Ministry of Higher and Secondary Specialized

Education. Vocational–technical education is under the State Committee of the USSR Council of Ministers for Vocational and Technical Education.

For our purposes we would need to examine briefly the function and the policy guidelines of the USSR Ministry of Education.

The USSR Ministry of Education was set up in 1966 in order to synchronize the educational structure and to ensure uniformity of academic standards, curricula, syllabuses, textbooks, and teaching methods. Its principal tasks are:

1. Ensuring communist education of children and youth, and providing for their spiritual, physical, and aesthetic development (socio-political);
2. Management of pre-school education, primary and secondary general education, and adult education;
3. Promotion and co-ordination of educational research in the country;
4. Elaboration and carrying out of measures on the further development and improvement of the system of people's education and presenting the corresponding proposals for the consideration of the Government;
5. Specification of targets for the current and long-term educational plans in collaboration with the Council of Ministers of the republics;
6. Determination of the content of general secondary polytechnic education and labour training of the pupils;
7. Improvement of the educational curricula for secondary schools of general education;
8. Preparation and publishing of school textbooks;
9. Rendering assistance to the republics of the Union in improving the management of schools and pre-school and adult educational establishments;
10. Fostering improvement in the professional skills of teachers and other workers in education;
11. Development of foreign relations in the field of education.[3]

[3]The USSR Ministry of Education. *On the Main Trends in the Field of Education in the USSR in 1968–1970*, Moscow, 1970, pp. 25–27. The USSR Ministry of Education, *Public Education in the Soviet Union*, Moscow, 1967, pp. 46–47.

1.3. FINANCING AND PLANNING OF SOVIET EDUCATION

Sixteen per cent of the 1974 annual budget was allocated to education. The details of expenditure on education in the Soviet Union are given in Table 6.

TABLE 6. *Expenditure on education and science (in billions of roubles)*

Budget	1940	1965	1970	1971	1972	1973	1974	1976
Education and science (total)	2.3	17.5	24.8	26.3	28.0	29.8	31.5	32.1
% of the budget	12.9	17.2	16	16	16.1	16.2	16	14.9

Source: *Narodnoe khozyaistvo SSSR v 1974 g.*, Moscow, 1975, pp. 756–7; *Narodnoe khozyaistvo SSSR za 60 let*, Moscow, 1977, p. 755.

The details of the distribution of educational expenditure are given in Table 7.

Finance for education comes from seven major sources: the Union, republican, and local budgets (the republican and local budgets con-

TABLE 7. *Distribution of expenditure of education (in millions of roubles)*

Selected items	1965	1970	1971	1972	1973	1974	1976
1. Pre-school education	1695	2600	2756	2923	3168	3329	3713
2. Children's homes and boarding and special schools	363	411	426	447	483	506	549
3. Primary and secondary education	5778	6953	7197	7605	8286	8460	8766
4. Cultural–educational work	424	703	752	805	873	926	1035
5. Tertiary education	1483	1188	2296	2465	2704	2840	3108
6. Secondary specialized education	829	1221	1274	1412	1647	1711	1848
7. Vocational–technical education	840	1313	1409	1554	1684	1926	2254
8. Mass media	360	748	826	911	981	1117	1322
9. Science	4126	6425	6916	7301	7502	7899	7897
Total	16,928	21,562	23,852	24,423	27,528	28,714	33,791

Source: *Narodnoe khozyaistvo SSSR v 1974 g.*, Moscow, 1975, p. 759; *Narodnoe khozyaistvo SSSR za 60 let*; Moscow, 1977, p. 755.

54   *Education in the USSR*

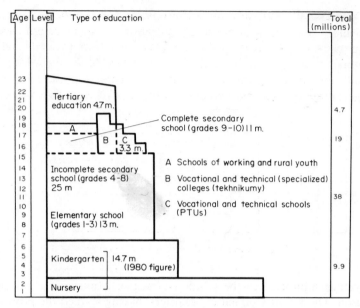

FIG. 3. *Structure of the Soviet educational system (1978).*

tribute the lion's share of 90%); parents, who pay for the maintenance of their children in crèches, kindergartens, pioneer camps, and boarding schools; social security (trade unions) and State economic organizations.[4]

Educational planning is dependent on the development of the national economy. The growth of Soviet industry, agriculture, and commerce requires the preparation of sufficient numbers of vocational–technical trained personnel. As Tomiak notes: 'educational planning had to be closely integrated with economic planning, particularly at the levels of vocational–technical secondary specialized and higher education.'[5] All educational institutions, together with administration, ministries, Party, trade union, and Komsomol organizations following the guidelines of the USSR State Planning

[4]Unesco International Institute for Educational Planning, *Educational Planning in the USSR*, Paris, 1969, p. 164.
[5]Tomiak, J., *The Soviet Union*, London, 1972, p. 51.

Commission (Gosplan) submit proposals for the development of primary, secondary, and tertiary education. Gosplan determines the quota of the different kinds of professional training in all educational establishments. In particular, it specifies the number of students to be admitted and trained in vocational–technical schools, secondary specialized colleges, and tertiary institutions.[6] The final version of the

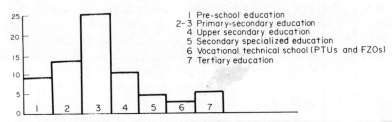

I   Pre-school education
2-3 Primary-secondary education
4   Upper secondary education
5   Secondary specialized education
6   Vocational technical school (PTUs and FZOs)
7   Tertiary education

FIG. 4. *Total enrolments (in millions) in different types of schools.*

draft is submitted to the USSR Council of Ministers for consideration. The USSR Council of Ministers, having studied the proposals, submits the long-term educational planning to the Central Committee of the CPSU for approval, which, if approved, are adopted at the Congress of the CPSU. Short-term educational planning is approved by the Economic Committee of the Soviet of Nationalities and the Budget Committees of the Soviet of the Union and of the Soviet of Nationalities.

Nearly 90 million people, or almost one in every three, were studying in 1975. Of these, 49 million attended polytechnic schools, 3.3 million attended vocational and technical colleges, 4.5 million attended secondary specialized colleges, 4.8 attended tertiary institutions, and 29 million adults attended in-service education. Nearly 8 million students were enrolled in pre-tertiary vocational and technical colleges—twice as many as in tertiary institutions. Of the 5 million who completed secondary education in 1975, over 1 million were admitted into secondary specialized colleges (technikumy), and just under a million were admitted into tertiary institutions. Tertiary education is avail-

[6]The USSR Ministry of Education, *On the Main Trends in Education in the USSR in 1968–1970*, Moscow, 1970, p. 81.

able for one in every five Soviet matriculants. The majority enter professional and technical schools or join the labour force.

The aim of this study is to examine social, moral, and political aspects of Soviet education during the 1970s and to evaluate them in the light of the educational policy of the Brezhnev group. It has been argued in this work that Soviet education is political in nature and that it is a highly efficient and necessary instrument of political socialization. However, political socialization is merely one important aspect of Soviet education. Educationalists in the USSR place an equal emphasis on social and moral aspects. The role of Soviet education is to assist in the formation of a communist society or, as Brezhnev put it, 'we must train the appropriate personnel, large contingents of new specialists capable of tackling ever broader and more complicated problems of building communism'.[7]

The Soviet educational system is one of the most massive, uniform socializing agencies in the world. The system, created after the October Revolution of 1917, is a Marxist–Leninist challenge to traditional education in bourgeois society. The ideal of a universal and compulsory ten-year secondary education for all Soviet youth adopted in principle in 1951, has been achieved in 1975. The USSR is one of the few countries where, to use Lenin's words, universal productive labour has been wedded to universal education. The most remarkable feat of Soviet education is its high degree of uniformity of curricula, textbooks, and teaching methods. The ten-year school curriculum is identical throughout the Soviet Union. Such uniformity makes it possible, among other things, to maintain comparatively similar educational standards in all republics. Every schoolchild, irrespective of his abilities and needs, receives the same quantity and quality of instruction. This uniformity, at least in theory, is supposed to give equal opportunity for all Soviet matriculants should they decide to enter a college or university.

The Soviet educational system embraces the principle of unity and continuity of all levels of public education (Figs. 3 and 4). Thus the USSR claims to have established a single, centralized system of public education from the kindergarten to university.

---

[7]Brezhnev, L., *Our Course: Peace and Socialism*, Moscow, 1975, p. 190.

2. The School System

2.1. PRE-SCHOOL EDUCATION

Makarenko believed that if a student was badly brought up, his teachers were largely to blame. Today this view is still upheld. Upbringing and the officially sanctioned communist education is the most important task of education and rearing for citizenship.

Pre-school education in the USSR offers the unique opportunity for early socialization, which represents the first phase of carefully planned and closely supervised political socialization, to be followed up and continued in secondary and tertiary institutions.

In the USSR there are two kinds of pre-school institutions: nursery (yasli) and kindergarten (detski sad). Nurseries accept children between 6 months and 3 years of age. The children are normally divided into small groups according to their age; they are looked after by trained nurses and sisters. Although nurseries are not free, the fee is very moderate—up to 10 roubles a month.

Kindergartens accept children from 3 to 7 years of age. They are not merely an expedient solution to the problems of working parents but also a vital agency in preparing children for their future in a communist society. It is here that children receive their first taste of collective life, discipline, and regimentation. 'The precious feeling of collectivism begins right here', explained one director of a large Moscow kindergarten.[8] The fundamental difference between a Soviet kindergarten and ours is that the former is a formal institution controlled by the State, whereas the latter is a government-sponsored community effort. Soviet kindergartens perform three distinct and interrelated functions. They provide baby-sitting facilities, political socialization, and early education. Since 1960, when the Institute of Pre-school Education was established, Soviet educationalists increasingly stress the importance of early socialization and moral education in pre-school upbringing. Their views are expressed on the pages of the monthly journal *Doshkolnoe Vospitanie* (*Pre-school upbringing*) which has been coming out since 1928.

Kalinin (1969) defines the aims of pre-school education as easing the burden of the new school curriculum. He believes that the new

[8]Jacoby, S., *Inside Soviet Schools*, Hill & Wang, New York, 1974, p. 46.

primary school curriculum requires rather complicated analytical and synthetical activity and great volitional effort on the part of children.[9] He is, clearly, preoccupied with academic learning in the pre-school education. Some pre-school educationalists fear that an academic bias may ignore the child's social, emotional, and aesthetic development.[10] The 1976 pre-school curriculum in the USSR was based on physical, intellectual, moral, and aesthetic rearing of pre-school children in accordance with the 'developmental and individual psycho-physiological traits'.[11] If there is any bias in the Soviet pre-school curriculum it is political rather than academic. The kindergarten (detski sad) is a model of communist upbringing of children.[12]

Soviet pre-school educationalists claim that the age group from 0 to 4 years is the period of the most intensive physical and intellectual development of a child. Hirst, a prominent British moral philosopher, believes that man, from the time he is born, is socialized by patterns of thought, emotions, attitudes, values, and psycho-motor skills.[13]

Although the idea of public pre-school education was developed, among others, by the great English Utopian thinker Robert Owen, it was in Russia under Lenin that it was institutionalized. Since then it has become the most elaborate programme of collective upbringing in human history. It began in November 1917 with the decree on pre-school education, which stated that all public education of children was to take place in the first few months of life. Nadezhda Krupskaya, an eminent moral educationalist in the 1920s and 1930s (Lenin's wife), wrote that if pre-school upbringing and instruction were academic, the primary school would be raised to a higher level. Originally, in the 1919 educational reforms, pre-school education was to fulfil two tasks: (1) improve elementary education of children and, above all, (2) emancipate women. Lenin also reminded Russia that pre-school institutions were the shoots of communism.

The 1969 kindergarten curriculum attached great importance to the relation of pre-school training to life, and it took into account the

[9]Kalinin, A., *Pre-school Education in the USSR*, Moscow, 1969, p. 41.
[10]Ashby, G. F., *Pre-school Theories and Strategies*, MUP, 1972, p. 41.
[11]*Programma vospitaniya v detskom sadu*, Moscow, 1976, p. 4.
[12]Ibid., p. 19.
[13]Kalinin, op. cit., p. 21.

child's age and his psycho-linguistic and physiological characteristics. The curriculum emphasized the uniform character of education and rearing, which aimed at the all-round physical, intellectual, aesthetic, and moral development of the child, which may not be readily available at home.[13] The 1976 curriculum continues and reinforces all previous kindergarten curricula. In the introduction it is claimed that societal pre-school vospitanie (upbringing) is an integral part of the educational system and that it must, together with the family, guarantee communist vospitanie of children and prepare them for school.[14] The manual gives a series of prescriptions for mental, moral, aesthetic, and physical education applicable to children between the ages of 0 and 7. Moral education receives a special treatment in the kindergarten. The child is introduced to various aspects of Soviet reality. Love and respect towards Lenin, the Motherland (Rodina), the native land, and the village are the highlights of political socialization.[15]

Societal and family upbringing of infants is, states the manual, organically linked. The manual, which is obligatory for all kindergarten teachers, defines political and social aims as follows: 'The kindergarten must become a model of communist upbringing of children. In every pre-school centre vospitanie of the child's identity must be interwoven with the formation of the collective and relations within the collective.'[16]

What, then, is the nature and the methods of child rearing in the Soviet kindergarten today? On their arrival at the kindergarten, children are divided into different age groups which correspond to four developmental stages as indicated in Table 8.

Bronfenbrenner, Professor of Human Development and Family Studies at Cornell University, in his study, which was based on his visits to the Soviet Union between 1960 and 1967, claims that child rearing in the first year of life is based on two major principles, namely early experience in collective living and regime. He has observed that by 18 months of age the children are toilet-trained and are learning more complex skills such as dressing themselves. During the first year of life, language training for speech becomes a means for

[14]*Programma vospitaniya v detskom sadu*, Moskva, 1976, p. 3.
[15]Ibid., p. 7.
[16]Ibid., p. 19.

TABLE 8. *Kindergarten groups*

			Age (years)	Activities/lessons
Stage 1	1st group	} Babies	0–1	Games, etc., 10 min in duration
	2nd group		1–2	
Stage 2	1st group	} Junior pre-school group	2–3	Games, etc., 10 sessions weekly, 10–20 min in duration
	2nd group		3–4	
Stage 3	1st group	} Middle pre-school group	4–5	Games, etc., 10 sessions weekly, 10–20 min in duration
	2nd group			
Stage 4	1st group	Senior pre-school group	5–6	Games, etc., 13 sessions weekly, 15–20 min in duration
	2nd group	School group	6–7	14 sessions weekly, 20–30 min in duration

Programma vospitaniya v detskom sadu, Moscow, 1976

developing social, moral, aesthetic, and political behaviour. During this age and the period that follows, the child is at the most impressionistic and suggestible age.

Early speech training, positive attitudes of social behaviour, early collectivism, and accelerated character development are some of the main features of the kindergarten curriculum. Pre-school upbringing in the Soviet Union is based on a number of hidden assumptions, some of which are: that the child prefers work to play; that he prefers to work in a collective rather than alone; that he is capable of a high level of sustained concentration and thus accelerated learning; that he loves ritual repetition, and order; that he is able to grasp elementary social mores.

That speech is emphasized before play is demonstrated in the *Programme of Upbringing in the Kindergarten* (1964), the officially prescribed manual on pre-school education. It says: 'The instructor exploits every moment spent with the child [0–12 months] for the development of speech. In order that the infant learns to discriminate and understand specific words, the instructor speaks to him in short phrases, emphasizes by her intonation the main words in a given sentence.... The speech of the instructor should be emotional and expressive and should reflect her loving, tender relation to the child.[17] The baby is shown different toys and objects and is encouraged to pick out from a collection the one that is named. The game of hide and seek is used to teach the names of adults and other children. The child is also taught to associate phrases with certain actions (clap your hands, etc.). The manual describes how to cultivate in the baby positive attitudes of social behaviour; the chief one being, clearly, collective behaviour. If the instructor is not sufficiently attentive, warns the manual, negative relations may arise among the children. As an example it mentions the attempt by one child to take a toy held by another. Such expressions of egoism, individualism, and selfishness are not tolerated. To off-set these negative, better still, individualistic manifestations, the instructor frequently refers to communal owner-ship and collective play. 'Mine is ours; ours is mine' (Moe eto nashe, nashe moe) becomes the first most fundamental credo of collective socialization that is to influence the child, at least in theory, for the first seventeen years of his life.

As soon as children are able to express themselves, the adult gradu-ally withdraws from his role of game leader so that a self-reliant collective may develop. 'In his third year', states the manual, 'the child should be trained in the following skills and habits: washing his hands before meals, eating neatly and using his right hand predomi-nantly.... He should say thank you after the meal, wash and dry his hands by himself, put on and take off various items of clothing and footwear.'[18] A number of American observers, according to Jacoby, have been forcefully struck by early collectivism and accelerated character development, as children are expected to master a 'variety of skills at a much earlier age than American children'.[19] Many

[17]Bronfenbrenner, V., *Two Worlds of Childhood: US and USSR*, New York, 1972, pp. 20–21.
[18]Chauncey, H., *Soviet Pre-school Education*, Vol. 1, New York, 1969, p. 38.
[19]Jacoby, op cit., p. 62.

parents and teachers feel that early collectivism, accelerated character development, and academic preparation of children for school is too rigorous and that it takes away their childhood. It appears that the notion of baby-adults is not approved by some parents, and yet paradoxically there is a steady demand for placements in kindergarten. Between 1965 and 1975 the number of children attending kindergartens rose from 6 million to 10 million. The latter included 9 million children aged 4–6, which represented two-thirds of all children in that age group in the Soviet Union.[20] Despite these figures, demand exceeds supply of places in kindergartens. *Sovetskaya Pedagogika, Narodnoe Obrazovanie*, and other educational journals commented on the shortage of kindergartens in 1976.

Apart from fulfilling educational needs, the Soviet kindergarten—and this could be the reason for its popularity—offers closely supervised, round-the-clock care for children of working parents. As wages are low and consumer goods expensive, both parents need to work. The usual length of daily care is nine to ten hours, which corresponds to the eight-hour working day in industry. Thus children spend far more time in Soviet kindergartens than elsewhere in the world. The nursery is normally opened at 7 for working mothers, but most children arrive between 8.30 and 9 o'clock. Between 9 and 10, children play collective games, and at 10 o'clock they have a breakfast and play outside until lunch time (1 o'clock). After lunch more communal work and play follows until 3 o'clock when children take a two-hour nap. More games and outdoor play follow and at 6 o'clock they have a supper, to be followed by more games and departure. Departure time varies from child to child. Some children are picked up by their parents after work between 5 and 7 o'clock, others go home at 7 o'clock or later. Children attending the nine- to ten-hour groups receive three meals daily, and those in twelve-hour and round-the-clock groups receive four meals daily. The fee varies from 2 to 12 roubles a month according to one's income.[21] As the teacher's average monthly salary in 1974 was 126 roubles the fee does not seem to be prohibitive.[22] In 1975 more than half of all children under the age

[20]Darinsky, A., Nepreryvnoe obrazovanie, *Sovetskaya Pedagogika*, No. 1, 1975, p. 18.
[21]Kalinin, op. cit., p. 49.
[22]*Narodnoe khozyaistvo SSSR v 1974 g.*, Moscow, 1975, p. 563.

TABLE 9. *The kindergarten summer time-table (5–6 years)*

1. Morning gymnastics, games, check-up	7.00–8.25
2. Breakfast	8.35–9.00
3. Games (outdoor) and work sessions	9.00–12.15
4. Sponge baths	12.15–12.30
5. Lunch	12.30–13.00
6. Afternoon nap	13.00–15.00
7. Games	15.00–15.25
8. Afternoon snack	15.25–15.45
9. Games (outdoor) and work on kindergarten plot	15.45–18.10
10. Supper	18.25–18.45
11. Games, departure	18.45–19.00

of 7 were enrolled in nurseries and kindergartens. Despite some strong criticism from certain parents, the authorities are convinced that the process of political, moral, aesthetic, and intellectual upbringing in kindergartens is extremely effective.

Educating the youngest citizens for a communist way of life becomes the most important task of Soviet kindergarten teachers. Not only do they follow essentially a prescriptive manual of instruction in the kindergarten, but they also adhere to a model regime. Table 9 illustrates one such regime for children aged 5 and 6 during the summer months.

Russian children aged 4–7 sleep, on the average, ten hours during the night (9 p.m. to 7 a.m.) and two hours during the day (1 p.m.–3 p.m.), a total of thirteen hours daily. Table 10 shows a typical daily programme for children aged 4–5 in the Soviet kindergarten.

The principle of work and play is strictly observed: children aged 3–4 would normally have ten short lessons (15–20 min) weekly and children in the senior group (ages 5–6) receive fourteen lessons in literacy, numeracy, art, music, physical education, and practical work. Table 11 illustrates the kindergarten curriculum for 1976.

As children are exposed to early schooling and regime in a Soviet kindergarten they adjust more readily to collective life and school discipline. Because kindergarten-trained children are better behaved their teachers have fewer discipline problems and are able to concentrate their efforts on the demanding and formidable academic curriculum of the Soviet primary school.

TABLE 10. *The kindergarten programme (4–5 age group) in 1976*

Admission and inspection; games; physical education	7.00–8.25
Breakfast	8.25–8.55
Games	8.55–9.20
Activities on the plot	9.20–9.40
Games, observation, physical education	9.40–11.35
Return to the kindergarten. Games	11.35–12.00
Lunch	12.00–12.35
Daytime sleep	12.35–15.10
Getting up. Games	15.10–15.25
Afternoon tea	15.25–15.50
Going for a walk. Games	15.50–18.00
Return to the kindergarten	18.00–18.15
Supper	18.15–18.45
Games. Departure for home	18.45–19.00
At home	
Going for a walk with parents	19.00–20.30
Returning home, quiet games, getting ready for bed	20.30–21.00
Sleep	21.00–7.00

The authorities in the Soviet Union are more than convinced, following extensive research in pre-school education theory between 1932 (when the first uniform curriculum for the Soviet kindergarten was issued) and 1975, of the immense social, political, and cultural implications of upbringing before the child commences his formal schooling. 'Modern pedagogical experiments', writes Kalinin, 'show that the pre-school child's intellectual abilities are markedly greater than it was believed. It has been proved that from the age of four children under definite conditions are able to assimilate not only

TABLE 11. *Pre-school curriculum (1976)*

Activities	3–4 years	4–5 years	5–6 years
Introduction to nature and development of speech	2	2	3
Introduction to mathematics	1	1	1
Creative games and work	2	2	3
Art	1	1	2
Physical education	2	2	2
Music	2	2	2

factual information about objects and phenomena, but information of a more generalized character.'[23] Makarenko went so far as to say that up to 90% of the entire educational process takes place before the age of 5. Kalinin further claims, that 'on the average children entering school straight from kindergarten are better developed and make better progress than those brought up in the family. Their intellectual level is generally higher and they are better developed physically.'[24] It is important to notice that one of the aims of the new curriculum is to prevent the children from developing a purely consumer attitude towards life. Moral education in the kindergarten fosters the development of such positive attributes as politeness, truthfulness, modesty, kindness, responsiveness, love of the Motherland and people, love of nature, and respect towards working people.

Substantial changes of political and academic nature have been made in the new kindergarten curriculum. For example, in teaching speech the main emphasis is placed on developing the child's auditory skill and the child is taught to analyse words phonetically. In mathematics the child learns to count and to understand abstract concepts pertaining to quantity and form. Children also receive extensive vocational training so that they may develop a positive attitude toward labour and semi-skilled work in particular. Bronfenbrenner calls it 'role-playing in real-life social situations'.[25] Children are appointed as monitors, to take care of pets and plants, serve at table, clean up and to do gardening. Children, clearly, enjoy this role playing, and many give an impression of 'self-confidence, competence, and camaraderie.'[26] Since the 1950s the growth of pre-school institutions in the Soviet Union has been spectacular (Table 12). In 1970 30 tertiary institutes and 200 colleges trained more than 75,000 new kindergarten teachers.

2.2. PRIMARY AND SECONDARY EDUCATION

Administration of the Soviet School

The director and his deputy (zavuch) are responsible to the State for education of their pupils, particularly in achievement and high

[23]Kalinin, op. cit., p. 35.
[24]Ibid., p. 36.
[25]Bronfenbrenner, op. cit., p. 24.
[26]Ibid., p. 25.

66   Education in the USSR

TABLE 12. *The growth of nurseries and kindergartens between 1950 and 1975*

Year	No. of kindergartens and nurseries	Population	Staff
1950	25,600	1,168,000	92,000
1955	31,600	1,730,000	144,000
1960	43,600	3,111,000	243,400
1965	67,500	6,207,300	453,300
1970	83,100	8,099,700	576,300
1971	87,000	8,463,000	603,000
1972	89,000	8,871,000	636,000
1973	93,000	9,360,900	670,000
1974	96,000	9,906,000	702,000
1977[a]	115,000	11,500,000	—
1979[b]	120,000	13,000,000	
1980[c]	–	14,700,000	—

[a]The 1977 figures are quoted by Prokofiev in *Semya i shkola*, No. 5, 1977, p. 2.
[b]*Uchitelskaya gazeta*, 14 June, 1979, p. 1.
[c]Ibid., 4 December, 1979, p. 1.

pass rates, and general administration of the school. Their particular duties are:

1. Supervision of the ideological and political aspects of education and upbringing of the pupils.
2. The implementation of the official curricula and the quality of instruction.
3. Guiding and assisting their staff.
4. Assisting the youth organizations at school (the Pioneers and the Komsomol).
5. Directing the work of the parents' committee.
6. Submitting reports on the work of the school to higher educational authorities.[27]

The director is a powerful member of the school committee. He can hire and fire his staff. He can also expel problem pupils from his school. In consultation with the local government he can recommend that a problem pupil be sent to a corrective school. The director is,

[27]Listed by Tomiak, op. cit., p. 64.

normally, a party member. If he has failed in one of the duties listed above he could be demoted by the local organ of the Party.

Teachers

The Soviet teacher has a more clearly defined status, role, and duties than his American counterpart. Some Western writers have commented on the high prestige accorded to the teaching profession. Teachers are greatly admired and respected in the Soviet Union and they speak with authority to parents. They are commonly regarded as intellectual leaders in the community. They tend to be more authoritarian in dealings with their pupils, and the barrier between teachers and pupils is more pronounced in the Soviet school.

The Soviet primary teacher fulfils educational, socio-political, and moral roles. She must teach, indoctrinate, and inspire her pupils for life within a Soviet collective. Education and communist upbringing are the two main tasks of the Soviet teacher.

A Soviet teacher is expected to be a model for his pupils. Ushinsky wrote in 1864 that only as a model could the teacher have 'an ethical influence on the children and his schoolwork be truly effective'.[28] Kalinin referred to teachers as engineers of the human soul. This is how he saw the teacher's role in 1938:

Of course, a teacher's main work is to teach his particular subject, but apart from everything else he is copied by his pupils. That is why the teacher's world outlook, his conduct, his life, and his approach to each phenomenon affect all his pupils in one way or another.... It can be safely said that if a teacher enjoys great authority, some people will bear traces of his influence throughout their lives.[29]

The regulations of the Secondary General School (1970) adopted by the USSR Council of Ministers stated that the teacher's basic duties include, among other things, instructing pupils in the 'spirit of communist morality.'[30]

Because of their importance in the process of communist education and upbringing, Soviet teachers are regarded as one of the 'most important' groups in Soviet society.[31]

[28]See *Khrestomatiya po pedagogike*, Moscow, 1967, p. 311.
[29]Kalinin, M. I., *On Communist Education*, Moscow, 1950, p. 76.
[30]*Soviet Education*, Nos. 3–4, 1971, p. 110.
[31]Tomiak, op. cit., p. 121.

TABLE 13. *Primary and secondary schools*

	1965–6	1970–1	1971–2	1972–3	1973–4	1974–5	1977
Schools (in thousands)	190.4	174.6	169.5	165.0	160.1	154.8	144.7
Primary (grades 1–3)	94.4	74.5	68.5	63.7	58.4	53.0	43.4
Eight-year schools	62.4	53.8	53.4	51.4	51.3	49.6	46.0
Ten-year schools	31.9	44.2	45.5	46.7	48.1	49.9	52.8
Schools for mentally and physically handicapped	1.7	2.1	2.2	2.2	2.3	2.3	2.5
Total enrolments (in millions)	43.4	45.4	45.2	44.8	44.3	43.5	41.5
Primary schools	3.8	2.4	1.9	1.6	1.4	1.2	0.9
Eight-year schools	16.6	12.5	12.0	11.4	10.6	9.7	7.9
Ten-year schools	22.7	30.2	30.9	31.4	31.9	32.2	32.3
Schools for mentally and physically handicapped	0.3	0.3	0.4	0.4	0.4	0.4	0.4

Source: *Narodnoe khozyaistvo v 1974 godu* Moscow, 1975, p. 679; *Narodnoe khozyaistvo SSSR za 60 let*, 1977, p. 577.

Organizational structure

The organizational structure of the Soviet school is rather simple: a three-year elementary education is followed by a seven-year secondary education for all. Table 13 provides a statistical summary of enrolments and schools in 1975.

Table 13 shows that 41.5 million students were enrolled in 144,700 day-time schools during the 1977 school year. Another 5.5 million attended part-time evening schools, of whom 359,000 attended the eight-year school and 4,558,000 were completing the ten-year school.[32] In sum, more than 46 million attended schools of general education of all types in 1977.

The greatest change has taken place in elementary schools which have been reduced by nearly 30,000 between 1970 and 1977 and three times as few pupils attend them. Instead, the pupils in most places, except in remote settlements, are encouraged to enrol in eight-year and ten-year schools. Correspondingly, the number of ten-year schools, which cater for complete secondary education for all, has risen by 9500 or 43% in the last decade.

[32]5,162,000 completed grade 10 in 1978, representing 97.8% of those who entered grade 1 in 1968 (*Uchitelskaya gazetá*, 20 Feb., 1979, p. 2).

The ten-year general educational labour polytechnic school or the polytechnic school for short, combines both primary and secondary schooling in the USSR. The polytechnic school, the unrealized dream to link schools with life since the 1920s, is now the basic institution of learning for all Soviet schoolchildren. The paradoxical dichotomy between primary and secondary education, which is peculiar to the Western World, does not exist in the USSR. One obvious advantage of such a system is that it ensures a continuity of the school curriculum.

The polytechnic school is characterized by a functional education in that it fulfils the prescribed norms of the economy as envisaged by the State Planning Commission. To express it more simply, education is directly related to vocational training and employment. The main socio-economic goal of the Soviet school is to train and prepare youth for socially useful labour, to use the current phrase, in either industry or agriculture. Despite its vocational bias towards blue-collar and semi-skilled professions, the Soviet school curriculum is academically oriented with emphasis on science and mathematics. This is, clearly, the result of demands of the planned economy on the curriculum. Soviet schools, as observed by Jahn (1975), maintain the delicate balance between supply and demand.[33] The future economy and communism of technicians and scientists necessitates, no doubt, technological and scientific rather than humanist education.

Another functional characteristic of the polytechnic school, which serves the societal need, is political socialization. The school is to ensure that its pupils develop an increasingly sophisticated Marxist–Leninist belief system. A total devotion and unquestioned loyalty and obedience to communist morality is aimed at. Socialist patriotism, which is a love of the Motherland, and proletarian internationalism are among the two most commonly mentioned ideals of communist morality for schoolchildren.

Thus the Soviet school is the most important socializing institution which plays an important role in maintaining the political structure of the USSR, the monolithic ideology, and hopefully, the *status quo*. It is clear that the social, economic, and political structure of the USSR owes its existence to a well-designed and all-encompassing

[33]Jahn, H. R., USA/USSR: two worlds apart, *Comparative Education Review*, Oct., 1975, p. 460.

system of socialization. The ten-year curriculum is academic, vocational, and socio-political, and the school is co-educational, comprehensive, and unstreamed throughout.

The first three years of schooling in the USSR, denoting the primary phase of general and polytechnical education, corresponds to the six-year primary schooling in the United Kingdom and the United States.

All Soviet children begin their formal education at the age of 7, when they are admitted into grade 1. Those who have not reached the required school age either attend pre-school centres, which prepare them for school, or, hopefully, they are taught literacy and numeracy at home by their parents or grandmothers (babushka). It is expected that children will be instructed by their parents in the three Rs before they come to school. For this purpose, special teaching manuals, which define the tasks of pre-school education, may be obtained by the parents in their local bookshop.

The school year commences on 1 September, with a national celebration. On this day, the newcomers come to school and they bring flowers for their teachers. Education is treated very seriously in the USSR. Every year, Soviet teachers tell their first-graders that they are little adults who have to prepare themselves for the serious business of life and make an important contribution to society.[34]

Curriculum

The elementary school curriculum is particularly demanding as it attempts to introduce the children to reading, writing, and mathematics. During the first three years thoroughness is the rule, and a great deal of emphasis is placed on memorization and hence, rote learning. Although the elementary syllabuses have been changed considerably during the past sixty years, the main emphases in the curriculum are what they have always been—the insistence on the three Rs, including a very thorough grounding in Russian. Russian grammar, in particular morphology, must be thoroughly mastered. Homework was never abolished, and children are given regular homework in grade 1.

The academic load in non-Russian schools in the fifteen republics

[34]Jacoby, op. cit., p. 73.

TABLE 14. *The curriculum for elementary and secondary schools (1975 versus 1965)*

Subjects	Hours per week in classes: 1975/1965									
	1	2	3	4	5	6	7	8	9	10
1. Russian language	12/6	11/7	12/7	6/6	6/5	4/3	3/3	2/4	0/2	1/2
2. Russian literature	—	—	—	2/3	2/3	2/3	2/3	3/3	4/3	3/3
3. Mathematics	6/6	6/6	6/6	6/6	6/6	6/6	6/6	6/6	6/6	6/5
4. History	—	—	—	2/2	2/2	2/2	2/2	3/3	4/4	3/3
5. Social studies	—	—	—	—	—	—	—	0/1	—	2/2
6. Nature study	0/2	1/2	2/2	2/2	—	—	—	—	—	—
7. Geography	—	—	—	—	2/2	3/3	2/2	2/2	2/2	—
8. Biology	—	—	—	—	2/2	2/2	2/2	2/2	1/0	2/2
9. Physics	—	—	—	—	—	2/2	2/2	3/2	4/5	5/5
10. Astronomy	—	—	—	—	—	—	—	—	—	1/1
11. Technical drawing	—	—	—	—	—	0/1	1/1	1/1	—	—
12. Chemistry	—	—	—	—	—	—	2/2	2/2	3/3	3/3
13. Foreign language	—	—	—	—	4/4	3/3	2/2	2/2	2/2	2/2
14. Art	1/1	1/1	1/1	1/1	1/1	1/1	0/1	—	—	—
15. Music	1/1	1/1	1/1	1/1	1/1	1/1	1/1	0/1	—	—
16. Physical education	2/1	2/1	2/1	2/1	2/1	2/1	2/1	2/1	2/2	2/2
17. Work training[a]	2/1	2/1	2/1	2/2	2/2	2/2	2/2	2/2	2/3	2/3
18. Military training	—	—	—	—	—	—	—	—	2/0	2/0
19. Practical work days	—	—	—	—	5/6	5/6	5/12	—	22/24	—
20. Elective courses	—	—	—	—	—	0/2	2/2	4/2	4/4	4/4

Source: *Sbornik prikazov i instruktsii Ministerstva Prosveshcheniya RSFSR*, No. 8, March 1974, p. 29.

[a]Since December 1977, work training has been doubled (from two to four hours weekly) in all grades.

is even more demanding as children are required to study three or more languages—their native tongue, Russian, and a foreign language, usually English. Table 14 compares the 1965 and 1975 ten-year elementary and secondary school curricula in the Russian Republic (RSFSR).

The 1975 curriculum is not much different from the 1965 version. In elementary grades the core subjects are, as in the past, Russian language and literature (twelve hours or 50% of the curriculum), mathematics (six hours or 25% of the curriculum), and practical subjects like art, physical education, music, and work training (six hours in all or 25% of the curriculum). Mathematics and science continue to receive the greatest emphasis in the curriculum, and in grade 10 they occupy over 50% of the yearly programme. The ten-year school curriculum is, clearly, academic in content, with emphasis on mathematics, physics, chemistry, biology, and science electives. The humanities and social sciences combined represented only one-third of the 1975 curriculum, a marginal increase on the 1965 figures. The mathematics–science bias of the curriculum suggests that the Soviet economy and technocracy is making gigantic leaps towards the year 2000, when the technocratic and communist society would become a reality. It is obvious that to maintain its present rate of industrialization, the Soviet Union needs a vast army of technicians of all kinds. Work training and vocational training receives a great deal more attention in the Soviet school today. Work training is a characteristic, if not unique, feature of the Soviet elementary and secondary curriculum. It begins in grade 1 (two hours weekly throughout the year up to 1977 and four hours today) with paper-cutting, modelling, sewing, and gardening. By the end of grade 8 the pupils have had workshop sessions in metalwork and woodwork, gardening, machine shops, (repairing trucks and tractors) agriculture (rural schools), and maintenance. There is no specialization as such in Soviet schools, but work training is compulsory for all students. In a new society the average worker, in order to be socially productive, apart from mastering literacy and numeracy, will need to have a good background in abstract sciences, in particular in physics, chemistry, and biology. The educational planners, aware of the continuing spiral rise of knowledge and competence required in the majority of occupations, are beginning to plan retraining courses for those in employment, particularly teachers. Teachers have to refresh and upgrade their knowledge of physical sciences, methods of teaching, and educational theories in order to fulfil the demands imposed on them by the rapidly changing society, knowledge, and the economy.

The decree of 1972 'On completion of the transition to universal secondary education of youth and further development of the general education school' was a landmark in Soviet education and social history. The ten-year schooling becomes the minimum general education for the masses. The increase in compulsory schooling after 1972 from eight (pre-1972) to ten years complete secondary education is the most significant educational reform in Russian history. The far-reaching consequences of the decree are: a higher level of literacy throughout the nation; a more sophisticated culture; and more efficient workers. The 1972 decree was by necessity rather than by choice. The whole future of the Soviet economy rests on the well-educated and trained Soviet man.

The 1972 decree, which was initiated by Kosygin in 1967 at the Twenty-third Party Congress, affected the entire structure of the ten-year school curriculum. As already mentioned, elementary schooling was reduced from four to three years. Grade 4, which previously was the final year of elementary education, now becomes the first year of secondary schooling, when the teaching switches over to subject specialization. In addition to Russian, mathematics, history, geography, biology, physics, and chemistry, a modern language and politics will be studied in depth. Physics, history, social studies, and chemistry have picked up additional hours at the expense of Russian, which dwindles from twelve hours a week in grade 1 to four hours in grade 10.

The concept of guiding the pupil into the right type of education, which characterizes education in the United Kingdom and France, does not apply to Soviet education. Selecting the pupil for the right type of education, which will eventually result in the right kind of employment, does not pose any problems in the USSR. The fact that all children must be educated up to the age of 17 precludes selection or any form of streaming by ability.

In 1975 96% of students continued their secondary education beyond grade 8, the year that in the past served as a leaving certificate for early school-leavers.[35] This figure rose to 97.8% in 1978. This indicates that the eight-year compulsory schooling introduced in 1959, which provided co-education for children aged 7–15, was successful.

The fact that universal secondary education became possible in 1975 in the country, which, less that sixty years ago, was 70% illiterate, is, undoubtedly, a magnificent achievement. The transition from the eight-year compulsory education to universal ten-year (complete secondary) education during the 1970s was not an easy one. Many obstacles had to be overcome—low educational standards in rural

[35] Panachin, F., *Narodnoe Obrazovanie*, No. 1, 1976, p. 8.

areas, abundance of incomplete secondary schools in many regions, reluctance of some senior students to continue with their secondary education beyond grade 8, opposition from teachers to inflate grades for school-leavers in order to meet the target set by the Ministry of Education, fluctuations in academic standards from region to region, and so on. Panachin reassures us that rigged passes in grades 8 and 10 did not exist, and that students were passed solely on their merit.[36] At the same time he concedes a serious discrepancy between the school certificate (grade 10) results and performance at the university's entrance examinations (konkursnye ekzaminy).

The majority of students do not need an incentive to continue with their secondary education beyond grade 8. There are two reasons for this. First, there is a high correlation between the level of education and occupation attained. Second, the choice of occupations is remarkably narrow for early school-leavers who do not possess professional–technical training.

Kashin, Director of the Research Institute of Teaching Methods, in the Academy of Pedagogical Sciences, has stated that all schools were using new syllabuses in the 1974/5 school year and that the transition took almost ten years to accomplish. He mentioned that 103 new standardized textbooks have been used in schools throughout the Union.[37]

What, then, are these radical changes in the Soviet school that so much has been written about in educational periodicals between 1975 and 1976? Panachin, Deputy Minister of Education of the USSR spoke of the triune function of the school in the 1975/6 academic year, which he saw as being the synthesis of political, moral, and labour upbringing.

The four new decrees which spearheaded educational reforms in the 1970s were: 'On completion of the transition to universal secondary education of youth and further development of the general education school', 'On further improvements of the vocational–technical education', 'Measures for further improvements in higher education', and 'Measures for further improvements in working conditions of the rural general education school'. Thus, working towards universal co-

[36]Panachin, F., *Narodnoe Obrazovanie*, No. 1, 1976, p. 4.
[37]*Izvestiya*, 22 Apr., 1976, p. 5.

education for children and adolescents aged 7–17, and improving educational processes in vocational–technical colleges, tertiary institutions, and rural schools are the main tasks of Soviet educational policy after 1975.

The new curricula and syllabuses for the ten-year (elementary and secondary) school, prepared by a joint commission of the USSR. Academy of Sciences, the USSR Academy of Pedagogical Sciences, and the Party, defined educational goals of the Soviet school as follows:

1. To provide a solid knowledge of the fundamentals of sciences.
2. To assimilate the principles of a communist view of life.
3. To provide labour and vocational (polytechnic) training in accordance with the needs of society and the abilities and wishes of pupils.
4. To offer moral and aesthetic education and physical culture.

The above shows that educational process in the USSR is shaped and guided by economic, social, political, moral, cultural, and educational factors, all of which are closely interwoven with each other.

Educational reforms emphasized a modern approach to how, why, and what in teaching. Aims and objectives, the content and methods of teaching, bearing in mind the fast-approaching twenty-first century, had to be up-dated with the latest developments in all fields of human knowledge. It is believed that by the year 2000 the volume of knowledge will have increased 15–25 times compared with 1960.[38]

The Stalinist school curriculum was criticized for being dogmatic, pedantic, scholastic, formalist, and sterile. Unrealistically heavy programmes, excessive homework, and demanding examinations resulted, in many cases, in rote-learning, superficial knowledge, and mechanical rather than creative thinking. The new reforms, hopefully, would remove these and improve the quality of learning.

In their pursuit of mastery of school disciplines, Soviet educationalists have cause to accept the notion that each subject can be reduced to its shell, the nucleus, which is the essence of knowledge. Markushe-

[38]*Soviet Education*, Dec., 1974, p. 18.

vich, Vice-President of the USSR Academy of Pedagogical Sciences, who has put forward his nucleus theory of knowledge, said:

> It is my conviction that it is possible to identify a nuclear core, a shell in the syllabus of any school subject. . . . This massive, relatively stable nucleus consists of knowledge and skills that have acquired, what I would call, a classic character. This knowledge and these skills must accompany a person through his entire lifetime. On the other hand, the shell, which is considerably smaller in mass, contains ideas and facts that are more or less confined to the scientific and cultural 'topics of the day'.[39]

The new elementary curriculum was a bold educational reform, which stipulated that only three years (instead of four) were required to complete primary schooling. The survey, undertaken by the Academy of Pedagogical Sciences (the research institute of curriculum and teaching methods) in May 1973, was to test the knowledge of elementary pupils at the end of their schooling who have been taught by the new syllabuses since 1970. In particular, investigators wanted to find out whether the knowledge of grade 3 pupils was equivalent to that of grade 4 pupils under the old system, and whether the new pupils were ready for systematic study of basic disciplines in grade 4. Reading, writing, and mathematics or the three Rs were tested. Six thousand children in each skill were tested. The received data indicates that the three-year primary school gives a fully satisfactory preparation for secondary schooling.[40] Two significant claims are being made here. Firstly, traditional four-year (six years in England) education in the elementary school has been reduced to three years without any setbacks to academic standards. Soviet educationalists claim that the new three-year elementary school gives a satisfactory training in the three Rs. This, if it is true, could be a break-through for those who continue working with the six-year elementary school curriculum. Secondly, it is asserted that the ten-year pupil, who had completed the new three-year elementary curriculum in 1973, is well prepared for secondary education, which emphasizes a systematic and serious study of major disciplines in science and the humanities. In particular, this kind of learning takes place at the age of 14 (form 3), if not later. One thing is clear, if the pupil commences secondary schooling after grade 3 and, for the next seven years he is engaged in

[39] *Soviet Education*, Dec., 1974, p. 19.
[40] Kashin, M., Ob itogakh perekhoda . . . , *Sovetskaya Pedagogika*, No. 3, 1976, p. 25.

a systematic study of core disciplines, he is bound to learn more than his American and British counterparts.

The new elementary curriculum envisages a more complete utilization of abstract knowledge, and a more intensive study of the material in the syllabus, and a greater use of the pupil's mental powers.[41] The basic three Rs—reading, writing and arithmetic—together with grammar and nature study, constitute the main educational goals of the elementary school. The Soviet three-year elementary plan of learning is seen as the foundation stone of the entire educational system. It is argued that secondary and higher education depend on the degree of perfection achieved by the *elementary school*.[42]

The new secondary curriculum devotes much more attention to the study of the humanities and social sciences. Literature is one of the most powerful instruments of moral, social, political, and aesthetic upbringing in the Soviet Union. The ideological bias of literature was summed up aptly by Brezhnev in his report to the Central Committee of the CPSU at the Twenty-fourth Congress: 'With the advancement of our society along the road of communist construction, a greater part is played by literature and art in the formation of the world view of the Soviet man, his moral convictions and spiritual culture.'[42] It could well be that due to a rapidly changing image of the Soviet youth during the 1960s under the impact of Westernization and consumer goods, the partymindedness (partiinost) and patriotism needed a powerful boost in the troubled 1970s, the worldwide phenomena of declining morality, and ideological confusion. Prokofiev, Minister of Education, in line with the Party's ideological stand on upbringing, pontificated on the role of literature in contributing to the pupil's development of communist and Marxist–Leninist morality.

History and politics, which go hand in hand in the secondary school, being ideal for political socialization, became the two core disciplines in moral education. The new seven-year history curriculum places a far greater stress on Lenin. The course is designed to rear children in the spirit of Soviet patriotism and internationalism and imbue them with a deep understanding of the worldwide historical significance of the achievements of socialism in the USSR. The most fundamental

[41] *Soviet Education*, Dec., 1974, p. 22.
[42] Ibid., p. 38.

role of history is to 'teach pupils a deep understanding of Party policy and a correct assessment of historical events, from class and Party positions'.[43] The course 'History of the USSR' and other history courses are designed to deepen ideological and political indoctrination of schoolchildren, the future builders of communism. The subject politics (obshchestvovedenie—social science) is taught in grades 8 and 10. Buryakova, a method lecturer (Moscow Institute for In-service Teacher Training) writes that the subject social science develops the following four links: the Marxist–Leninist doctrine, analysis of the current events, the politics of the Communist Party, and ideological and communal participation.[44] Politics consists of a detailed study of documents and materials of the CPSU, the Party Congress, and its resolutions and decrees. It is meant to be a serious, intelligent study of Marxism–Leninism and the CPSU. In order to ensure that this is so, the Academy of Pedagogical Sciences had published a special methodological guide, *The Study of the Materials of the Twenty-fifth Congress of the CPSU* (1976), for teachers of social sciences.

A new course, 'Fundamentals of the Soviet Government and Law', was introduced in grade 8 in the 1975/6 school year. The course is designed to reinforce moral education in the Soviet school. Juvenile delinquency, judging by articles in educational journals and the press, is becoming a serious social problem in the USSR. The authorities hope to overcome the problem by intensifying socio-political indoctrination and moral education.

The above shows that one significant outcome of the reforms was the increase of direct, systematic instruction in politics (from the Marxist–Leninist point of view) and morality. A mere conformity to the ideology is no longer sufficient. What is needed is a new Soviet man who would internalize communist ideology and implement undeviatingly the Party's moral code of the builder of communism.

Assessment

Academic curriculum, rigid asessment, excessive homework, group competitiveness, strict discipline, and polytechnical training were characteristic features of the Soviet school in 1975.

[43] *Soviet Education*, Dec., 1974, pp. 39–40.
[44] *Narodnoe Obrazovanie*, No. 10, 1974, p. 41.

The Soviet system of assessment is so formal and so meticulous that it needs to be considered here. Soviet teachers do not suffer from internal doubts as to the reliability and validity of formal assessment for small children. Most of the Russian teachers, writes Jacoby, laughed when they were told that Western educators were increasingly dubious about the value of grades and examinations for small children. One Russian teacher, and I am sure that this comment would apply to most teachers, had this to say about assessment:

> As teachers, we naturally have a good idea of how well a child will do in an examination. But the child—well, he might go on thinking he was doing very well when he was only average. The examination keeps him in touch with reality, and it gives us something to show the parents. If I talk to a mother about a child's reading difficulty, she won't understand. But if she sees a 2 on a paper, she will understand and be concerned.[45]

Assessment has not been changed in the last fifty years. The way that I was assessed and examined in the secondary school in the 1950s, so pupils are assessed in 1980. Every pupil has a special daily report book (dnevnik), which is like a diary. It contains the pupil's daily assessment for oral and written work and the teacher's comments on his achievement and conduct in the class. The teacher opens his class journal (zhurnal), and he calls out a name. I never knew how he worked out who should be asked to come to the blackboard. Since I did not want to be caught unprepared I had to study every night. The pupil whose name was called out, would get up and proceed to answer the teacher's main question, say in history, which may be followed by two or three supplementary questions. 'Tell me, Boris, what do you remember of Napoleon's invasion of Russia, which we talked about last week?' If Boris gives a complete and correct answer, and to be correct it had to be almost word by word from the textbook (rote learning), the teacher is satisfied that Boris knows his material and gives him 4. The mark is entered in his journal and he asks Boris to bring his daily report book where, in the right column, he enters 4. Normally, two or three pupils may be examined in the first ten minutes of the lesson. During a mathematics lesson, the pupil may be asked to work out a given algebraic formula and solve one or two problems on the blackboard. Speed is essential. The slightest

[45] Jacoby, op. cit., pp 75–76.

hesitation may be fatal as the teacher may think that the pupil is uncertain and thus unable to solve the problem. Having assessed in this manner the pupils' acquisition of knowledge, he proceeds to lecture or instruct on the new topic.

At the end of the six-day school week the pupil's daily report book must be signed by his parents and countersigned by his form teacher. This means that both his parents and form co-ordinator are aware of the progress on a day-to-day basis. This, no doubt, is a Soviet answer to continuous assessment.

Each lesson is followed up by substantial homework, which is prescribed by the regulations, according to the grade level's maximum load, ranging from one hour a day in grade 1 to four hours a day in grade 10. In practice, however, this is exceeded in many cases as children are given exercises which are time consuming. Excessive homework is, indeed, a heavy burden for both children and parents. Parents are still complaining about excessive homework as their children are forced to sacrifice outdoor play for homework. One parent said that her eight-year-old son brings home three hours of work a day.[46] In order to relieve the burden of homework, the Ministry of Education had to issue a special decree in 1970 on limiting homework to a maximum of one hour a day in grade 1 and up to four hours a day in grade 10. But this, too, by our standards, especially in the primary grades, is excessive. Soviet educationalists obviously believe that regular homework must reinforce learning.

The school's academic year is divided into four terms, totalling thirty-five six-day weeks. At the end of each term, oral and written tests are set to be followed by the final examination at the end of the year. Thus the pupil's certificate contains six grades for each subject: four term marks, the end-of-year examination mark, and the final exit mark, being the average. Promotion is not automatic as it is in some countries. If the pupil receives unsatisfactory marks (2—dvoiki) in more than two subjects, he must repeat the year. Those who repeat grades may leave the school if they are over 15.

The pupil's conduct is treated much more seriously in the Soviet school than it is in the United States. The pupil's certificate has a subject called conduct (povedenie), which is marked out of 5. Unsatis-

46Jacoby, op. cit., p. 76.

factory marks for conduct, which are indeed very rare, may result in the pupil's expulsion. It is taken for granted that the pupil will observe the Rules for Pupils, which insist on 'diligence, punctuality in attendance, unquestioning obedience, full attention during lessons, modest and respectful behaviour towards parents, and loyalty to the school.'[47]

What measures are taken against failing pupils? Normally, the teachers try to pass as many as they can, for having a good pass-rate means less trouble from the local educational authority as well as having better chances for promotion, salary rises, and so forth. Both teachers and parents are held responsible for the pupil's education (obrazovanie) and upbringing (vospitanie). To the Ministry of Education, which does not accept IQ factors or heredity, a low pass-rate means ineffective and bad teaching. Streaming by ability as we know it simply does not exist in the Soviet Union. It is taken for granted that one makes progress through hard work, concentration, diligence, and perseverance.[48] Those who fail go through a personal hell. The school, from the director (the principal) down to a Pioneer group leader, the parents, and class mates exert a great deal of psychological pressure on these pupils. Sometimes unpleasant comments are written in the pupil's weekly report book until the parents take some action. The pupil cannot be admitted into the ranks of Pioneers, where all his friends are. If he is a bad Pioneer who keeps getting unsatisfactory marks, the grade's Pioneer leader will call a meeting and discuss the unsatisfactory progress of one or two members. If no improvement is made, the next stage is to ridicule these lazy pupils publicly in the grade's wall newspaper. A typical cartoon would depict the lazy pupil, untidy, dirty, carrying a school-bag full of unsatisfactory marks. If all these measures do not work then the director would get in touch with the parents' employer (the boss—nachalnik). The employer is asked to co-operate, and he does so by rebuking the parent in his office for having failed in his parental duty in bringing up the child to the glory of the Motherland. This may sound somewhat incredible, but this is exactly the ideological ground for criticizing the parents' method of upbringing. Failing all this, the parents are

[47]Tomiak, op. cit., p. 62.
[48]Ibid., p. 63.

openly criticized during parents' and teachers' meetings for neglecting their civic duties. As a final punishment, the pupil is not promoted into the next grade and he will stay in that grade until he obtains satisfactory marks in most of his subjects. The pupil who has failed in one subject may be asked to study during summer vacation and sit for a supplementary examination, an ordeal that was dreaded by everyone. The 1973 figures by Danilov indicate a considerable decline in the number of drop-outs, being fewer than 1.5%.[49]

Differences and similarities between Soviet and American schools

The basic difference between Soviet and American students is their exposure to political socialization. Indoctrination, and rigid at that, is the inherent characteristic of Soviet education. No attempt, by and large, is made in the United States to indoctrinate schoolchildren. The ever-present moral–political education in the Soviet school, affecting all spheres of the pupil's development, contrasts sharply with the moderate political socialization in American schools.

The Soviet pupil has no choice in his selection of the school and the curriculum, as all decisions concerning education are made for him by the local educational authority or the school administration. Parents may, if they so desire, place their children in special language schools, where foreign languages are taught from grade 2 through grade 10. The ten-year school curriculum, with minor modifications, is compulsory for all students. As already noted, the general core curriculum of the Soviet school includes the entire spectrum of disciplines, ranging from the humanities to science. The curriculum is very demanding, as mathematics and science are taught as separate disciplines after grade 3. The student must cover prescribed courses in history, social science, geography, literature, politics, chemistry, biology, physics, mathematics, and modern language. In this sense, the Soviet ten-year school resembles the three track German Gymnasium (the humanities, modern languages, and science) all combined in one.

Unlike his American counterpart, the Soviet student must pass all core subjects to be promoted to the next grade. Promotion is not

[49]Danilov, A., Schools in the Russian Federation . . . , *Soviet Education*, Vol. 16, 1974, p. 5.

automatic in the Soviet elementary school—as is the case in most lower grades in American elementary schools. The Soviet teacher is, however, held responsible for the pass-rate in his grade. Low pass-rates mean more work with the weaker pupil after school.

Rigid assessment, end-of-year examinations, and excessive homework impose restrictions on Soviet education. As soon as they enter grade 1 Soviet children are subjected to academic curriculum and competitive assessment.

Another difference between the Soviet and American students is that the former is judged according to his participation in what is called socialist competition, which affects the whole curriculum, namely academic achievement, moral conduct, sport, work training, community involvement, and youth group activities.

2.3. VOCATIONAL AND TECHNICAL EDUCATION

As the ten-year schooling is now obligatory for all Soviet children and if they are to receive comprehensive, polytechnic, and academic education, which doors are opened for them? The school is not a vocational one despite its rather suggestive name. It does not really prepare individuals for life and socially useful labour as it was supposed to. Instead, individuals, having been exposed to an academically biased curriculum, which Rosen 1971 compares with a German real gymnasium type (emphasis on mathematics and science), wish to enter tertiary institutions.[50] The ten-year polytechnic school is still the most direct road to university.

A vast network of vocational and technical colleges offers training in many thousands of professions ranging from junior technical personnel to schoolteachers. Who enrols at these colleges today? After reading a number of articles on social stratification in the Soviet Union one is tempted to say that the vast majority of the students are those who simply failed to gain admission into university or tertiary college. Some Soviet educationalists are trying to convince parents and students that this is not the case, and that even the students with

[50]Rosen, S., *Education and Modernization in the USSR*, Addison-Wesley, London, 1971, p. 69.

excellent grades enrol in vocational colleges, often against their parents' wishes.

In actual fact, polytechnic colleges (tekhnikumy), vocational colleges (uchilishcha), and technical colleges (PTUs) occupy the middle position between the ten-year school and university (see Fig. 3 on p. 54).

The two most common institutions which offer vocational and technical training are secondary specialized schools (srednie spetsialnye uchebnye zavedeniya) and technical colleges (professionalno–tekhnicheskie uchilishcha or PTU for short).

Secondary specialized schools consist of polytechnic and vocational colleges, both offering vocational–technical education for those who have completed their basic eight-year school. These colleges, which could be compared with Australian TAFE colleges, offer training for semi-professional and professional occupations ranging from toolmaking to nursing.

Admission is by a competitive entrance examination, and the courses vary in length between three to four years. Polytechnic colleges, which are larger training establishments, offer a combination of general education (complete secondary) and vocational training for highly skilled blue-collar or white-collar occupations. Basically, polytechnic colleges offer courses in the following three categories:

1. Senior courses in certain specialization in industry, transport, construction, and communication.
2. Courses in public health, physical culture, education, economics, and art.
3. Agriculture, geology, industry, and farming.[51]

Typical professions which polytechnic or vocational colleges offer are:

1. Toolmaking, radio-technical, communication, automation of production, power technology, construction, machine building, lumbering, and woodworking—four years.
2. Mining, metallurgical, chemical, and transport—four years.
3. Geological, geodetic, cartographic, and meteorological—four years.

[51]Tomiak, op. cit., p. 75.

TABLE 15. *Enrolments of students in secondary specialized education institutions (by group of specialities in thousands)*

	1966	1971	1972	1973	1974	1975	1977
Industry and construction	1623	1931	1929	1914	1907	1903	1956.0
Transport and communication	318.8	379.5	385.8	392	395.6	403.9	419.6
Agricultural science	584.9	692.7	709.1	730.5	738.5	753.3	784.8
Finance—economics and law	397.5	476.1	485.8	489.7	489.4	489.4	500.7
Health and physical education	344.5	433.8	427	418.1	414.6	415.5	418.1
Education	304.4	367.5	367.9	374.9	381.7	388	417.0
Art and cinema	86.2	107.4	115.4	118	121.3	123.9	126.5
Total	3659	4388	4421	4438	4448	4478	4623

4. Technological training for production of consumer goods and food products–four years.
5. Agricultural industry and science—four years.
6. Finance–economics and law—three years.
7. Medicine (health care), physical education, and sports—three years.
8. Education.

Table 15 demonstrates the extent of the popularity of certain professions in polytechnic colleges.

Table 15 indicates that polytechnic colleges cater mainly for heavy industry, construction, agriculture, transport, and communication, where nearly two-thirds of all students are enrolled.

On completing polytechnic and vocational colleges, the students obtain two certificates—a certificate of secondary education, which is equivalent to a British GCE, and a diploma. Students can technically continue in tertiary education, but only a small percentage of them do so; the majority go to work.

Vocational–technical schools, or PTUs as they are commonly known in the Soviet Union, have been in vogue lately. Soviet educational periodicals and the press describe PTUs very favourably in the hope of attracting more school-leavers.

The main task of PTUs is to train skilled workers and junior technical personnel for all branches of the national economy. PTUs

TABLE 16. *Enrolment in vocational–technical schools* (1965–75)
(in thousands)

	1966	1971	1972	1973	1974	1975	1979[a]
PTU enrolments	1701	2600	2700	2900	3100	3300	3500

[a]*Uchitelskaya gazeta*, 23 June 1979, p. 1.

are growing in significance as the State needs more and more skilled workers. The Soviet Union could experience a shortage of skilled workers unless PTUs supply an adequate number of workers in such skills as mechanics, electricians, and computer engineers.

Vocational–technical education, established in the 1930s, is now under the State Committee of the USSR Council of Ministers for Vocational and Technical Education. Since 1959 vocational–technical schools have been divided into urban and rural institutions. Vocational–technical schools have nearly doubled in the last decade from 1,701,000 (1965) to 3,300,000 (1975) students. By 1979, 3.5 million students attended these institutions (Table 16).

On completion of the course, which could vary from six months to three years, the student is awarded a diploma in his given specialty.

The curriculum in vocational–technical schools, as in secondary specialized schools, is based on a uniform and compulsory courses of study. The curriculum is dominated by production and technical training (up to 80%) and only 20% is spent on general education subjects. Rosen writes that trade-school courses are academically inferior to those at secondary specialized schools.[52]

Of all post-secondary institutions, vocational–technical schools (PTUs or trade schools) have, by far, the lowest social status. Unlike the graduates of polytechnic and vocational colleges, who are able to advance themselves socially by continuing their studies in tertiary institutes, PTU diplomates find it extremely difficult to enter similar establishments.

Education in the Soviet Union is, clearly, a means of upward social mobility. This may well explain the growing popularity of polytechnic colleges where there has been an increase in the proportion of full-time students (from 53% in 1961 to 60% in 1975). Nearly one-third of

[52]Rosen, op. cit., p. 77.

TABLE 17. *Enrolments in secondary specialized schools (in thousands)*

	1966	1971	1972	1973	1974	1975	1977
Full-time students	1835	2558	2641	2690	2725	2762	2867
Part-time students							
(a) Evening classes	629	645	603	571	545	532	554
(b) Correspondence	1196	1185	1177	1177	1178	1184	1202
Total	3659	4388	4421	4438	4448	4478	4623

the students in secondary specialized schools in 1974 were enrolled by correspondence or on a part-time (evening) basis (Table 17).

The State vocational training system has been in existence for over thirty years. Vocational–technical schools have been the main means of training skilled workers.[53] Vocational education of youths after they have completed eight years or ten years secondary schools continues to be difficult for the State Committee for Vocational–Technical Training. Rapidly changing technology necessitates flexibility of the otherwise standardized and rigid vocational–technical curricula. The monolithic Soviet secondary education system continues to emphasize the academic aspects of education at the expense of many non-academic-oriented students. The second problem is that of upgrading the vocational–technical schools. Attempts are made to improve not only the image of the PTU but the quality and the level of instruction, which would make it equal with the polytechnic college.[54]

2.4. SPECIAL SCHOOLS

Soviet schools not only satisfy the need of the economy for an educated and trained working force, but they also are responsible for social mobility by providing unlimited opportunities for the acquisition of adult status. It is true that the school as a socializing agency can fulfil or impede individual aspirations, ambitions, and desires. The school, by its methods of selection, streaming, assessment, and

[53]Oglobin, I., *Vocational Training in the USSR*, Moscow, 1967, p. 13.
[54]Tomiak, op. cit., p. 81.

teaching methods, can influence the whole future of the child. Some schools more so than others. In a mobile Soviet society, education has become the main determinant of adult status.

This is particularly true of the better secondary schools located in major cities or the schools for gifted children. Side by side with the ordinary polytechnic secondary schools there are to be found special schools, which are academically, vocationally, and socially biased, and which accept only small, selected groups of children.

Schools for gifted children in ballet, music, drama, mathematics, and science seem to indicate an undesirable departure from the comprehensive labour–polytechnic school. It could be maintained that such schools are élitist.

Talent scouts select the most talented children on the basis of competitive tests for outstanding talent. The Russians have a particular adulation for ballet and music. The best-known ballet and music schools in the Soviet Union are the ballet schools in Leningrad, Moscow, and Kiev and the Central Music School in Moscow. Nationwide competitions are regularly held in the fine arts, sciences, and sport. The winners, usually after grade 1 for ballet, are accepted to these schools. The curriculum consists of normal general subjects, and an intensive vocational training in ballet, dancing, music, or singing. If the child's aptitudes do not fulfil the teacher's expectations, he or she is transferred to an ordinary secondary school. If successful, pupils graduate as ballet artists (artist baleta), concert violinist, and soloists. They become the élite if one is to judge them according to their income, power, privileges, and status.

Special schools for gifted pupils in mathematics and sciences have come into being in the 1960s. They were originally proposed by Professor Keldysh, the President of the Academy of Sciences of the USSR, and Professor Lavrentiev, the President of the Novosibirsk branch of the Academy. They argued that in the interest of progress, pupils in mathematics should be given an opportunity for intensive study of the subject early in their lives. Mathematical olympiads are organized to select the most talented pupils. In August every year, during the school holiday, some 800 winners of the olympiad are taken to the University of Novosibirsk and about half of them are finally admitted, after a series of tests, to the university-run school.

The school is like a senior high school, for it consists of the three upper grades—8, 9, and 10. The winners of the mathematical olympiad are normally accepted into grade 8. The curriculum is like any other secondary school curriculum but with greater emphasis on mathematics, physics, and chemistry. Another distinct advantage is that the pupils are taught by university professors and members of the Academy of Sciences.

Other special schools in mathematics, physics, and chemistry exist in Moscow and other major cities. The introduction of these schools is difficult to reconcile, as correctly observed by Tomiak, with the principle of universal secondary education up to the age of 17. The polytechnic principle seems to conflict with the highly selective and over-specialized schools discussed above.[55] The very existence of such schools in the Soviet Union indicates that political, educational, and scientific maxims sometimes contradict each other.

One should also mention the existence of military boarding schools which prepare officers for service in the Soviet armed forces. Created in 1943, these schools were originally intended for the orphans of military and other personnel killed during the Great Patriotic War. To be admitted, the boys had to reach the age of 10 and had to complete primary education.

Today, preference is given to secondary trained applicants who are the sons of army and navy personnel. Selection is by competitive entrance examinations in Russian language, mathematics, and a foreign language. The course at the Suvorov School lasts for three years, and cadets study general secondary subjects but with an emphasis on a foreign language. The army cadets sit for a final examination which would give them a qualification in military interpretership. Those who have completed the course with honours or gold or silver medals for academic excellence may enter, without entrance examination, tertiary military technical institutes or military academies. In 1967 there were nine Suvorov schools in major cities.

The navy cadet schools prepare cadets for naval colleges. The Nakhimov school, located in Leningrad is the only major establishment training naval cadets. The battleship *Avrora* is used as a training base.

---

[55]Ibid., p. 83.

At the Nakhimov school, English is of paramount significance. Presumably, the aim is to train bilingual Soviet naval officers.

From the above it is clear that the authorities must find it politically expedient to pick, to use Khrushchev's words, 'from among capable pupils at the existing schools particularly gifted children.'[56] This is, clearly, in contradiction with the theory of equal opportunity for all in comprehensive and unstreamed education. Although Soviet educationalists do not accept hereditary intelligence they seemed to have grown accustomed to the idea that some children, given the same environment for all children, are substantially more gifted in a particular discipline than the rest. The problem of a highly motivated and exceptionally talented pupil in a comprehensive, labour–polytechnic environment has been partially solved by the organization of schools for the gifted.

So far, schools as the conformist agencies of socialization and social control have been described. What happens to the nonconformist or the deviant pupil? Assuming that some pupils deliberately reject the cultural goals and values, what forms of constraint are used? An absence of socially accepted norms in some pupils calls for a quick action. Deviance must be checked before it can threaten social order. Controls on behaviour, which are built into the social structure—and Soviet society is no exception—begin to operate. They may range from the 'trivial to the severe, from an annoyed glance to ritual expulsion from the school.'[57]

The regulation of deviant behaviour is taking place in special schools for Soviet juvenile delinquents. Special, 'closed' schools accept serious problem children aged 11–18. A serious problem child is defined as a systematic school discipline breaker who is responsible for disorganizing schooling and who has a negative and anti-social influence on other pupils.[58] The school council, having tried all possible forms of deterrent to correct the pupil's bad behaviour, may, as a form of punishment, recommend to the local branch of education department that the pupil be sent to the special school (spetsshkola). The special school is a cross between a boarding

[56]Quoted from Grant, N., *Soviet Education*, Penguin, 1968, p. 91.
[57]Shipman, M., *The Sociology of the School*, London, 1975, p. 71.
[58]*Pedagogicheskaya entsiklopediya*, Moscow, 1968, Vol. 4, p. 742.

school (shkolainternat) and a corrective labour colony (trudovaya koloniya).

The curriculum is based on the ten-year primary and secondary schooling. The main feature of schooling is the labour–polytechnic principle or the accent on vocation and socially useful labour. The trainees (vospitanniki) spend up to four hours daily, depending on their age and physical development, working in various workshops or on agricultural plots. They are closely supervised round-the-clock. Parents may visit their children once per term but they are not allowed to bring gifts. In special cases, some children, who show signs of conformity, are allowed, and this is a form of reward to encourage correct behaviour, to spend their summer vacation with their parents.

The Soviet special school is a corrective institution and the main task is to correct bad (deviant) behaviour and to encourage good (conformist) behaviour. Here, moral education is socialist through and through. The ideals of conscientious discipline, the collective, and the love of labour are the main features of upbringing.

If a problem child is socially resurrected he may be released to continue his education in a normal school. If he persists with his deviancy up to the age of 14, he is then transferred to another closed school, the special professional and technical school. Here the deviant pupil spends another four years while undergoing a fresh dose of ideological, social, and moral retraining (perevospitanie). There he continues with his secondary education, works, and receives blue-collar training.

The corrective labour colony (ispravitelno-trudovaya koloniya) is a corrective institution for children up to the age of 18 who have been sentenced by juvenile courts. This labour colony should not be confused with Makarenko's (open) labour colonies during the 1920s. There are three types of corrective labour colonies for youth, according to the degree of crime committed.[59] For instance, the corrective labour colony with a strict regime is only for criminally inclined juvenile delinquents. The corrective labour school, like any other educational establishment, offers secondary polytechnic education, moral education, and intensive on-the-job work training.

[59]Ibid., p. 320.

Some of the special schools are successful in fulfilling their aim—to retrain children and return them to their families and schools. The Primorsk special school is a remarkable example of successful upbringing of problem children. Its director, Fiodor Tikhy, believes that teachers must treat the trainees as normal people. 'Let them, for the time being, digress. They are however, normal and everyday people.' Tikhy tried to convince his colleagues to start believing in their pupils: 'It is important that the teacher himself believes in his pupils and in the fact that they can study well and behave normally.'[60] Trust is the key moral force of Fiodor Tikhy: 'Trust was what these children needed, and whose biographies had much in common: disturbed homes, no desire to learn, running away from homes....'[61] Kolya is mentioned as a typical example of a bad pupil turned good:

> Kolya, like many others, did not want to study. Generally, such things don't surprise us here. Sometimes we get children who have unsatisfactory marks (dvoiki) in all subjects. For them it is important to understand that here they would be helped to overcome that which they did not want or could not overcome at home. Kolya did not want to force himself to work. I would find him during lessons either outside or I would drag him from under the bed. The first three months of school were difficult for him. Our task was to make him believe in his own potential. It may well be that this faith began to mature with a chess game. Kolya was not a bad player. He was praised and rewarded. Later, during the spring, Kolya and his grade helped the government collective farm (sovkhoz). I saw him trying and the previous docility was not there. When he was thanked in front of his detachment, he was literally blooming with happiness. In June we decided to accept him into the ranks of prefects and send a letter to his parents.[61]

Three months later, Kolya becomes a senior prefect, which is the highest symbol of leadership. During his record year he joined the 14-year-olds club, which prepares members for the Komsomol. For the first time in the history of the school for problem children, the boys were invited to join the Komsomol. Kolya left the school as a Komsomolyets (a Komsomol member) and is now studying at a PTU (vocational–technical college). In most cases, however, the boys sent to a special school are branded by the society. The ex-special school pupils are walking the tight rope. At the slightest sign of trouble, the boys are threatened with another term at a special school.

[60]Meshchersky, S., Preodolenie, *Semya i Shkola*, No. 2, 1977, p. 14.
[61]Ibid., p. 15.

TABLE 18. *The growth of tertiary institutions between 1927 and 1977*

Year	No. of institutions	No. of students (in thousands)
1915	105	127.4
1927	148	168.5
1940	817	811.7
1950	880	1247.4
1960	739	2396.1
1970	805	4580.6
1973	834	4671.0
1975	856	4800.0
1977	859	4950.0

2.5. HIGHER EDUCATION

Soviet higher education, unlike that of French and other systems, has a simple pattern called the VUZ or the higher educational establishment. Although a large number of tertiary institutions mushroomed after the revolution (Table 18), the pattern remained distinctly monolithic. As the State is totally in control of all university matters and, clearly, all academics are affected by this, the Soviet university enjoys nowhere near the same degree of autonomy and freedom as that of English and French universities.

In 1975 4.8 million students were enrolled in 856 tertiary establishments. Of these, 963,000 were enrolled in their first year. The rate of growth between 1950 and 1970 was very high, as the number of students doubled itself every decade since 1950. However, since 1970 the rate of growth has slowed down to 1% per annum. The Brezhnev regime attaches great importance to higher education, which trains highly qualified professionals for all sectors of the national economy. The degree of importance that the Government attributes to this sector of education is best seen, as Tomiak correctly observes, in the light of the officially declared aims of higher education.[62] These aims have not changed greatly in the last two decades. The 1961 decree on

[62]Tomiak, op. cit., p. 89.

the higher educational establishments of the USSR emphasized political, economic, and scientific aims of higher education. Some of these were:

(i) To train highly qualified specialists educated in the spirit of Marxism–Leninism, well versed in both the latest achievements of science and technology at home and abroad and in the practical aspects of production, capable of utilizing modern technology to the utmost, and of creating the technology of the future.

(ii) To carry out research that will contribute to the solution of the problems of building communism.

(iii) To disseminate scientific and political knowledge among the people. ...[63]

According to Article 41 of 'Osnovy zakonodatelstva o narodnom obrazovanii' (1973), the main tasks of higher education are:

1. Preparation of highly qualified specialists who are trained in Marxist–Leninist doctrine, solid theoretical knowledge, and practical aspects of their speciality and organization of massive political and rearing work.

2. Inculcating the students with high moral qualities, communist awareness (soznatelnost), culture, socialist internationalism, Soviet patriotism, readiness to defend the Socialist Motherland, and physical training of students.

3. Constantly perfecting the quality of training of the specialists, taking into consideration contemporary industry, technology, culture, and perspectives of their development....[64]

The future specialists, according to Grechishkin (1976) receive fundamental knowledge according to their profession, are armed with Marxist–Leninist theory and they pass through a serious practice of societal activity. A systematic study of social studies at the university enables the students to learn Marxism–Leninism as a purposeful and structured system of philosophical, economic, and socio-political views, and to 'develop a Marxist–Leninist view of life and communist conviction'.[65]

[63]Grant, op. cit., p. 110.

[64]For further details see Osnovy zakonodatelstva soyuza SSR i soyuznykh respublik o narodnom obrazovanii, Article 41. *Narodnoe Obrazovanie*, No. 10, 1973, pp. 4–13.

[65]Grechishkin, V. A., *Sotsializm i Obrazovanie*, Moscow, 1976, p. 123.

Most of the decrees concerning higher education deal with two items—improving training and indoctrination of the students. The outcome of these reforms was the introduction of the All-Union examination in scientific communism in all tertiary institutions.[66]

Administration of tertiary education

Soviet tertiary education is under the jurisdiction of the Ministry of Higher and Specialized Secondary Education. The Ministry is responsible for all curricula, syllabuses, textbooks, entrance examination requirements, as well as the planning of professional training. Administratively and financially, tertiary education may be subordinated also to respective republican ministries or Union ministries. Most of the tertiary institutions are supervised by the Ministry of Higher and Specialized Secondary Education, which co-ordinates other ministries responsible for certain areas in tertiary education. For instance, medical institutes are controlled by the Health Ministry of the USSR, and agricultural colleges are under the administration of the USSR Ministry of Agriculture. The uniformity of academic standards are formulated and regulated by the Ministry of Higher and Specialized Secondary Education. Regular inspection tours undertaken by the State inspection (under the Ministry of HSSE) of tertiary establishments ensure that directives, regulations, and laws are being observed and fulfilled and that lecturing and academic qualifications of lecturers are of a required level. Tertiary inspection of Soviet universities is an inseparable part and an effective means of influencing all aspects of teaching research and other related activities.[67] The main task of these inspections is to disseminate advanced methods of teaching and thereby eliminate existing shortcomings.

The Soviet version of our universities commission is the All-Union Council for Higher Education, a permanent administrative body set up to deal with the fundamental problems of tertiary education. Its main tasks are:

1. To study and assess the prospects of development of higher

---

[66]Ibid., p. 124.
[67]Yelyutin, V., *Higher Education*, Novosti Press, Moscow, 1976, p. 45.

education for a period of 3–5 years and, in a more general way, 10–15 years ahead.

2. To work out recommendations concerning organization of the study process.
3. To define ways of promoting research in the basic sciences and on key applied problems, and of developing methods of teaching and student research work.
4. To determine the ways of raising the qualifications of the teaching and research staff.
5. To make recommendations concerning the financial and everyday needs of students and their physical training.
6. To make recommendations on improving the administration of the country's system of higher education.[68]

At the local level, tertiary education is co-ordinated by Rectors' Councils. These councils are established in eighty-two large cities. All rectors of tertiary institutions of a given city would form a Rectors' Council, which would co-ordinate tertiary education in that city. They are concerned mainly with the curriculum process and professional training, and they have to submit annual reports to the USSR Ministry of Higher and Specialized Secondary Education.

Tertiary education is free and 75% of university students receive State stipends, which are small—40 roubles monthly[69] (the minimum basic wage in the Soviet Union in 1971 was 70 roubles and the average wage of the worker 120 roubles[70]).

The Soviet VUZ (higher educational institution) may be a university, a polytechnic institute, or a specialized (vocational) college.

Universities

In 1976 the Soviet Union had 63 State universities with a total enrolment of 600,000. Degree (diploma) courses are offered in sixty areas of study, including philosophy, medieval history, archaeology, ethnography and anthropology, and the history of the Soviet society. The university has a dual function—to prepare skilled per-

[68]Yelyutin, V., *Higher Education*, Novosti Press, Moscow, 1976, p. 46.
[69]Smith, H., *The Russians*, Sphere, London, 1976, p. 242.
[70]*Sovetskii Soyuz*, Spravochnik, Moscow, 1975, pp. 231–2.

sonnel for the Soviet economy and to prepare academic staff for various tertiary establishments. Student numbers are adjusted to meet the demands of the economy. The demand for university places, especially in major cities, continues to be very strong, and every applicant must sit and pass an entrance examination for the faculty of his or her choice. The entrance examinations, although based on secondary school curriculum, present a major hurdle for Soviet students. There are four examinations and the subjects depend on the faculty chosen by the student. The applicant's secondary school record is also taken into consideration but it has little influence on the final decision of the admission committee. Those who are admitted are the top students of the entrance examinations. Special concessions are made to top secondary students who hold gold medals for academic excellence. They need to pass only one examination. The authorities do try to ensure equal admission opportunities. Tutoring for university examinations is available in 600 tertiary institutions. Theoretically, this intense preparation for entrance examination is supposed to eliminate great gaps between urban and rural students, between white-collar and blue-collar workers. In practice, the ruling élite is institutionalized. Failure to enter the university was regarded as a serious blow, for despite all the propaganda about communist labour, vocational, and technical training for blue-collar professions and, ultimately, the workers' Utopia, Soviet sociological polls, as mentioned by Smith, among secondary students, show the strong preference for intellectual occupations and the low prestige of blue-collar professions.[71] In 1973 the MGU (Moscow State University), inspired by the ideal of egalitarianism, made an effort to give workers' and farmers' children a better chance. The University was ordered, presumably by the Ministry, to admit 70% from workers' families. Of the 40% who qualified for admission, very few were able to get good results at the University in their first year. Their academic performance was so poor that the University decided to disregard the social background requirement entirely and went by admission results alone. The workers' and the kolkhozniki' family contingent was drastically reduced by the natural process of elimination. Richard Dobson, a Harvard sociologist, claims that Soviet sociology studies indi-

[71] Smith, op. cit., p. 239.

cate that children of the intelligentsia had a two to eight times better chance of being admitted than workers' or kolkhozniki' children. A Soviet dissertation showed that children of white-collar parents constituted nearly 80% of the MGU first-year enrolments in 1970.[72]

The university curriculum is very demanding by our standards. A university student has between 4500 and 5500 hours of instruction in twenty to thirty-five subjects or units during his five-year period of study for a university diploma, his first academic qualification. The duration of studies at the VUZ varies from four to six years. The MGU offers five-year courses in the humanities and six-year courses in medicine. Courses in teacher education are normally five years.

During each semester the students take five or six units from their strictly fixed diploma curriculum. Up to thirty-six hours of weekly instruction in the first year is not uncommon. At the end of each semester the students must obtain satisfactory results for their essays and seminar papers as well as pass four or five semester examinations. At the end of the final year, students upon a successful completion of three or four examinations and satisfactory defence of a diploma thesis before a State Examining Board, are awarded university diplomas. After graduation, the graduate is normally assigned his or her first job in industry.

The university curriculum consists of the core subjects, which are fragmented into twenty-odd units during the five-year period of study, a foreign language, politics, military training, physical education, work training, and optional units.

Throughout their tertiary training, Soviet students receive the following five (full-year) units: dialectical materialism, historical materialism, the history of the Communist Party of the Soviet Union, scientific communism, and the stages of capitalism and socialism.

Political education is designed to increase the political socialization of the students and to make them active participants in building a new society. The authorities would like to see that every student acquires a thorough grasp of the principles of Marxism–Leninism and the political aims of the Party and society. 'Our aim,' writes

[72]Quoted from Smith, op. cit., p. 240.

Yelyutin,[73] 'is to instil into every student the Marxist–Leninist doctrine which is to become his deeply held conviction and guiding principle in life and in work.'[74]

Political socialization, together with work training, is supposed to deepen the students' knowledge of Marxist–Leninism and develop their social and political image and awareness.

> The Soviet specialist today [said Brezhnev], is one who has mastered well the fundamentals of the Marxist–Leninist teaching, who is well aware of the political aims pursued by the Party and the country.... A Soviet specialist today is an efficient organizer able to apply in practice the principles of scientific organization of labour. He knows how to work with people, values collective experience.... And, of course, a specialist today is a highly cultured and broadly informed, erudite person, a real intellectual of the new, socialist society.[75]

Brezhnev also spoke of loyalty to Marxism-Leninism and proletarian internationalism, but he particularly stressed that only by mastering Marxism–Leninism could one creatively master one's job and thus become an active builder of communism. The study of scientific communism was seen by Brezhnev as being an indispensable part of any specialist's knowledge, regardless of his occupation. Paradoxically, as it seems, academic learning goes hand in hand with communist education.[76]

Political education at the tertiary level, judging by recent reports and comments made in educational journals, is not infallible. Some students are cynical about the tenets of Marxism–Leninism, but most of them appear to be neither radical nor progressive. The political atmosphere of every facet of Soviet life makes it unthinkable, if not impossible, to oppose the official ideology. The silent majority of Soviet students are loyal, obedient, and conformist.

The university curriculum is biased towards inculcating scientific and technological skills often at the expense of the humanities and fine arts. For instance, during the ninth five-year plan period (1971–5)

---

[73]V. Yelyutin (b. 1907–) is the USSR Minister for Higher and Secondary Specialized Education, a member of the Central Committee of the CPSU, and a Deputy of the USSR Supreme Soviet.

[74]Yelyutin, op. cit., p. 39.

[75]Brezhnev, L., speech delivered at the All-Union Rally of Students, 19 Oct., 1971.

[76]Brezhnev, L., *Our Course: Peace and Socialism*, Novosti Press, Moscow, 1975, pp. 193–4.

12 new universities, 21 engineering, and 5 economics institutes were opened.

The number of tertiary establishments (universities, polytechnics, and other specialized institutes) in the academic year 1978/9 was 866 or 163 more than in the 1964/5 academic year. During the 1970s, 42% of all the graduates were in the humanities, half of whom were secondary teachers. The remainder was divided into engineering (42%) agriculture (8%), medicine and sport (7%), and fine arts (1%).[77]

The 1974 curricula reforms in tertiary education was an attempt to up-date various courses and to bridge the gap between over-specialization in either the humanities or science. Non-humanities students are obliged to take extra courses in the humanities and vice versa. Soviet curriculum experts argue that science, technology, and the humanities are becoming increasingly integrated with social problems. Hence, the engineering student has to study the history and laws of social development, and his background knowledge in the humanities is supposed to immunize him against dogmatism, scholasticism, and other social evils of over-specialization. Likewise, a philosophy student is required to study higher mathematics (for his logic), physics, chemistry, biology, and physiology in order not to become too narrow in his outlook on life.

Among the newly introduced compulsory courses are economic cybernetics, biophysics, biochemistry, automated management systems and the use of computers in engineering and economic–mathematical models and methods, scientific management principles, and analysis of economic performance in economics. Courses in psychology and education have been added to the core university curriculum.

Tertiary graduates spend a year as trainees in order to acquire the necessary practical and managerial skills which will make them efficient at their jobs. Prolonged periods of practice in industrial and other organizations is the outcome of the 1974 tertiary education curricula reforms. The on-the-job training and graduate vocational training particularly applies to doctors, engineers, agronomists, lawyers, and teachers.

[77]Yelyutin, op. cit., p. 16 and *Narodnoe Khozyaistvo SSSR v 1978 g.*, Moscow, 1978, p. 472.

Polytechnic and specialized tertiary institutes

Tertiary establishments other than the universities consist of sixty-eight highly specialized polytechnic institutes and well over 700 monotechnic institutes in education, medicine, law, agriculture, economics, visual arts, and physical education.

The current developments in Soviet economy require a complex structure of polytechnic education, which should enable the future engineer to avoid over-specialization and comprehend the production system as a whole. The Soviet polytechnic institutes are major educational and research establishments, many of them very famous and large, which train technologists and, in particular, engineering personnel, in all the key fields of modern technology. The Kharkov Polytechnic has fifteen faculties training technologists in thirty-eight subjects. The Soviet polytechnic offers refresher and in-service courses (every five years) for teachers, scientists, and engineers. The average enrolment in a polytechnic is between 10,000 and 15,000. Specialized institutes have about 3000–7000 students (about the size of our smaller universities) and they prepare specialists in a particular branch of Soviet economy. Over 200 monotechnic institutes (more than one-quarter of all tertiary establishments) train specialists in a particular branch of industry, construction, transport, and communications. Ninety-nine agricultural institutes prepare specialists for different branches of agriculture and forestry. Eighty-three medical institutes train over 25,000 doctors annually. Over 200 teacher colleges train teachers but only six law institutes prepare lawyers.[78]

Higher degrees and research

A uniform system of accreditation of Soviet graduates has been in existence in the USSR since 1934. Two academic graduate degrees are conferred upon successful masters (aspiranty) and doctoral (doktoranty) degree students. The master of science (kandidat nauk) is awarded after a three-year period of study. The aspirant has to pass a set of examinations known as the kandidatskii minimum and publicly defend his or her thesis. The thesis is normally published in advance.

[78]Ibid., p. 16.

The size of an MSc dissertation is about 150 typed pages. A good Soviet MSc thesis is equivalent to a good American or English master's dissertation, both representing the culmination of a three-year full-time research. Grant argues that a Soviet MSc thesis is equivalent to our PhD. This is highly speculative and not empirically verifiable. Having read a number of MSc and doctorate dissertations in education published during the 1970s, I have noticed that these are more than often equal to our master's major dissertation in the humanities and education. It is interesting to note that Soviet translators do translate kandidat as MSc. However, the Soviet doktor nauk, being the highest academic degree (particularly in the sciences), is higher than our science PhD. The doktor nauk consists of a major dissertation, and work on it may well last up to ten years. The finished product is ready in every respect for publication, and after it is published the thesis is submitted to the academic council. A secret ballot is taken to decide whether the degree is to be awarded. The doktor nauk is equivalent to the *doctorat d'état* rather than the *doctorat de l'université* or a PhD. In education and humanities a good American PhD can be equated with a good Soviet doktor nauk dissertation.

Like ourselves, the Soviet Union is also experiencing the inflation (inflyatsiya) of graduates with higher degrees. In 1950, 4093 graduates obtained a candidate's degree, but the number rose to 25,810 in 1969.[79] In 1975 there were more than 100,000 graduate students.[80]

In the section, concerning the demands that are made on dissertations of the procedure for awarding academic degrees document (3 July 1972), we read:

> The topics of doctorate and candidate dissertations must conform to the tasks entailed in the contemporary development of science, to the practice of communist construction, to the demands of the struggle for the development and purity of Marxist–Leninist theory, and to the demands for intolerance of bourgeois ideology, and must be based on the needs of our country's national economy and culture....[81]

It is clear that even in graduate work it is impossible to escape the Marxist–Leninist doctrine. This political imperative must necessarily

[79]Tomiak, op. cit., p. 102.
[80]Yelyutin, op. cit., p. 21.
[81]Order No. 525 of the USSR Ministry for Higher and Secondary Specialized Education, 3 July, 1972 (*Biulleten Ministerstva Vyshego, Srednego Spetsialnogo Obrazovaniia SSSR*, No. 8, 1972).

restrict creativity and autonomy. To present dissertations in the humanities or the sciences, which must first and foremost express the experience of the Party's and the people's struggle for the victory of communism and creatively elaborate the key problems of modern times and the basic patterns of developed socialist society and of its transformation into communism, poses a dilemma indeed.[82]

3. Conclusion

The Soviet educational system is, to a large extent, based on the polytechnic principle which can be observed to function in pre-school, primary/secondary, and tertiary education. In comparison with the United Kingdom, France, and the United States, the Soviet educational structure is relatively monolithic, especially at the primary/secondary level. A common core curriculum is characteristic of the ten-year polytechnic school. The one and only schooling offered for the majority (excluding special schools for the gifted pupils) is general, comprehensive, and vocational. The most recent curriculum reforms indicate a concerted effort to raise the level of education in every grade. Substantially revised curricula in grades 1–10 in most core subjects have been adopted by schools since 1970. The next five years (1970–5) were the years of changing over to new curricula, syllabuses, and textbooks.

Why would the authorities want to give so much education to so many so quickly? Could we interpret this as an ideological motive on the part of the CPSU to diminish and, eventually, bridge the gap between blue-collar workers and the intelligentsia by giving every person, irrespective of his future career, a sound, academic, and poly-technic secondary education?

Matriculation (attestat zrelosti) has now become the minimum educational qualification as an entrance requirement for most jobs. This must raise the overall social status of blue-collar professions. As far as income is concerned, workers are already equal if not superior when compared with the poorly paid members of the lower intelligentsia. The following is an extract from a conversation between a 23-year old

[82]*Soviet Education*, June, 1973, p. 63.

mechanic (diesel engines) and his employer:

'Do you plan to complete your secondary education?'

'I can manage. Valka Gorokhov, my childhood friend, after his five years at the institute, having dried up from study, gets 120 roubles. But I, with my eight grades can earn 200 roubles anywhere!'[83]

A good construction worker can earn, on the average, 350 roubles, which is nearly three times the salary of a tertiary trained teacher.[84] The only qualitative difference between the lucky person who enters university and the one who misses it and is forced to enrol at a trade school is that the former gets slightly better results at the matriculation examination.

However, if all school-leavers are to complete secondary education in the future and if some of them are to become tradesmen, then their education and wages are likely to make them equal to the lower ranks of the intelligentsia.

It seems that it is possible for most candidates to complete successfully the upper grades of secondary school. Assuming that there are weak students who are struggling with academic subjects, how do they manage to pass one of the most competitive end-of-the-year examinations in the world? The teacher, for one, is held responsible for the overall achievement in his discipline. It is expected of him that he will obtain a very high pass-rate, as near to 100% as possible. A low pass-rate may result in visits from inspectors, questions being asked, and close scrutiny by the school administration. It is conceivable that to meet these requirements of the Ministry of Education, teachers inflate their marks. It is also possible for the teacher to coach his students as he can obtain sets of test questions published by the Ministry of Education. Much of this kind of instruction is examination oriented and it encourages a great deal of rote learning.

A booklet of thirty-two samples in the Russian literature oral examination (1970) contained the following test (bilet):

1. Blok's poem 'The twelve'. The idea, composition, lexicology, and rhyme.
2. The civic work of N. G. Chernyshevsky.

[83]Sanin, V., V lovushke, *Znamya*, No. 9, 1976, p. 19.
[84]*Russkii Yazyk Za Rubezhom*, No. 3, 1976, p. 89.

The 1975 edition of the *Soviet Literature and Nineteenth-century Russian Literature* contained similarly structured questions, politics being the added element.

1. The Twenty-fourth Congress of the CPSU and the growing role of literature in communist upbringing of the working class.
2. The portrayal of a revolutionary democrat in the works of N. A. Nekrasov.

The 1975 examination in history of the USSR and Social Studies included the following questions:

1. Lenin's struggle in founding the Marxist proletarian party in Russia between 1900 and 1903. The Second Congress of RSDRP and its historical significance.
2. Labour relations under socialism.[85]

The above questions seem to test the lower levels of Bloom's taxonomy, namely knowledge and comprehension. Analysis, synthesis, and evaluation is not specifically tested.

The educated youth can influence the ideology and the political structure of Soviet society. Marxism–Leninism, over the last sixty years, has evolved into a sophisticated philosophy of positivism and rationalism. The result is the so-called scientific communism. Communist clichés, which were used for propaganda work during the ideological struggle of the 1930s, had served their purpose and have been worn out with time. The educated youth of today and tomorrow are becoming more aware and increasingly critical of the vast abyss between theory and practice of Marxism–Leninism. In theory, the October Revolution had abolished all social class differences and there was to be an egalitarian society and a uniform and universal educational system that provided equal opportunity for all. Whether the Soviet society is egalitarian or not is a controversial question. Some critics maintain that, fundamentally, communist ideology is closer to capitalist (Western industrial societies) society than we care to admit. Anderson (1959) talks of a new Soviet élite as one of educational dilemmas. It is clear that there is more than one class in an allegedly classless Soviet society. There is, for example, a high degree

[85] *Sbornik Prikazov Instruktsii Ministerstva Prosveshcheniya.*

of correlation in occupational ranking between the Soviet Union, the United Kingdom, the United States, France, the Federal Republic of Germany, Poland, and other Western societies. In these countries the professional groups often rank higher than other occupational groups. Inkeler and Baur found out that there was a high correlation between the level of education and occupation attained in the Soviet Union and the United States.)[86] Education is still, unfortunately, seen by many as a means towards social mobility. The other apparent social contradictions of Soviet education include inequality of educational opportunity based on social status and geographic location, the dichotomy between intellectual and manual labour, and, in general, the drift between theory and practice. These were the same capitalist contradictions that Marx had spoken of.

The educated Soviet youth cannot but be aware of the above stated social contradictions. Despite all this, the authorities believe that the educated communist youth, who voluntarily and conscientiously accept the ideology, will make better and more enlightened communists.

Critical attitudes towards the doctrine may, eventually, lead towards a gradual liberalization of the once rigid tenets of scientific communism and which, in the past, the majority had accepted with a grain of salt.

Another inherent contradiction expressed in Soviet education is in the very concept of the polytechnic school. The unified labour school, as it was known during the 1920s, was created in order to 'eliminate social class divisions and give labour a dignified place in the society'.[87] The unified labour school was to be the symbol of a classless educational system oriented towards socially useful labour.

But by 1934 the Lunacharsky's protected unified labour school had turned into an élitist ten-year school that was characterized by an academic curriculum based on a systematic study of the sciences, firm discipline, selective examinations, group competitiveness, vocational training, and public terminal examinations. The Soviet ten-year polytechnic school, far from what it intended to be, despite polytechnic education, equal opportunity for all, and the link between

[86]See Kazamias, A. M. C., *Tradition and Change in Education*, 1965, p. 49.
[87]Ibid., p. 101.

intellectual and manual work, has failed to eliminate social class divisions as well as to give the slogan socially useful labour a dignified place in the society.

A more delicate problem which faces Soviet educationalists today is how to maintain a delicate balance between academic, comprehensive, and vocational curricula, and how to preserve the polytechnic school from the prevailing influence of academic and theoretical curriculum.

CHAPTER 3

Moral Education and Political
Socialization of Soviet Schoolchildren

I. COMMUNIST MORALITY

In 1958 a group of American educationalists visiting the Soviet Union concluded that Soviet educationalists had failed to develop 'a rational and reflective morality'.[1] This statement, if it ever was true, is certainly not true today, as moral education occupies one of the leading places in the Soviet school curriculum.

Teaching in the spirit of communism and developing a Marxist–Leninist philosophy of life are some of the aims of the Soviet school. This was confirmed by the USA study missions between 1965 and 1971, which, having examined the Soviet educational system, recommended that American education, following the Soviet model, should develop the new American citizen—'one who is highly moral, deeply principled, ethical in his relations with others...', and that 'greater emphasis should be placed in schools on teaching moral and ethical values'.[2]

It is clear that Soviet education not only imparts knowledge and skills but it also instructs the child into the norms and values of communism. Political socialization in Soviet society is a ubiquitous process which enables the political élite (the ruling Communist Party) to inculcate in the youth loyalty to the communist regime and to the ideals of Marxism–Leninism, mastery of the environment, the acceptance of authority, love of the socialist Motherland, collectivism, conscientious labour for the good of society, a high moral sense of public

[1]Bereday, G. Z. F., et al., The Changing Soviet School, Boston, 1960, p. 418.
[2]Chabe, A. M., Soviet education: its implications for United States education, The Educational Forum, Nov., 1976, p. 17.

duty, an uncompromising attitude to the enemies of communism, and so on.[3] Complete and utter devotion to the communist cause is, clearly, the leitmotiv of political socialization in the Soviet Union today.

Major characteristics of political socialization are, no doubt, reflected by the communist ideology as defined in the Programme of the Communist Party of the Soviet Union. The inculcation of a collectivist philosophy of life or the collective ego pervades Soviet society.

The Soviet school is an ideological institution, and as such it is obliged to instil a communist world outlook in the pupil by means of prolonged and constant work.[4] A vivid example of this is an editorial in *Semya i Shkola*, which boasted of 10.5 million Soviet pupils writing the essay 'We follow the example of Communists'.[5]

The aim of a socialist system of education is to develop a many-faceted and harmoniously expressed identity that is ideologically armed and ready to participate actively in the creative labour of the nation in the building of communism.[6]

The teaching of communist ideology, which has been described by Rosen as militantly anti-capitalist, anti-individual, and anti-religious, is present at all levels of the Soviet educational system.[7] The school curriculum, especially humanities disciplines, contribute substantially to the development of a Marxist–Leninist morality. The morality taught is fundamentally Leninist for it is based on a famous formula: 'The whole task of the upbringing, education and teaching of contemporary youth should be the rearing of communist morality.'[8] It is argued that a communist morality is more than a conglomeration of ideas, principles, and rules. Morality becomes an active ideology, a force that inspires man to work and struggle for the good of mankind.

Prior to examining political socialization and its effect on the formation of personality, let us consider what Soviet educationalists

[3]*Programme of the Communist Party of the Soviet Union*, Moscow, 1961, p. 108.
[4]*Uchitelskaya gazeta*, 30 Dec., 1961.
[5]*Semya i Shkola*, No. 11, 1976, p. 2.
[6]*Uchitelskaya gazeta*, No. 142, 1977, p. 1.
[7]Rosen, S. M., *Education and Modernization in the USSR*, 1971, p. 132.
[8]Lenin's speech, Zadachi Soyuzov Molodiozhi, 2 Oct., 1920, in *Khrestomatiya po Pedagogike*, Moscow, 1976, p. 72.

have to say on the nature of communist and moral upbringing in the 1970s. This will enable us to determine the main aspects of political culture and various problems associated with moral education in Soviet schools. Examining Marxist ethics which, among other things, perpetuates the dignity of manual labour, one finds it difficult to conceptualize Soviet moral philosophy in the traditional sense. The elaborate definition of ethics is provided by Lenin's statement on morality:

> We say that our morality is entirely subordinated by the intèrests of the class struggle of the proletariat. We say: Morality is what serves to destroy the old exploiting society and to unite all the tools around the proletariat, which is creating a new, communist society.[9]

If moral philosophy is described as above it is bound to result in serious semantic difficulties which would render it almost impossible to make valid comparisons between communist and capitalist morality.

The Marxist system of morality does emphasize conformity to the laws of nature and the laws of society, and particularly to the great laws of evolution. Soviet moral philosophy can be reduced to rigid conformity to a set of customs, laws, and codes. The CPSU, unmistakably, is in control of morality and it exerts a profound influence over the entire child-reading process in school.[10] The underlying purposefulness of Soviet educational philosophy is to accomplish the Party's goal of building the material base for a communist society and developing the new communist man.

1. Soviet educationalists on communist morality

Tselikova describes a communist ideal as a moral absolute (moralnoe vysshee), having borrowed the term from Lenin's *Filosofkie Tetradi*. She states that communist morality is based on the humanist principle, which also happened to be the credo of the Programme of the CPSU: 'All in the name of mankind and all for the good of man' (vsyo vo imya cheloveka, vsyo dlya blaga cheloveka).

'The Communist ideal is', writes the author, 'a fusion of the societal

---

[9]Lenin, V. I., *Polnoe Sobranie Sochinenii*, Vol. 41, pp. 309, 311.
[10]*Soviet Education*, Apr., 1976, p. 3.

morality, moral values of aspirations, material needs, and the moral image of one's self and behaviour.' Furthermore, the unity of the objective and the subjective is another characteristic feature of a communist moral ideal.[11] Tselikova states that the questions 'What do you value most in people?' and 'What brings you the greatest joy?' were mostly answered as 'love towards labour' and 'creative work and labour achievements of the Soviet people'.

Shchukina contends that the formation of a new, socialist type of identity constitutes the main aim of communist upbringing and thus reiterating the accepted version of doctrinal prescriptions in the present-day educational system. She bases her entire argument on the 1973 major educational decree 'The basis of law of the Soviet Union and allied republics on public education'. This massive educational document is one of the major sources of moral education. It lists the aims of Soviet education as preparation of highly educated and fully developed active builders of communism, active participation in communal and state affairs, and so on. In the light of these aims, Shchukina discusses the content of moral education in the school under the following headings:

1. Formation of moral traits which determine the relationship of man towards society.
2. Formation of a communist attitude towards labour.
3. Formation of ethical (moral) attitudes towards people.
4. Formation of moral attitudes of people towards their behaviour.
5. Cultivation of moral values within one's family.

Shchukina further claims that moral attitudes of the new man manifest themselves in such ethical attributes as Soviet patriotism, citizenship, and proletarian internationalism. Clearly, morality and politics are necessarily interwoven in doctrinal prescriptions of Marxism–Leninism. Shchukina, in fact, quite openly and forcefully argues that Soviet patriotism is the most significant feature of communist morality.[12] Hence militant patriotism, which features prominently in Soviet educational journals during the 1970s and which is an important stage of moral education, will be discussed later.

[11] *Sovetskaya Pedagogika*, No. 10, 1974, pp. 97–102.
[12] Shchukina, G. I., in *Sovetskaya Pedagogika*, No. 11, 1974, p. 94.

Shchukina also believes that proletarian internationalism facilitates the development of human attitudes in schoolchildren and understanding of class solidarity with people in other countries.[13] The communist attitude towards labour occupies a special place in communist morality today. One of the resolutions of the Twenty-fourth Congress of the CPSU stated that developing in Soviet people a new, communist attitude towards labour was of utmost importance to the Party.

The school, argues the author, is to maintain the development of collectivism (kollektivizm) and socialist humanism. It is suggested that patriotism, humanism, proletarian internationalism, communist labour, and discipline are based on the concept of collectivism. Other attributes of communist morality include the ability to replace one's private interests with those of the State, truthfulness, sincerity, comradeship, and mutual respect.

Boldyryov, fellow of the research institute of general education (the Academy of Pedagogical Sciences of the USSR) discusses in his article the historical and humanistic roles of communist morality in upbringing of schoolchildren.[14] The author makes a claim that Marxist–Leninist morality is relative rather than absolute: 'There cannot be morality applicable for all times.' He uses Engels to back up his argument. Engels wrote that the criteria of good and evil change so much throughout the ages that they often contradicted one another.[15]

Next, communist morality is discussed as the highest level of man's morality. A characteristic feature of this morality is a profound optimism. Having stated Brezhnev's summary of communist morality—diligence, honesty, modesty, comradeship, mutual respect, etc.—the author proceeds to show how communism is the basis of moral education. The result is that the reader gets a new definition of Marxist–Leninist ethics as a dialectical synthesis of psychology, philosophy, sociology, politics, and education. How is this to be carried out in practice? By means of socially useful labour, suggests the author. He states that moral education necessitates a close tie

[13]Shchukina, G. I., in *Sovetskaya Pedagogika*, No. 11, 1974, p. 95.
[14]Boldyriov, N. I., in *Sovetskaya Pedagogika*, No. 9, 1974, pp. 92–105.
[15]Ibid., p. 93.

between education, life and communist construction.[16] He refers to Lenin to prove this thesis, for Lenin has stated: 'To be members of the Union of Youth means to give one's work, one's strength for a common cause. This is the essence of communist upbringing. Only through such work does a young boy or girl become a communist.'[16] Hence, the author concludes that communal life and collective labour by means of different types of pupil's work brigades should bridge the gap between theory and practice.

Professor Monoszon, member of the Academy of Pedagogical Sciences and a prominent Soviet educationalist, writes that Marxist–Leninist morality necessitates an active and creative attitude towards nature. He defines the communist Weltanschauung in terms of:

1. Dialectic and materialistic method in explaining the phenomena of nature.
2. Irreconcilability of and opposition to an idealist, metaphysical, and bourgeois philosophy of life.
3. Optimism based on coexistence of the interests of the working class.
4. Humanism, socialist patriotism, and internationalism.
5. The unity of theory and practice and the inseparable link between Weltanschauung and the construction of communist society.
6. Revolutionary nature of a communist world outlook.
7. Militant atheism.
8. Non-tolerance of bourgeois ideology.[17]

Having defined so neatly the characteristic features of a communist philosophy of life, the author discusses the Marxist–Leninist theory of formation of personal identity. He argues that man is conditioned by his environment and that man develops his identity during active social life.

Professor Monoszon is, at the same time, aware that moral education has failed to reach all schoolchildren. He writes that some school-leavers do not possess a sufficiently developed philosophy of life.

---

[16]Boldyriov, op, cit., p. 102.
[17]Monoszon, E., in *Narodnoe Obrazovanie*, No. 9, 1974, p. 111.

They do not always consciously master the most significant theses of the Marxist–Leninist teaching.[18] The author sees the necessity for raising the degree of ideological and political maturity among all schoolchildren. He regards the 11–15-year-olds as being the most critical phase in political socialization. He describes problems associated with rearing. The child's identity is conditioned by social interaction and there is a need to remove the antagonism between the individual and society. It is suggested that a conscientious assimilation of communist outlook by the child is far superior to that of rote learning. The method used is the method of conviction. Schoolchildren should be convinced rather than told of the truth of Marxism–Leninism. The author argues for the necessity of teaching all subjects against the background of Marxism–Leninism. He places great hopes on social studies (politics) in grade 8.

Arguing from Marx, Monoszon postulates the two-level cognition of Marxism–Leninism by schoolchildren, namely of everyday or practical communism and of theoretical or rational communism. He sees the school's task as that of elevating practical communism to the heights of abstract Marxism–Leninism.[19]

To enable the child to accept communist morality it is necessary, according to Monoszon to isolate in each discipline the sum total of basic theoretical concepts and generalizations concerning the outlook on the world and, consequently, reveal the essence of phenomena of nature, life, man, and society.

The last problem examined is that of the transfer of theoretical knowledge into personal convictions. Mirovozzrenie (a philosophy of life), argues the author, becomes a 'real conviction when it permeates the whole life and action of man'.[20] This idea is based on the teachings of Kalinin.

The problem of transfer is also linked with morality. The author claims that the child's attitude and behaviour towards the real world is significant if one is to teach the right kind of morality. A transfer of knowledge into beliefs can only take place if the right morality of the communist-oriented personal attitudes towards nature, society, work,

[18]Monoszon, E., in *Narodnoe Obrazovanie*, No. 9, 1974, p. 113.
[19]Ibid., pp. 113–18.
[20]Ibid., p. 121.

and friends is achieved on the basis of the organic fusion between the intellectual, emotional–volitional, and actively practical spheres.[21]

In another article Monoszon examines some theoretical problems associated with defining the pedagogical basis of the pupil's world outlook. He claims that some teachers limit themselves (and which is incorrect) to a philosophical interpretation of mirovozzrenie. The programme of the CPSU defines mirovozzrenie as a system of knowledge based on philosophical, economic, and socio-political modes. The author, quoting from Ushinsky, dispels the myth that moral education should begin in the upper grades. 'Every grade', wrote Ushinsky, 'beginning with the elementary one, ought to have a rounded outlook that takes into account the age of pupils.'[22]

In the recently published monograph by the Academy of Pedagogical Sciences, the authors maintained that character education begins at the pre-school level.

Monoszon stresses that the most important prerequisite for the formation of communist mirovozzrenie is to base the teaching of all school disciplines on the Marxist–Leninist methodology.[23]

Among the more influential works on communist morality is Shchukina's *Teoriya i Metodika Kommunisticheskogo Vospitaniya v Shkole* (*The Theory and Methods of Communist Rearing in Schools*). The book is prescribed for all tertiary teachers' institutes and was prepared by a group of authors from the Academy of Pedagogical Sciences. Consisting of fourteen chapters on the peculiarities and principles of rearing, formation of the collective and its influence on the pupil's identity, moral upbringing, general features of child-rearing methods, and so on, the text is an authoritative reference on communist upbringing. One of the fundamental aims of the book is to equip teachers with methods of child rearing and to show alternative models in the inculcation of moral values in the pupil. School discipline is a necessary prerequisite for the successful implementation of moral education and political socialization. In the Soviet Union, school discipline is used to improve the overall effectiveness of moral, social, and political indoctrination. Shchukina mentions four

[21]Ibid., p. 123.
[22]Ibid., p. 12.
[23]Ibid., p. 16.

principles that influence the process of formation of communist morality in schoolchildren. They are:

1. Comprehending the essence of ideas concerning a particular world view.
2. The pupil's attitude towards the acceptance of ideas should be both positive and active.
3. Systematic internalization of experience of communist relations (participation in the Pioneer and Komsomol organizations) is the most important condition of communist upbringing.
4. Significance of the age factor as the greater part of moral education is taking place between the ages of 7 and 17.[24]

Commenting on the role of moral norms in the behaviour of schoolchildren Bogdanova (1973) wrote:

> Moral norms are an element of social consciousness. They perform various functions: they embody the model and the reference point for behaviour; they regulate one's relations with society and its members and monitor individual behaviour. Moral norms are a form of standard by which social behaviour is evaluated (positively or negatively).[25]

To Bogdanova, moral norms are a means of controlling and assessing behaviour. Following N. K. Krupskaya and the more recent Soviet educationalists, Bogdanova asserts that the pre-school age is visualized as a period of intensive imitation of adults and that children show a heightened interest in the content of the moral rules and behaviour. Using Petrova's text *Instilling Culture in Pupils in Grades 1–3* (1972) as a guide, Bogdanova implies that the schoolchild is a natural moralist. For instance:

> Little boys are not ashamed to follow rules of politeness towards little girls and towards their elders since they see the rules as a basis for politeness and decorum. Among very young children there is as yet no negative attitude towards the rules of morality, such as manifested in teenagers. They do not yet entertain any doubts concerning their necessary and obligatory nature.[26]

Not only children can be moralists but they can be uncompromising and merciless moralists. Sometimes the nature of the offence and

---

[24]Shchukina, G. I., *Teoriya i metodika kommunisticheskogo vospitaniya v shkole*, Moscow, 1974, p. 94.
[25]*Soviet Education*, Nov. 1974, p. 22.
[26]Ibid., pp. 23–24.

the degree of punishment which the children demand for the accused are too severe. Bogdanova uses the example of a little boy who would not let his friends touch his notebook as an illustration of the above. His class accused him of being greedy, complained to the teacher, and demanded that he be expelled from the Octobrists on the grounds that he was unfriendly. On another occasion a first grader forgot to bring a game to an Octobrist meeting as he had promised. The children saw this as a serious deviation from the school rules and demanded that he be punished—that he should be summoned to appear before the Principal and that his parents should be notified so that they might punish him also.[27]

Krupskaya in her article 'On the question of children's books' stressed that the child between the ages of 8 and 13 years wants to know what is good and what is bad and in this way he develops his ethical principles.[27] Children's games could be employed to teach morality. Vygotskii believed that nowhere was the behaviour of a child so regulated by rules as in games, and that nowhere did it assume such a free and morally instructive form as in games.[28]

The above pronouncements on communist morality by some of the most eminent Soviet educationalists today indicate that some of the main aims of upbringing in the Soviet schools are:

1. The formation of a new, socialist type of identity.
2. The preparation of highly educated and fully developed active builders of communism.

The main characteristics of communist morality as defined by Soviet scholars in numerous monographs and articles published after 1970 could be listed as: dialectical materialism, humanism, collectivism, proletarianism, communist labour, patriotism, internationalism, and atheism. Of these, militant patriotism and communist labour, to be discussed in the next chapter, have received the greatest emphasis in Soviet educational periodicals of the 1970s.

2. Soviet interpretation of Marxist ethics

So far we have looked at some of the articles on communist mor-

[27]Ibid., p. 25.
[28]Vygotskii, L. S., *Educational Psychology*, Moscow, 1926, p. 237.

ality. Now we shall consider an official, Soviet interpretation of Marxist ethics. This will enable us to determine the extent to which Soviet educational philosophy is based on Marxism.

In *Marksistskaya Etika* (1976) the authors argue that collectivism denotes a communist morality, whereas individualism characterizes a morality of the West. The authors discuss moral principles of socialism and communism under the following headings: devotion to the communist cause; communist humanism, collectivism, and solidarity; conscientious attitude towards labour and its significance for a creative perfection of the identity; patriotism, and internationalism.[29] Having assumed that devotion to the communist cause is the key moral principle of communist morality, the authors argue that the principle gives birth to a moral substance (ideinost). Devotion to the cause does not mean, the authors point out, the negation of personal for the sake of communal interests. Instead, it necessitates a fusion of the self and the collective. The authors warn the reader that communist moral substance must be humanist in essence if it is to avoid fanaticism and the belief that ideas and principles are superior to people. Now, basing their argument on Marx, they claim that communism is humanism.[30] Communist humanism is viewed as being universal (vseobshchii), active (deistvenny), and real (realny). Humanism in a Marxist interpretation is, claim the authors, a 'struggle for man, and his free and many faceted development'[31] Communist humanism is directly opposed to capitalism, which is looked upon as a social evil that enslaves and exploits mankind. In their attempt to link the terms communist humanism and collectivism, the authors argue that since the true meaning of a Marxist humanism is revealed by its imposition of demands for the all-round development of the identity of every individual, then a Marxist solution of the problem of the relationship between man and society is to be realized in the principle of collectivism.[32]

Collectivism as a principle of communist morality is a concrete, all-proletarian, all-socialist, and all-communist fusion of millions of

[29]Titarenko, A. I., *Marksistskaya Etika*, Moscow, 1976, pp. 183–218.
[30]Ibid., p. 193.
[31]Ibid., pp. 193–4.
[32]Ibid., p. 196.

wills into a single will.[33] Again, referring to Marx, the authors argue that socialist collectivism is a prerequisite for a complete development of the identity. Hence, a free development of identity is unthinkable outside the collective.[34]

Communist morality necessitates a communist attitude towards all forms of socially useful labour. Marx wrote that labour is the first fundamental condition of the entire human existence.[35] The authors argue from Lenin that communist labour is a free labour for the benefit of society, for the common good.[36] In a socialist interpretation, labour becomes a 'decisive moral condition by which society assesses man.[37] Hence, one of the most significant moral principles of communism is a 'conscientious attitude towards labour'.[37]

Concerning the place of patriotism and internationalism, the authors, referring to Lenin, argue that patriotism is man's deepest feeling and that internationalism is superior to nationalism.[38] The authors argue for unity between internationalism and socialist patriotism which would bring about a communist brotherhood of mankind.[39] Should there be a contradiction between the national and the international, then the international should be placed above the national. This argument is borrowed from Lenin who stated that in order to be a 'social democrat and an internationalist one has to think not only of one's own nation but also place above it the interests of all, their freedom and equality'.[40]

The *Marksistskaya Etika*, as a monograph designed for university students and those enrolled in the courses of Marxism–Leninism, attempts to appeal to wide audiences. In an attempt to popularize major principles of Marxism and limited by space, the authors were unable to present convincing arguments showing that communism is based on Marxist ethics. Instead, the above summarized views in Chapter 6 show that there are certain similarities between Marxist–

[33]Ibid., p. 198.
[34]Ibid., pp. 201–2.
[35]Ibid., p. 202.
[36]Ibid., pp. 205–6.
[37]Ibid., p. 205.
[38]Ibid., pp. 211–13.
[39]Ibid., pp. 214–15.
[40]Ibid., p. 214.

Leninist and Marxist ethical systems. Soviet educational philosophy is, clearly, closer to Marxism–Leninism rather than pure Marxism.

The book is a vivid proof that there exists an urgent need in the Soviet society for a meaningful and relevant system of ethics and value theory. The emphasis of the communist morality is on the formation of a communist world view in the broadest masses of working people, and their inculcation with the ideas of Marxism–Leninism. It highlights internationalism rather than nationalism, socialist patriotism rather than geographic nationalism, and socially useful labour rather than bookish ideology.

3. Towards a definition of communist morality

The key role of communist education is to prepare educated and ideologically committed individuals who have mastered the communist world view. This is done by raising the general educational and cultural level. It is assumed that higher educational standards will lead to a superior culture, which in turn should aid the construction of communist society. Since the very concept of communist society is Utopian there is something prophetic and optimistic about the aims in the education of the new man. To say that the aim of Soviet education is the struggle for the heart and mind of people, for their convictions, for their political orientation, for the orientation of their social, moral, and aesthetic ideals, is to suggest its transformational and metaphysical quality. For this kind of philosophy to succeed, communist morality must become the individual's inner need. Ideologically committed adherents of the Marxist–Leninist morality are described as being formed through labour, communal participation, and the struggle for the cause of communism, as being aware of, to use Brezhnev's words, 'one's labour as a minute part of the great common cause—the building of communism'.

Communist morality is defined as the scientific interpretation of the phenomena and processes of reality, a conscientious attitude towards labour, the steadfast observance of the rules of socialist society, fulfilment of the demands of the Soviet way of life, and of socialist internationalism and patriotism, and irreconcilability towards all negative phenomena in everyday life.[41] This particular definition describes rather succinctly the prescriptive nature of the Marxist–Leninist ethics, with its emphasis on commitment, loyalty, and fulfilment on the part of the individual.

The Marxist–Leninist ethic is viewed as a unity of knowledge, convictions, and actions, and Soviet educationalists argue that to be a committed Marxist–Leninist means to be actively involved in the practical implementation of the moral and socio-political principles stemming from the Marxist–Leninist ethic.

Marxist–Leninist ethics is functional, for it serves the State—the construction of communism and a communist attitude towards labour, being the highest moral norm, is a necessary condition for achieving the communist ideal. It follows that the concept of socially useful labour and the term partymindedness (partiinost) are of utmost significance in the Marxist–Leninist system of beliefs.

It could be concluded that the most important practical and ideological aim of moral education in the Soviet school is to unravel the individual's spiritual potential and to shape his 'thinking, tastes, inclinations, and aspirations in such a way that the struggle for the unflinching realization of the ideals of communism in all spheres of personal and social life and in spiritual and production activity' become his inner need.[42]

4. Trends in political socialization and moral education

So far we have considered theoretical issues of Marxist–Leninist ethics. Next we must examine the communist morality in practice in order to assess the degree of success of moral and political education in the Soviet school. Reference will be made to a few recent sociological surveys conducted in Soviet schools. The role of youth organizations in reinforcing the communist morality will be dealt with in the next section.

In 1974 a survey was conducted to determine the overall effectiveness of political socialization in the upper secondary grades.[43] A

[41]Ogorodnikov, I. T., *Pedagogika*, Moscow, 1968, p. 52.
[42]Tselikova, O. P., Kommunisticheskii nravstvenny ideal, *Sovetskaya Pedagogika*, No. 10, 1974, p. 98.
[43]*Vospitanie Shkolnikov*, No. 2, 1974, pp. 34–36.

random sample of 1168 students represented secondary schools of Moscow, Voronezh (500 km south-west of Moscow), Ulyanov (700 km south-east of Moscow), and Magnitogorsk (1400 km south-east of Moscow). Some of the questions asked were: From which sources do you most often receive political information? What is the nature of political information in your grade? Which forms of political information are the most popular? What place should it occupy in the upper grade? What do you regard as the main deficiency in its presentation?, and so on. The most telling answer was to the first question, which was answered thus:

the press	84.9%	journals	41.8%
television	79.3%	the school	29%
radio	58.1%	parents	25.2%

It showed that the mass media are far more effective in political socialization of the Soviet youth than parents and schools combined. The survey revealed many negative aspects of political information in the school and failures of political socialization. Political meetings were found to be irregular and superficial in quality. There was no permanent day set aside for such meetings. Instructors were poorly qualified and poorly involved form-teachers conducted their normal school administration, form meetings, and the day-to-day running of the form during the hour scheduled for politinformatsiya. Furthermore, there was no effective control of the Komsomol, which would normally be very involved in this kind of work. In short, on this occasion, political socialization via politinformatsiya sessions was a dismal failure in many secondary schools of the above-mentioned cities. One of the reasons why politinformatsiya had failed was the method itself. Less than one-third of the students were given the opportunity to analyse current affairs and the majority had used the pereskaz (retelling method) which they felt was dull and sterile. Many had felt that reading to the class of selected excerpts from *Pravda* was equally ineffective. Not all of the senior students read regularly political periodicals such as *Novoe Vremya* and *Za Rubezhom*, and only 53.8% read the *Komsomolskaya Pravda*. One of the major findings of the survey was the students' apathy towards political information sessions in the school was clearly the result of these inappropriate methods. Those who cared wished for more discussion and analysis, expressing their own views and attitudes to make their own conclusions. It is clear that the impact of political socialization will vary from one region to another. Soviet educational periodicals abound in articles enumerating various successful practices of political indoctrination in schools. For instance, Meshalkina, Principal of the Secondary School No. 14 in Severodvinsk (near Arkhangelsk), describes how it is done at her school. Political sessions are held on Fridays, between 8.30 and 9 a.m. Every Komsomol group in grades 8–10 has at least two political officers (politinformátor) who act as group leaders during political sessions. In the elementary grades (grades 1–3) political discussions are initiated by grade teachers. They base their talks on *Pionerskaya Pravda* and other children's periodicals. All teachers are involved in preparing material for politinformatsiya. They regard their work as a party task (poruchenie). Students are encouraged to write lectures on current affairs and the best ones are used for politinformatsiya work in grades 5–10. These gifted orators are the junior lectors (yuny lektory).[44] Every student is required to give 2–4 talks during the term.

A special study into the nature of ideological and political upbringing, conducted by the Volgograd teachers' college, revealed a growing influence of political school clubs and societies in the Volgograd region.[45] Curiously enough, the study discovered that senior students followed closely international relations and tended to ignore local politics. The more disturbing finding was the fact that students received most of their political information through the mass media and not the teachers. Demidov argues that it is, indeed, the teacher who should play a decisive and major role in the organization of political education. Clearly, there is a trend among some Soviet teachers to ignore their ideological role in political education.

Vilchko, in his survey, attempted to examine the nature of socialization at the secondary school No. 27 in Penza.[46] He hoped to

[44]Meshalkina, K., O sisteme politicheskoi informatsii, *Narodnoe Obrazovanie*, No. 8, 1974, pp. 59–60.

[45]Demidov, N., Vospityvat obshchestvenno–politicheskie interesy, *Narodnoe Obrazovanie*, No. 8, 1974, pp. 54–55.

[46]Vilchko, Ya. A., Kharakter deyatelnosti starsheklassnikov i formirovanie ikh mirovozzreniya, *Sovetskaya pedagogika*. No. 4, 1976, pp. 52–57.

discover some form of concrete manifestations of the influences of education on the student's activity and his attitude towards life. The students (grade 9) were divided into three groups. Group 1 consisted of the top academic stream, group 2 represented the average achievers, and group 3 had the weakest (under-achievers) students. The findings are shown in Table 19.

TABLE 19

	Group 1 (%)	Group 2 (%)	Group 3 (%)
1. Expressed positive views about the school	the maj.	—	—
2. Satisfaction with the curriculum	96	80	—
3. Community involvement (special tasks)	91.8	30	50
4. Performing socially useful labour	62.5	40	36.5
5. Ready to overcome difficulties	100	60	62.5
6. Helping other students	100	70	50
7. Helping parents with domestic tasks	80	—	50
8. The use of free time			
(a) Sport	16.4	—	—
(b) Self-education	79	60	37.5
(c) The theatre, cinema, television	45.8	60+	
9. The level of mirovozzreniya achieved			
(a) High	54.4		
(b) Average	45.6	Average	37.5
(c) Below average	—		62.5

Group 3 was characterized by a low degree of cognitive activity. Only 33% read books in their spare time, 70% spent their time being out with their friends, and 90% visited the cinema and watched television. Slightly more than 50% glanced at papers and only 33% regularly read journals. Almost 40% of the group was attracted to material comfort. It seems that the better students (group 1 and partly group 2) were nearly twice as much involved in the community, performing socially useful labour, assisting the weaker students with their school work, helping their parents at home and spending their spare time on self-education than the under-achievers in group 3. Paradoxically, it is the under-achiever who is the least interested in the community involvement and who remains indifferent to certain ideological issues. Character education and political socialization have failed to convert the under-achievers into convinced and committed young Marxist–Leninists. On the other hand, the academically gifted students exhibit exemplary attitudes towards the school curriculum, socio-political upbringing, and the communist morality. It could well be that in the atmosphere of militant Marxism–Leninism, which does not tolerate any deviation from the prescribed tenets of the doctrine, it is safer and more prudent to act as a satellizer, a conformist, and be rewarded with the social status and prestige. Acting out the role set of a committed, convinced, and conscientious young builder of communism would be a necessary condition for upward social mobility. Interestingly enough, nearly 80% of the sample hoped to enter a tertiary institution. Under the influence of their families, students came to regard higher education as the most significant factor in the development of one's identity.[47]

Perhaps the most crucial finding of the survey was the senior students' moral standards concerning the meaning of life. Labour, serving the society, and contributing to the happiness of others were for them the most important social and moral values which determined the purpose and meaning of life.[47]

5. Moral values as envisaged by Soviet pupils

A group of Soviet educationalists conducted a survey, the aim of which was to categorize, rank, and define variables in moral education. They proceeded on the assumption that such a set of variables would reflect the basic tasks of communist morality in the school curriculum.[48] Table 20 illustrates the pupils' ranking of values in moral education. Twenty-three different values were mentioned and ranked by the pupils aged 7–17. In their aggregate, they describe the model citizen, the ideal of the new Soviet man, the embodiment of a socialist type of personality. In short, they reflect the pupils' attitudes towards the reality surrounding them, towards work, towards society, and towards themselves.[48] From a practical point of view these moral attributes provide Soviet educators with a very quick checklist for

[47]Ibid., p. 54.
[48]*Soviet Education*, Nov., 1974, p. 65.

TABLE 20. The pupils' ranking of values in moral education. (*Source:* Sovetskaya Pedagogika, *No. 9, 1973, p. 63–70. This table was constructed by the author, being based on the mentioned article*)

	Group 1 Grades 1–3	Group 2 Grades 4–5	Group 3 Grades 6–8	Group 4 Grades 9–10
1.	Love of Motherland (patriotism)	Love of Motherland (patriotism)	Love of Motherland (patriotism)	Patriotism
2.	Comradeship and collectivism	Comradeship and collectivism	Communist awareness	Communist awareness
3.	Respect for elders	Respect for elders	Collectivism	Collectivism
4.	Kindness	Kindness	Humanness	Internationalism
5.	Honesty	Honesty	Honesty	Humanness
6.	Love of work	Love of work	Conscientious attitude towards labour	Honesty
7.	Thrift	Thrift	Discipline	Conscientious attitude towards labour
8.	Discipline	Discipline	Activism	Discipline
9.	Diligence	Self-sufficiency	Bravery	Responsibility
10.	Love of knowledge	Love of knowledge	Will-power	Commitment to principles
11.	Love of beauty	Love of beauty	Self-criticism	Purposiveness
12.	Physical fitness	Physical fitness	Modesty	Activism
13.			Love of knowledge	Love of knowledge
14.			Love of beauty	Love of beauty
15.			Physical fitness	Physical fitness

determining and assessing the extent of the impact moral education (or character training) and political socialization have on the pupil. It also enables the teacher to describe in concrete terms, the overall quality of moral education within the school curriculum. The study confirmed, which is remarkable, that moral, social, and political values were 'essentially the same for pupils of all ages'.[48] It also demonstrated that moral education in the Soviet school is concentric rather than linear, for many personality traits and value judgements were formed simultaneously in the pupil.

The most characteristic features of moral education in grades 1–3 were patriotism, collectivism, love of work, love of beauty, honesty, and discipline. On the other hand, students in grades 9–10 were more concerned with such attributes as communist awareness, internationalism, purpose in life, responsibility and commitment to the ideology. Activism, however, was not as popular with Soviet matriculants as it is with students in grades 6–8. It dropped by four points and moved into a low priority (No. 12) position. Since patriotism, collectivism, and a communist awareness received the highest ratings from the students, they could be seen as the three most fundamental political, social, and moral norms which define the identity of the new Soviet man.

Soviet educators believe that moral education commences as soon as the child enters a kindergarten. Some, including Bogdanova and Kairov, claim that it begins at birth.[49] The current view is that children aged between 7 and 10 are ideal material for 'a systematic and developmental moral education'.[50]

To determine the nature of moral norms and models of behaviour adhered to by the primary schoolchildren in grades 1 and 2, Bogdanova concentrated on the games children play. During her experimental study with the 7- and 8-year-olds she discovered that they followed a code of ethics of their own.

1. An eye-for-an eye principle or making concessions for concessions.
2. Taking turns and sharing in all kinds of games.

[49]Kairov, I. A., *et al.*, *Azbuka nravstvennogo vospitaniya*, Moscow, Prosveshchenie, 1975, p. 5.
[50]Ibid., p. 5.

3. Being faithful during an agreement, especially when playing a voluntarily assumed role in a game.

4. The rules of comradeship and lending a helping hand.[51]

Bogdanova observed that moral development of the child takes place amid a complex interaction of external influences (peer groups, opinions, fear of rejection by his/her peers) and internal motivating agencies (the feeling of shame, conscience, pride, etc.). She believes that children show a 'heightened interest in the content of rules governing behaviour and that they are "natural" moralists'.[52] Children, however, are not entirely aware that violating the moral norm leads to consequences. Bogdanova concludes that the child should be made aware by his/her teacher that violation of the moral norm is always associated with consequences for other people (his/her family, friends, the collective).[53]

The above seems to indicate that Soviet methods of child rearing (vospitanie) are successful in producing a child who not only conforms to adult standards of good conduct but who also loves his/her land and people and who sees the meaning of life to make others happy and to labour for the benefit of his/her society.[54]

II. THE ROLE OF THE SCHOOL CURRICULUM IN MORAL EDUCATION

Cary (1976) analysed the treatment of Marxist–Leninist ideology in history, geography, and social studies as taught in Soviet schools.[55] He hoped to discover how Soviet schoolchildren aged 10–17 acquire a Marxist–Leninist belief system. He knew only too well the emphasis that Soviet pedagogical literature places on political socialization. Among his findings were the following generalizations:

1. Marxist–Leninism is emphasized more in history than in any other subject in grades 5–9.

[51]*Soviet Education*, Nov., 1974, p. 27.
[52]Ibid., p. 24.
[53]Ibid., p. 35.
[54]Bronfenbrenner claims that Soviet children are more conformist than their Western counterparts and that they more readily adopt the adult values of good conduct (see *Two Worlds of Childhood*, Penguin, 1974, p. 76).
[55]Cary, C. D., Patterns of emphasis upon Marxist–Leninist ideology..., *Comparative Education Review*, Feb., 1976, pp. 11–29.

2. The higher the grade the greater the emphasis on Marxism–Leninism.
3. The greatest emphasis on ideology in the senior grades.

A computer analysis of seventeen school textbooks (11 in history, 5 in geography, and 1 in social studies) and their 5030 exercises of the type 'Tell about the fight of communist parties against revisionism, dogmatism, and sectarianism' or 'Why is our Motherland called socialist?,' and so on resulted in the eighty-three word dictionary of the concept of Marxist–Leninist ideology. These words and phrases were used 1635 times in the exercises. Cary concludes that between the middle (grades 4–7) and senior (grades 8–10) schools there is an intensification of both curricular and extra-curricular efforts to inculcate a Marxist–Leninist belief system and that senior students are expected to develop a sophisticated philosophy of Marxism–Leninism.[56]

Cary's findings concerning the continuity of political socialization in Soviet schools are valid in so far as they elucidate the Marxist–Leninist bias in social sciences. His conclusion that senior students are expected to develop a sophisticated philosophy of Marxism–Leninism does not necessarily spell out the success of political socialization in schools. Some students, despite the intensification of indoctrination, remain untouched by the rigorous political training, and some even manifest anti-Soviet and anti-social tendencies.

In *Literaturnaya gazeta* we read about the increasing rates of juvenile delinquency due to the fact that 'social life in many educational establishments suffers from the lack of emotional fulfilment.[57] Here are examples of deviant behaviour. Four schoolboys were returning home when they were approached by two drunk senior students. They asked the boys to empty their pockets and they took their money. One of the boys had no money which infuriated the attackers. They dragged him into the nearest entrance and began to beat him up. 'What do you think his three friends did?' asks the writer. 'They simply went home.' In another incident, a man heard a girl's cry for help. When he approached the company he was told to get.... He did not get very far. He was attacked by three youths who hit him in the

[56]Ibid., p. 29.
[57]*Literaturnaya gazeta*, 22 June, 1977, p. 12.

back with something heavy and as he fell down put their boots into action. Fortunately, but unfortunately for the attackers, our man was an ex-serviceman who still remembered unarmed combat. Our hero managed to repel the attackers but not without losing his briefcase and scarf. 'Good Lord,' exclaims the writer, 'could it be true, that these sympathetic, shy lads, who are neither illiterate nor stupid but educated, have, in the most savage manner, beaten up my friend?'[57]

The above-mentioned instances of juvenile delinquency in the Soviet Union must be fairly common if they get a mention in the most influential socio-political and cultural Soviet weekly *Literaturnaya gazeta.* It could be that the general weakening of moral standards in the Soviet society, the Westernization of the Soviet Union, particularly a growing demand for consumer goods and the apparent signs of materialistic tendencies, with a corresponding loss of spiritual values, forced the authorities to tighten up the instruction of young people in the values of Marxism–Leninism. It is clear that the image of Soviet society of the 1970s is vastly different from a Western cliché of the Stalinist society of the 1940s. There are obvious social and political indicators to validate this claim: (i) demographic changes—a spectacular growth of the urban population due to a continual migration from rural areas, a decrease in fertility, and the growing number of one-child families; (ii) upward social mobility and the prominence of an educated intelligentsia in the Soviet social structure; (iii) shortage of semi-skilled and skilled workers in all spheres of the Soviet economy; and (iv) changes in the ideology with its emotional commitment to patriotism, the collective, labour, and Marxist–Leninist doctrine. It is normal to expect that the values and beliefs presented to Soviet youth have changed, particularly during the last two decades after Stalin.

It is equally apparent that the school curriculum, witnessing the gradual socio-political and cultural transformation of the Soviet society plays a far greater role today than in the past. The latest monograph on moral education in schools stresses the ideological and political fibre (zakalka) of the young, and the communist philosophy is defined as a fusion of knowledge, convictions, and application.[58]

[58]Maryenko, I. S., *et al., Voprosy ideyno-vospitatelnoi raboty shkoly v svete reshenii XXV Syezda KPSS*, Moscow, Pedagogika, 1977.

In another work, Prokofiev writes that labour training (trudovoe vospitanie) occupies an important place in communist upbringing and that its satisfactory solution is not only the most important practical task of the communist construction but also the sphere of an acute ideological struggle.[59]

The Soviet curriculum as an agency of political socialization is a powerful weapon of ideological education. Improbable as it may be, Soviet educators often argue that all school disciplines should be used in moral education and political indoctrination. Obviously, some disciplines are more effective in the upbringing process than others. Literature, history, and social studies are particularly vulnerable to a Marxist–Leninist interpretation, and they play a key role in the teaching of a communist belief system.

1. The principles of moral education in the elementary school

The elementary school is regarded as the backbone of moral education. The character of moral education is both prescriptive and restrictive. It deliberately sets out to change behaviour by influencing the social and political attitudes of pupils in a specific and prescribed manner. It could be seen as being unethical and undemocratic as children are moulded into the set ideal of a socialist identity. They have no say in the planning of the content of moral education and they are not presented with the alternative models of behaviour. Thus they have no opportunity to select their own systems of values and clarify their own beliefs, feelings, and value judgements.

The main emphasis in moral education at the elementary school is on discipline (conduct), feelings, and beliefs rather than such cognitive skills as modes of moral judgement, ability to evaluate, ability to control impulses and to defer gratification, etc., which are left for the secondary schools. What the teachers are trying to do in grades 1–3 is to teach morality, which, if we are to adopt and modify Wilson's classification of the goals of moral education, would consist of:

1. Accepting other people's feelings and interests as one's own.

[59]Kuzin, N. P., *et al.*, *Sovetskaya shkola na sovremennom etape*, Pedagogika, Moscow, 1977.

2. Accepting moral imperatives which define one's own and other people's lives and interests.

3. Accepting the necessity to live by categorical imperatives, i.e. translating one's principles into action.[60]

By now one should be aware that in the Soviet Union moral education and the acquisition of political values or political socialization are interrelated and almost inseparable. The earliest signs of moral education in the Soviet kindergarten mark the beginning of political socialization. One of the first scholars to point this out was Bronfenbrenner (1972). In his monograph he stated that the aims of the Soviet school were concerned with the development of communist morality in children. He discussed the official manual *The Programme of the Upbringing Work of the School* (1960) as a definitive example of moral education and political socialization. He found the manual's prescriptions of the specific activities designed to develop the desired characteristics to be the most revealing information. For each grade level there were sets of aims, followed by procedures employed. They defined behaviour at school, at home, and in the community.

The content of moral education in the elementary school, which affects all pupils aged 7–11 was described under the following headings:

1. Communist morality.
2. Responsible attitude toward learning.
3. Cultured conduct.
4. Bases of aesthetic culture.
5. Physical culture and sport.[61]

Since 1960, with one or two additions, communist morality for the elementary pupils has emphasized the following traits:

1. Sense of good and bad behaviour.
2. Truthfulness, honesty, kindness.
3. Atheism: science vs. superstition.
4. Self-discipline.
5. Diligence in work and care of possessions.

[60]See Wilson, J., *Introduction to Moral Education*, Penguin, 1967.
[61]Bronfenbrenner, U., op cit., pp. 32–33.

6. Friendship with classmates.
7. Love of one's own locality and the Motherland.[61]

Strictly speaking, only the last objective hints of political socialization and, hence, communist morality.

Let us consider the nature of behaviour of the 7-year-olds (grade 1) at school, at home, and in the society as envisaged by the *1960 Manual of Moral Education*.

The school: all pupils are expected to arrive in the classroom on time. They also must 'greet the teacher and all technical staff by name, give a general greeting to classmates... keep one's things in order, obey all instructions of the teacher, learn rules of class conduct... learn and fulfil special classroom duties, such as those of monitor, sanitarian, class librarian, teacher's assistant, gardener, etc.'

At home, the pupil, upon rising, must greet his/her parents. He/she must also 'thank them after the meal or for any help received... take care of his/her own things (e.g. sew on buttons, iron, shine shoes, keep desk in order);... help with housecleaning, dusting, setting table and chairs in place, serving, clearing, washing dishes, growing and caring for decorative flowers, taking care of younger children... do homework; follow the rule "Job done—take a rest, then start another job".'

In society the pupil is asked to follow these rules: 'Behave calmly; obey all requests of elders; do not disturb others by loud noise or running; yield right of way to grown-ups; don't litter; dissuade friends in time from engaging in bad behaviour... visit local workshops, sovkhozes, kolkhozes, garages, etc., and become acquainted with how people work there for the common good....'[62]

The *ABC of Moral Education* (1975) is a practical manual for primary teachers.[63] How does the *1960 Manual of Moral Education* compare with the *ABC of Moral Education* published in 1975? In many ways the latter continues moral upbringing recommended by the 1960 and 1971 theoretical manuals. Both were published by the Academy of Pedagogical Sciences, the most scholarly educational establishment in the USSR. The *ABC of Moral Education* supplements the theoretical manual *A Model Guide for the Upbringing of*

[62]Ibid., pp. 30–36.
[63]Kairov, op. cit., pp. 1–319.

Schoolchildren (*Primernoe soderzhanie vospitaniya shkolnikov,* Moscow, 2nd edn., 1976). In the introduction, the authors point out that moral education is one of the most significant tasks of the Soviet school.[64] They describe communist morality in terms of the following attributes: industry, honesty, humility, friendship, mutual respect, personal dignity, love of the Motherland, patriotism and internationalism, collectivism, active attitude towards life, and profound respect towards working people. These characteristics indicate that Soviet moral education, like any moral education, is based on the following three constituent concerns: the self, others, and the relationship between the self and others.

The pupils' collective is the backbone of Soviet moral education, and the manual tells the primary teacher how to utilize the pupils' collective influence and how to direct children's relationships within the collective and how to make use of the collective as the most powerful and the most effective means of refining the child's identity. 'It is necessary', write the authors, 'to help the children to perceive the collective as a whole. . . . . The collective must care about each comrade.' Use is made of 'Rules for pupils in grades 1–3', which provide a viable basis for life within the collective.[65]

The *ABC of Moral Education,* like the *1960 Manual,* discusses moral education as a three-way process: moral inculcation at school, at home, and in the community. The direct moral education takes place during most lessons. Extra-curricular activities reinforce morality taught by the school. These include the Octobrist's meetings, moral education through play, excursions, and clubs.

In grade 1 the teacher's energy and effort is directed towards organizing the pupils' collective in his/her classroom, which will become an active unit of the communist youth organization. Moral education in grade 1 takes place at school, during reading, art and work-training lessons, and outside the school.

Reading and discussing articles, stories, poems, and tales from prescribed readers enable the children to comprehend and appreciate moral behaviour of adults. Children discuss stories which raise problems concerning man's character, his behaviour, and his attitudes

[64]Kairov, op. cit., p. 3.
[65]Ibid., p. 9.

towards society, nature, and the State. The notions of justice, honesty, friendship, loyalty, patriotism, and internationalism are taught in grade 1. As the 7-year-olds are quite naive about these concepts, it is the teacher's duty to explain in the most concrete terms the morality of good and evil. It is no longer true to claim that children are unable to comprehend didactic stories. Stories on moral and psychological themes are, according to Kairov, meaningful to children in grade 1.[66]

The primary school reader used in moral education is divided into the following four sections:

1. V. I. Lenin as the high ideal of man.
2. On good and sympathy.
3. You are not alone in the world.
4. Loving all living things.

The section dedicated to Lenin is of crucial significance to moral upbringing of the schoolchildren. Krupskaya argued that the image of Lenin should be authentic rather than artificial. She claimed that the 10-year-olds were capable of comprehending social evils, especially the impoverished and miserable life of the working class.[67] The same argument is used to justify the inclusion of Lenin's life in the primary school.

Citizenship and man's humanity to man, which is reminiscent of the golden rule principle, is, clearly, the key moral precept in grade 1. The section 'on good and sympathy' contains eight stories dealing with such character traits as honesty, bravery, comradeship, kindness, humanness, collectivism, modesty, and so on. The text that follows is a typical moral story concerning comradeship.

> Once Vasya brought with him in the yard a fire engine.
> Seryozha quickly ran to Vasya.
> 'We are friends! Let's play together as the firemen.'
> 'Let's,' agreed Vasya.....
> Other children came.
> 'We are also the firemen.'
> But Seryozha hid the car from the children.
> 'I am Vasya's friend! I alone will play with his car!'

[66]Ibid., p. 22.
[67]Krupskaya, N. K. O buchebnike i detskoy knige dlya I stupeni, in *Pedagogicheskie Sochineniya*. Vol. 3, Moscow, 1959, p. 240.

> The children were hurt and they left. Next morning Borya brought with him a toy train with carriages to play with.
> Seryozha ran to him. 'I am your friend! We are friends! Let's play as the train drivers.'
> 'Let's,' agreed Borya.
> They began to play as the train drivers. Vasya came.
> 'Can I join?'
> 'No, you can't,' said Seryozha.
> 'Why not?,' asked Vasya surprised. 'But you are my friend. You said so yourself only yesterday!'
> 'That was yesterday,' replied Seryozha. 'Yesterday you had a fire engine but today Borya has a train and carriages. Today I make friends with him.'

Presumably the story is read to the grade by the teacher. The questions to be answered are:

1. Why did Seryozha at first call Vasya his friend and later Borya?
2. Can we call Seryozha a real friend?

Children are encouraged to love nature and the story that follows is one of the five tales making up the section 'Love the animals'.

> The dog barked viciously.... Right in front of it sat a little frightened kitten. It had its mouth open wide and it meowed pitifully. Two boys stood nearby and waited to see what would happen. The woman looked through a window and she hurried out. She chased the dog away and in an angry voice shouted to the boys:
> 'Aren't you ashamed of yourself?'
> 'Why should we be ashamed? We haven't done anything!'
> 'That's why it is bad', replied the woman in an angry voice.

The children had to answer the following two questions.

1. Why was the woman angry?
2. Why didn't the boys feel guilty?[68]

The tasks of moral education in grade 2

Having established a good, effective pupils' collective in grade 1, the teacher must now develop further the notion of ethical ideal (nravstvenny ideal).[69] More moral stories are studied in the class.

[68]Kairov, op. cit., p. 116.
[69]Ibid., p. 121.

They are simple, concise, and with a moral truth. For instance, the following story could be read:

> The summer season had come. Raspberries had ripened in the forest. The three friends—Vasya, Mitya, and Misha—had decided to bring home a basket each of ripened berries. They walked in the forest for a long time. They had eaten enough of the raspberries and filled their baskets. Suddenly, Mitya noticed that the key from his house was missing. He decided to return and search where the raspberries were collected. Misha sighed, felt sorry for his friend and went home. But Vasya....

Exercise: Write what Vasya should have done.[70]

During their reading sessions the children are taught to understand and evaluate basic moral problems. The stories are used to develop basic loyalties, positive qualities of character, and a philosophy of life. Children are taught to be honest, kind, truthful, and trustworthy. Such qualities as true friendship, sympathy, sensitivity, fairness, justice, and mutual assistance are taught during all sessions in grade 2. Here, Soviet pedagogues refer to Ushinsky's pronouncement on children's literature: 'A literary work that is moral compels the child to love a moral deed, moral feeling, and moral thought expressed in that work.'[71]

During art and craft sessions the child is further taught to develop a correct collective relationship towards labour. The main task in art is to teach the child to express in his/her drawings his/her attitude towards different events, people, and nature, so that he/she should be able to understand the good and evil in everyday life.

The tasks of moral education in grade 3

In grade 3 children are subjected to more academic and sociopolitical pressures. Their work-load becomes heavier and they are expected to take their obligations in the collective seriously. In grade 3, more than in elementary grades, the child's personality is shaped by his/her active participation in the collective and by academic performance. The pressure on the child in grade 3 is greater than in the

[70]Kairov, op. cit., p. 122.
[71]Ushinsky, K. D., *Sobranie Sochinenii*, Vol. 5, Moscow, 1949, p. 349.

preceding grades because it is the last year of primary schooling and, by now, the child has become a Pioneer.

During literature and art and craft sessions, the teacher is expected to inculcate in the children love of the Soviet country, people, workers, and nature. Supplementary material on humanism and collectivism is provided by the *The ABC of Moral Upbringing* (*Azbuka nravstvennogo vospitaniya*). As before, the section on Lenin and his activity is of crucial importance in moral education in grade 3. Not only the legend is kept alive, and with it the heroic era that is removed further and further by the veil of history, but also the Pioneers, being the grandchildren of Lenin, are encouraged by the teachers to model themselves on Lenin. Children are meant to develop the following moral traits: kindness and goodwill, friendship and comradeship, justice, and personal responsibility.[72] Moral discussions are introduced for the first time in grade 3. The following moral discussions (eticheskie besedy) have been recommended in the manual: Term I (On friendship and comradeship); Term II (About collectivism; learn to keep your word and your promise); Term III (On goodwill and indifference; On courtesy); and Term IV (How to become socially involved).

One of the multiple socio-political roles that Soviet teachers perform is that of a moralist. Grade 3 teachers are expected to judge and appraise in a moral context the pupils' attitudes, classroom behaviour and conduct, and discipline. The basic function of this moral appraisal is to explain to the children the meaning of what is right and wrong and to continue guiding them through the artificial maze of good and evil, moral and immoral. In making moral judgements, the teachers are warned not to commit a common error and shift the focus of their attention from the child's conduct to his/her identity. There is, clearly, a vast semantic and philosophical difference between 'Fedia, you haven't learnt the lesson and in doing so you make it worse for yourself and you have upset me' and 'Fedia you are a bad boy!'[73] As soon as the unfortunate Fedia is labelled by the teacher as a bad boy, the class may soon treat him as one.

[72]Kairov, op. cit., pp. 200–1.
[73]Ibid., p. 197.

2. The place of ideology in the secondary curriculum

Kuzin's remarks that the new history curriculum is a major ideological achievement of Soviet education could easily apply to the Soviet curriculum as a whole.[74] The new curriculum was introduced in 1966 and the transition took ten years. Educational reforms in humanities and social sciences are, according to Kashin, of 'a great importance in the formation of the communist outlook and the moral aspect of youth, as well as understanding of politics of our Party and social and political events within the country and the international arena'.[75] The new curriculum reflects the Party's concern for a more intense political socialization and moral education. Let us consider briefly the role of literature, history, and social studies in ideological education.

2.1. LITERATURE AND MORAL EDUCATION

The new literature curriculum in the secondary school indicates the intensification of ideology.[76] For instance, the prescribed textbook for literature in grade 4 (1972), which is a product of three major revisions in the last twenty years, contains nearly one hundred pages (or 30%) dealing with the Civil War, the Great Patriotic War (1941–5), the October Revolution, and Lenin. The 1958 edition contained only twenty-five pages (11%) and the 1962 edition published during the de-Stalinization period, had twenty pages (8%) dedicated to the patriotic and revolutionary theme. As a result of the inclusion of revolutionary and war literature in the 1972 edition, the textbook has increased by more than 100 pages. In addition to such famous Soviet writers as Fadeyev and Simonov there were A. Gaidar (*Timur and his Team*), V. Katayev (*The Son of the Regiment*), A. Tvardovsky, and N. Tikhonov. The difference between these stories and those in the 1958 edition is that they are masterpieces of Soviet prose. They were written specially for the 11-year age group and they clearly appeal to their feelings, emotions, and ideals.

[74]*Sovetskaya Pedagogika*, No. 3, 1976, p. 49.
[75]Ibid., p. 36.
[76]Ibid., pp. 26–27.

The study of literature in grades 4–10 is meant to make the pupil aware of the Motherland (Rodina). The principles of historicity and party mindedness (partiinost) dominate the teaching of literature. The students in grades 8–10 understand the ideological meaning of literary works and they correctly evaluate the role of literature in the society. They approach literature from the angle of communist ideals.[77] The students, however, do exhibit a fragmentary and superficial knowledge and shallow judgements during literary discussions.[78] Lenin's articles and the Party decrees on literature occupy a prominent position in the textbook for grade 10. Although the students are closely familiar with these documents some of them are unable to use them in their analysis of literary texts.[79]

A sample of 250 pupils in grade 4, representing four secondary schools in Moscow and Kaliningrad, were asked to name the happiest and saddest moments in their lives.[80] One-third thought of their families, friends, and acquaintances. The other third mentioned their own personal successes and failures at school, etc. (egocentric), and the last group included trivial things like 'couldn't get a ticket to the cinema', and so on. The question established that only one-third of the fourth graders are capable of experiencing compassion for other people. Thus the need for moral education in grade 4 was established. The most common method of teaching moral principles is the method of hero-worship. The pupils compare their own behaviour with that of their heroes and as a result develop or reexamine already existing moral criteria.[81] Kudriashev taught that literature sessions 'should, above all, evoke aesthetic feelings, which in themselves had an enormous implication for character training'. 'The aesthetic feeling,' he wrote, 'if it is genuine and profound, carries with it a vast moral principle.'[82] The main themes emphasized in the study of

[77]Kurdiumova, T., Zadachi prepodavaniya literatury, *Narodnoe Obrazovanie*, No. 9, 1973, p. 50.
[78]Ibid., p. 50.
[79]Ibid., p. 52.
[80]Meshcheriakova, H. Ya., *Nravstvennoe vospitanie uchashchikhsya na urokakh literatury, v 1V–V klassakh*, Moscow, Prosveshchenie, 1975, p. 6.
[81]Ibid., pp. 6–7.
[82]Kudriashev, N. I., *Za tvorcheskoe izuchenie literatury v shkole*, Moscow, 1968, p. 28.

Russian literature in the Soviet school are Soviet patriotism, bravery and militarism, and communist labour.

Some Western critics are very dubious as to whether literature in the Soviet school is an effective weapon of moral and political instruction. Political socialization seems to be reasonably successful, for the majority of students, judging by their examination scripts in literature, readily accept communist morality. A random analysis of 250 examination compositions from six different Moscow schools indicated that only one-fifth selected the free topics. The rest wrote on the prescribed topics 'I love you Russia, my Soviet land' and 'It is our good fortune, children, to march under the Red Banner'.[83] The over-emphasis on ideology became apparent when the 1969 survey of the Russian literature oral examinations involving a sample of over a hundred tenth-graders from seven Moscow schools showed that the students knew and understood Soviet literature much better than Russian classical literature. They were thoroughly familiar with Lenin's articles on literature and so on.[84] But in an earlier survey (1964) involving 1139 compositions from grades 9–11 it was discovered that the most popular authors were Granin (*I go into the Storm*), Bondariov (*Silence*), and Aksionov (*Colleagues; A Ticket to the Stars*). Of these, Aksionov, a young author, with his unorthodox prose describing the Soviet drop-outs, topped the list. Only thirty-four pupils (13%) discussed Solzhenitsyn's *One day in the Life of Ivan Denisovich* and an equal number discussed Sholokhov's *Virgin Soil Upturned*. In discussing the works mentioned, the students 'rejected the established stereotypes and favoured a direct and honest description of reality without embellishment'.[85] The authorities could not allow questioning and, at times, an outright rejection of the basic concepts of socialist realism and other accepted norms to go on. Thus there was every reason to believe that the penetration of bourgeois philosophy was, indeed, taking place during the early sixties. For the first time the Soviet youth felt alienated from dictatorship of the proletariat, and although they wrote in an elated manner about

[83]Shneidman, N. N., *Literature and Ideology in Soviet Education*, Lexington Books, Toronto, 1973, p. 13.
[84]Ibid., p. 15.
[85]Ibid., p. 18.

marching under the Red Banner their essays lacked a feeling of truly patriotic fervour.[86] Nearly a decade ago a certain writer stated that his inspection of the Russian Republic schools revealed that the tenth-graders had very vague notions concerning partiinost and narodnost* in literature and that they had mastered only superficially the ideological and class struggle role of literature.[87] There are at least three factors that could have minimized the overall effectiveness of ideological training in the Soviet school. Methodology is certainly the key factor. Any method, based on the formal approach to the teaching of literature with a predetermined ideology and the one and only principle of literary analysis, is limiting and not necessarily successful. Secondly, it is possible that Marxist–Leninist highly theoretical principles are too abstract and too remote to capture the imagination of secondary students, let alone to be meaningfully interpreted by them. It is not so much their age factor as their attitude towards truth and their priorities in life that contribute towards their alienation from the Marxist–Leninist ideology. Finally, the teachers themselves may be either unwilling or unsuccessful in converting their pupils to a communist world view. It is difficult to imagine that all teachers would play the role of an agitator.

2.2 HISTORY AND IDEOLOGY

History in the Soviet curriculum does play a very important role in political socialization of schoolchildren aged 10–17. History has at its core a central tenet of Marxist–Leninist ideology–historical materialism. In history, the average emphasis upon ideology is greater in the senior grades (8–10). What is even more interesting, the emphasis upon Marxist–Leninist ideology in history is similar to that of social studies, the latter being an overtly indoctrinating subject.[88] Commenting on the role of history in the formation of a communist world view in the pupils, Kuzin said: 'History lessons enable us to demonstrate...[to the pupil] the inspiring and organizational role of the Communist Party in the revolutionary transformation of the

---

[86]*Literatura v shkole*, No. 6, 1968, p. 59.
[87]*Uchitelskaya gazeta*, 4 Sept., 1969, p. 1.
[88]Cary, op. cit. p. 23.
*See Glossary.

world....[89] He also pointed out that the history curriculum is inseparably linked with the 'development of a Marxist–Leninist history'.[89] Evans claims that there is no radical change in emphasis in history in grade 10. According to him the overall emphasis on class struggle has remained about the same, but sections on post-war history stressed economic and technological achievements.[90] Evans also notes the emphasis on class struggle in the 1973 textbook was somewhat higher than in 1952. Although there have been quantitative shifts in history textbooks between 1952 and 1973, there were no qualitative changes. 'Symbols of class struggle and social reconstruction', writes Evans, 'predominated consistently in treatments of the Revolution, the Civil War, early industrialization, and the collectivization of agriculture....'[91] National defence appears to be the principal theme in the interpretation of the war. In short, the Soviet ideology is characterized by social transformation, economic development, and national defence. The central message (or ideology) of the history texts is:

> ...the period of social reconstruction is past; the required framework of society has been erected; the Party is seeing to the completion of the material–technical base; all that remains is for the individual to do his part in economic construction, and through the Party's guidance to emulate the shining example of the heroes and heroines of the Revolution and War....[92]

In the new history curriculum the student is taught that the romantic–heroic era of the October Revolution, the Civil War, and the Great Patriotic War is 'past—long past'.[93] It would seem that there is a subtle shift in the Soviet ideology in the history texts since 1953.

Since the communist regime has achieved secure acceptance it need no longer challenge large-scale organizations. It therefore focuses on the individual instead. In this manner the regime creates an artificial tension between 'a person's behaviour (influenced by the practical dictates of institutions) and his expectations for himself (established

---

[89]*Sovetskaya Pedagogika* No. 3, 1976, p. 50.
[90]Evans, A., Trends in Soviet secondary school histories of the USSR, *Soviet Studies*, No. 2, 1976 pp. 234–5.
[91]Ibid., pp. 237–8.
[92]Ibid., p. 239.
[93]Ibid., p. 238.

by the Utopian requirements of an ideology)'.[94] Thus the regime makes the individual responsible for remaining imperfections in the ideology. This, clearly, would explain the current emphasis on such values as a conscientious attitude towards labour, a communist morality as deep inner conviction, being a convinced Marxist–Leninist, and an ideologically committed individual.

'The depth of understanding of Lenin's scientific heritage', remarked V. N. Stoletov, President of the Academy of Pedagogical Sciences, 'is found to be in direct proportion to the depth of knowledge of history.'[95] Perhaps the most prominent feature of the new history curriculum is the increase of attention to the study of Lenin's works, fundamental documents of the Party, and so on. These are regarded as being of primary importance to the formation of a communist outlook.[96] The new edition of the history text in grade 4 contains a substantially revised and rewritten essay 'The Communist Party of the Soviet Union is leading us to communism' and an entirely new topic 'Citizen of the Soviet Union'.

To summarize, maximum attention is being paid to the history curriculum in the patriotic and international indoctrination of pupils according to the 'heroic labour traditions of the working class'.[97] Both patriotic and international upbringing, together with scientific–atheistic indoctrination are regarded as being the necessary prerequisites in the formation of the new Soviet man. It is clear that the history teacher's task, as envisaged by the Party, is that of intensifying the 'international and patriotic, economic, legal, and atheistic indoctrination of schoolchildren'.[98] The overall aim of the history curriculum is to develop a materialistic world view and profound communist convictions in schoolchildren.[99]

2.3. SOCIAL STUDIES AND INDOCTRINATION

Social studies (obshchestvovedenie), which was added to the school

[94]Evans, A., Trends in Soviet secondary school histories of the USSR, *Soviet Studies*, No. 2, 1976, p. 239.
[95]*Sovetskaya Pedagogika*, No. 3, 1976, p. 53.
[96]Ibid., p. 52.
[97]*Soviet Education*, Aug., 1973, p. 8.
[98]Ibid., p. 13.
[99]Ibid., p. 12.

curriculum in 1962, is taught only in grade 10, and being in the last year of secondary schooling it attempts to polish the process of indoctrinating Soviet pupils in the values and symbols of Marxism–Leninism, the official Soviet belief system. The subject occupies a special place in upbringing as it is best suited for systematically explicating Marxist–Leninist ideology.[100] In contrast to instruction in history, literature, and geography, instruction in social studies explicitly treats the philosophical and theoretical questions of the ideology.[101] The main aims of the course are to 'arm students with the knowledge of the basic laws of development of nature and society, to teach them to link theory with the practice of communist construction, to instil the fundamentals of dialectical thinking, and to inculcate firm convictions, will, and other qualities'.[102] The course synthesizes various aspects of the ideology derived from other courses. It facilitates a deeper understanding of the problems of the Communist Party and its policy. It promotes upbringing of the pupils in the spirit of a communist consciousness. The most important stages in the process of imbuing the upper grade students with a scientific world outlook and communist convictions to be found in social studies are:

1. The study of the most important principles of a Marxist–Leninist theory.
2. A systematic and logical study of politics of the Communist Party and the Soviet Government.
3. The organization of active, ideological, and socially useful activities of the pupils.[103]

The study of documents relating to the Twenty-fifth Congress of the CPSU occupies the most conspicuous place in social studies. Seminar topics range from 'The characteristics of contemporary capitalism' to 'The Soviet multi-national State—the main weapon of communist construction'. One of the more popular teaching methods is the one based on comparing theoretical pronouncements of the

[100]*Narodnoe Obrazovanie*, No. 10, 1974, p. 41.
[101]Cary, op. cit., p. 13.
[102]Ibid., pp. 13–14.
[103]*Narodnoe Obrazovanie*, No. 10, 1974, p. 41.

Party's Congress with the relevant tenets of Marxism. For instance, the topic 'Gradual transformation of socialism into communism—an objective law of societal development' is studied against the background of Lenin's "The State and revolution" (Chapter 5).[104]

III. THE ROLE OF YOUTH ORGANIZATIONS IN MORAL AND POLITICAL TRAINING

Moral and political upbringing takes place in the Soviet school not only through the curriculum but also by means of a massive, communist youth movement. The Octobrist, the Pioneer, and the Komsomol youth organizations are huge Soviet collectives where the majority of schoolchildren and youth aged 7–17 are politically socialized. These collectives perform a vital role in character training, moral education, and political indoctrination. They reinforce and augment the Soviet ideology present in the school curricula.

Soviet youth organizations play such a major role in education and communist upbringing that without their valuable contribution the whole process of communist education would have been seriously undermined.

This chapter will deal with collective upbringing in the Soviet Union. Particular attention will be given to moral training and political socialization of children and youth. Child socialization is normally described as that type of behaviour during which the individual acquires the attitudes, values, ways of thinking, personal, and social attributes, all of which contribute to his development as a social agent.

In order to understand how collective upbringing works one ought to ask: What does it require, expect, and demand of the average member? What we really are asking is what Soviet society must have in order to survive and maintain its *status quo*. Political socialization and moral training are, no doubt, based on imperatives or the so-called functional requisites.

How, then, does Soviet society inculcate its required norms in the individual? Soviet socialization techniques amount to no more than

[104]*Narodnoe Obrazovanie*, No. 10, 1974, p. 42.

the imposition of discipline in early child rearing and the use of rewards and punishments.

Collective socialization in the Soviet school is institutionalized by means of such formal organizations as the Octobrists, the Pioneers, and the Komsomol. It is commonly believed that peer influence is the strongest within these groups. Unlike the United States, where peer socialization often undermines adult standards and society, in the USSR youth organizations reinforce the Soviet communist ideal. Hence the problem of role conflict of multiple loyalties and of overlapping conflicts, which normally characterize peer groups in an open society are not, generally speaking, applicable to the USSR. Having realized the strength of peer-group influence, Soviet educationalists control and manipulate them in order to teach a standardized morality, namely Marxism–Leninism.

The single most important difference between Soviet and American education is the degree of influence of agencies of socialization on the child and the rationale and methods used by both to inculcate an official role model. As the United States is an open society, one of its immediate problems is that attitudes towards moral instruction and political indoctrination will vary so greatly as to contribute towards a serious failure of socialization and perhaps even de-socialization. In the Soviet Union the entire process of socialization is standardized and controlled by the Party, working hand in hand with educational, vocational, and recreational institutions. In the United States the child is affected by a number of agencies of socialization which often question the socially accepted norms. The child spends a great deal of his free time in unsupervised play with his peers and he participates in autonomous grouping. In the USSR all socializing agencies, including the media, are subservient to the needs of the State and ideology. Child upbringing (vospitanie) outside the school is being emphasized and attempts are made to reduce the amount of time the child spends on unsupervised and wasteful activities. Youth organizations have expanded their extra-curricular activities so that in theory, at least, the child has little opportunity to play outside the collective.

The localization of primary responsibility in the upbringing of children is another major difference between socialization in the Soviet

Union and the United States.[105] It is assumed that the family plays the decisive part in primary socialization. In the Soviet Union, however, the role of the family in child rearing has been reinforced with yet other socializing agencies—youth organizations and the school. Both of these collective-centred agencies compete against the individual-centred family for the loyalty of the child.

Youth organizations, after the family, represent the most influential primary groups in the Soviet Union. They are characterized by communal activities, ritual behaviour, and symbolism—all of which are designed to promote loyalty, solidarity, and collectivism.

1. The Octobrists and Political Socialization

Collective socialization in the Soviet School begins in grade 1, when the 7-year-old pupils are prepared to join the Octobrist organization. Although membership is voluntary, all children are strongly encouraged to become little Octobrists and thus, become, symbolically speaking, the little grandchildren of Lenin. As a socializing agency, the Octobrist organization, like all Soviet youth organization, is based on Makarenko's moral imperative in the collective, by the collective, and for the collective. The classroom through its structure does necessarily socialize the child. In the USSR each classroom is a unit of the communist youth organization appropriate to that age level.[106]

The Octobrists accept pupils in the first three grades (ages 7–10). The little Octobrists have to understand and internalize the following five cardinal rules of the organization:

1. Octobrists are future Pioneers.
2. Octobrists are diligent children; they like the school and respect adults.
3. Only those who like work may be called Octobrists.
4. Octobrists are honest, brave, apt, and skilful.
5. Octobrists are friendly children who read and draw, play and sing, and live happily.

[105]Bronfenbrenner, U., *Two Worlds of Childhood*, Simon & Schuster, New York, 1972, p. 4.
[106]See Grant (1968), Bronfenbrenner (1972), and Bereday (1960).

The above five rules inculcate the social, moral, and political up-bringing of the Soviet child. They are very close to the teachings of Christianity: love thy neighbour, work hard, and be happy. The Octobrist organization, as the name implies, is an agent of political indoctrination. The Octobrist detachment is divided into smaller units of six pupils. Each such unit is called the little star (zvyoz-dochka). The life of children within the zvyozdochka both in and out of the school normally reinforces the official doctrine. Their communal activities from now on for the next ten years (in the ranks of the Pioneers and the Komsomol) are excessively ritualistic and rich in overt symbols. Octobrists meet regularly at a formal assembly, they sing patriotic songs, and learn about the life of Lenin. They participate in the official initiation ceremony during which they receive their badges—a little red star with a baby picture of Lenin. Octobrists observe various national holidays and anniversaries, including Mother's Day and the Day of the Armed Forces. The All-Union Octobrists' week (16–22 April) was introduced in 1972 and has been celebrated ever since.

The Octobrist rules express the major objectives of communist upbringing for the youngest school-age level group. Shlagina (Baku) suggests a school programme for internalizing the five rules of the Octobrists.

Rule 1. *Octobrists are future Pioneers.* For this rule the suggested plan of activities is:

1. Organizing an Octobrist game and visiting the land of the Pioneers.
2. Inviting Octobrists to Pioneer meetings.
3. A series of talks on the history of the Pioneer organization.
4. A series of talks about the Pioneer heroes.
5. Visiting a Pioneer centre.
6. Talks on the topic 'The rituals-of the all-Union Pioneer organiz-ation of V. I. Lenin'.
7. Competition: 'You are the future Pioneer.'
8. Introduction to traditions of a Pioneer regiment (druzhina).
9. Meeting leading Pioneers from other schools, suburbs, and cities.[107]

[107] *Nachalnaya Shkola*, No. 10, 1975, p. 36.

Rule No. 2. *Octobrists are diligent children, they like the school and respect adults*, the following programme is suggested:

1. Introduction to the pupil rules (grade 1).
2. The Octobrists' visits to the pupils' homes: 'The fulfilment of the pupils' rules at home' (grade 3).
3. Meeting with people of unnoticed professions: the school nurses, caretakers, and maintenance men (grades 2 and 3).
4. Composition on the theme 'The school as your native home' (grade 3).
5. A series of talks and meetings on the theme 'Your friend: mother'.

Rule No. 3. *Only those who like work may be called Octobrists* envisages the following activity: duty roster, book-binding for the school library, helping mothers at home, meeting people from all walks of life, visiting local industry, and the Octobrist reading conference on the theme of work.

Rule No. 4. *Octobrists are honest, brave, apt, and skilful*, stipulates a programme that begins with a morning talk 'About truth and lies'.

Rule No. 5. *Octobrists are friendly children; they read and draw, play and sing, and live happily*, emphasizes collective celebration of birthdays, competition in poetry recital, an art exhibition on the theme 'I look upon the world with vigilant eyes'.

Chesnokova, Secretary of the Central Soviet of the All-Union Lenin Pioneer organization, very quickly dispels our notion that the Octobrists ranks as an informal organization, being essentially a rather vague preparatory stage for entry into the Pioneers.[108] Her article 'On perfecting the work with the Octobrists' aimed at senior Pioneers, teachers, and parents, reaffirms the opposite, that the Octobrist's upbringing is a carefully planned process of political socialization. She argues that youth collectives, including 13 million Octobrists, represent the union of three generations which are true to revolutionary ideals. Communist morality unites all Octobrists from the very first days of their school life. The fifty-year existence of the

[108]Grant, N., *Soviet Education*, Penguin, 1968, p. 64.

Octobrists (1924–74) is, according to the author, a 'brightly lit page in the annals of the child–communist movement'.[109]

Chesnokova's article is, clearly, an attempt to systematize the Octobrist's upbringing in the school. In this she is guided by the following directive from the Ministry of Education of the RSFSR: 'During school hours, the formation of communist traits of the children's identity . . . is governed by the logic and content of school disciplines.' On the basis of a series of experiments in elementary grades in Moscow during the 1960s and the 1970s, which included nearly 300 primary teachers' collectives, it was possible to work out a manual *Suggested Planning of Upbringing Work for the Whole Year (Grades 1–3)*. The manual included the following major educational aims:

1. It is clear that the school . . . must utilize all its capacity to plan and organize the following aspects of the children's life outside the school: ideological, political, and moral upbringing; the collective life. . . .
2. The training of the rudiments of communist convictions and behaviour in every schoolchild will depend on his developing ability and habit to behave independently in the Octobrist way. . . .
3. It is necessary to direct the main attention to the everyday systematic work with the Octobrists' collective. . . .
4. Primary education helps to secure the organic unity of school and extra-curricular rearing work.
5. The main reason for uniting junior pupils in the Octobrists' collectives is to prepare them for membership of the Pioneers.
6. The development of spiritual and intellectual abilities can only take place when mental work is united with manual work.
7. The school is to have an increased major role in the system of communist upbringing.[110]

The author advocates the use of symbols in the Octobrist movement. The sharing of symbols like slogans, signs, and names for various links (the Red carnation, the Friendship, etc.) and participating in the All-Union march 'Always ready', brings about, no doubt, a

[109] *Narodnoe Obrazovanie*, No. 10, 1974, p. 121.
[110] Ibid., pp. 122–4.

feeling of solidarity, collectivism, and friendship at the 8–10 age group.

Acting out different social roles by the Octobrists is vital to the success of socialization. Each link or little star (zvyozdochka) has its own leader, medical officer, a librarian, a gardener, a foreman, a sportsmaster, and an organizer of games. These roles are exchanged among the pupils at least once each school term. During his three-year membership of the Octobrists the pupil would have had a multiple experience in internalizing the adult roles.

The Octobrist rules reinforce the pupil rules (grades 1–3). They also act as the first stage of moral education by providing values and shared beliefs about what is right or wrong, good or evil. The Octobrist rules facilitate the development of physical, intellectual, vocational, moral, and aesthetic upbringing.[111]

The Octobrist organization fulfils an important role in the socialization process. It has become, clearly, a massive process of moral replacement—a process in which the new generation acquires the values which not only must be socially acceptable but also reinforce Soviet adult standards. This is particularly evident in the article 'Familiarizing children with phenomena of civic life'. It is claimed that such activity should take place in the kindergarten and that children should be gradually made aware that they live in the Soviet Union, that the country is vast, mighty, and rich. No matter where the Soviet child resides he is to be introduced to the Russian Republic because there 'we find Moscow, the capital of the USSR, Leningrad, the Revolution city, and Ulyanovsk, the hometown of V. I. Lenin'.[112] Children are encouraged to collect in their scrap-books pictures depicting the workers, current affairs, ethnic groups, and so on. They are also encouraged to participate in the April communist Saturday (Subbotnik) when everybody works for the whole day without pay to help the country. The sense of esteem from participating in real deeds is very important for the rearing of civic feeling in the children. A series of talks is held during the year. They include such topics as 'The birth of Soviet land', 'Our Motherland', 'The Soviet Army', 'People of the USSR', 'Work and the workers', and so on. It is clear that

[111] *Nachalnaya Shkola*, No. 10, 1975, p. 36.
[112] *Doshkolnoe Vospitanie*, No. 11, 1975, p. 10.

the above talks could easily become indoctrination sessions, but it is not necessarily the case. Instead of being monotonous politinformatsiya* sessions they become stories with a political tinge. For instance, the instructor says: 'Look children. What a beautiful bouquet of roses I have. Where shall we put it? Yes, you are right Lena, let's place the roses near Lenin's portrait.'[113] The highlight of socialization is the October day celebration in the kindergarten. The main aim of the October utrennik[114] is to bring forth in the children a happy and elevated mood, and deepen their feelings of love towards the Motherland. At the form assembly, children recite poetry and sing songs about the October Revolution, the Motherland, and Lenin. They also see an excerpt (three minutes) from the film 'The October armed uprising' which shows the taking of the Winter Palace.[115]

The October organization is the primary phase of socialization of the pupils. In the October collective the pupils learn to do things independently or collectively, helping each other. The 7-year-old pupils normally become Octobrists on 7 November, the anniversary of the October Revolution and the celebration of the Red (Octobrist) Star. The Octobrists have new duties and rights. These duties include observance of the Octobrist rules and fulfilment of civic tasks imposed by the pupils' collective.

The primary group collective of the Octobrist organization is the link or little star (zvyozdochka). The zvyozdochka consists of five to six Octobrists. This enables the link leader (vozhaty) to work more effectively with his group. A small group facilitates rapid cohesion and friendship. Here, the children's collective becomes an influential moral force. Every member of the group is made aware that he or she is an important part of the collective.

Political upbringing is taken very seriously in the Octobrist organization. Children are given facts about local and international politics, and they celebrate important events. They are likely to be emotionally involved in social events. They are supposed to be impressed by

[113]Ibid., p. 13.
[114]A morning talk.
[115]Ibid., p. 14.
*See Glossary.

Lenin's revolutionary activity, rejoice at the nation's success in space exploration, and be intolerant of wars in other countries.[116]

In grade 2 the Octobrist organization becomes more ritualistic and symbolic. Children wear a red star and each link has its own flag. The school organizes Octobrist assemblies and the flag ceremony, which consists of bringing the flag out of the room, is an important ritual. More and more emphasis is placed on collective and communal involvement. Children are becoming more acquainted with the norms of life within the collective, which follows the Octobrist rules.

In grade 3 the Octobrists are being prepared to join the ranks of the Pioneer organization. Although membership is voluntary, the Octobrist must earn the right to become a Pioneer. The following three moral criteria are used to determine whether the Octobrist could become a good Pioneer:

1. Does the Octobrist wish to become a Pioneer?
2. Has he proved himself in participating in communal activity and did he fulfil the tasks of his collective?
3. Is he a good friend? Can he work and play in a friendly way with others? Does he tell the truth?[117]

Admission into the ranks of the Pioneers is gradual rather than simultaneous and it depends largely on the Octobrist's collective maturity. The child must do something, he must earn the privilege of being a Pioneer. He must accomplish something, no matter how simple it may look as it is important for his moral upbringing.

2. The Pioneers and Political Socialization

The Pioneer organization is regarded by the State as the most significant form of political upbringing. At the All-Union Congress of the Pioneer leaders in Moscow (18 May 1976) Brezhnev said: 'Youth in our country is closely related to the Pioneer organization, which carries the name of Vladimir Illich Lenin. In the Pioneer detachments and regiments millions of children undergo ideological, political, labour, and moral upbringing; they learn to live, work, and fight as

[116]Kairov, op. cit., p. 46.
[117]Ibid., p. 223.

the great Lenin bequeathed.' Addressing the Pioneer leaders Brezhnev concluded: 'Working with the Pioneers is a complex affair ... requiring a high pedagogical mastery, profound knowledge, and a big soul and heart. Insist on studying Marxist–Leninist theory.... Remember: Today they are children but tomorrow they are active builders of communism.'[118]

The Pioneer organization is, according to its statute, an 'organ of directing collective life of a detachment' and an 'organ of the collective Pioneer self-government'.[119]

The Pioneer meeting is an important form of political education. It represents the highest organ of the group, the organ of collective Pioneer self-government. It exerts a powerful socialization influence on children and it is full of Pioneer rituals, symbols, and traditions.

The Pioneer traditions include celebrating important dates (22 April—Lenin's birthday; 19 May–the birth of the Pioneer organization), conducting Lenin's symposium, competing for best readers on the theme 'Lenin, the Party and the Motherland', celebrating the Day of the Soviet Armed Forces (23 February), the Congress of young internationalists (8 February), the Victory Day (9 May), and so on. The military game zarnitsa* has become yet another important tradition. The Pioneers, apparently, love bright and colourful rituals with banners, flags, bugles, drums, and torches.[120]

The Pioneer political symbols (especially the banner, the emblem, and the red tie) are designed to promote communal activity, solidarity, and, clearly, adherence to the Marxist–Leninist doctrine. The red tie, for instance, worn by all Pioneers, symbolizes the 'indestructible union of the three communist generations. It is also a symbol of the Pioneer honour. It is a part of the Red Banner.' The red star on the Pioneer emblem, as in the flag, depicts 'solidarity of the workers of the five continents'.[121] The Pioneer salute is a symbol of greeting.

The All-Union Lenin Pioneer Organization is a massive communist organization of children and teenagers. It aims at fostering a communist philosophy of life—being true to the Party, and revolu-

[118]Brezhnev, L., *Pravda*, 18 May, 1976, p. 1.
[119]Kozlov, E. P., Pionersky Sbor ..., *Nachalnaya Shkola*, No. 10, 1975, p. 29.
[120]Igoshkin, V., Pionerskie ritualy, simvolika, *Vospitanie Shkolnikov*, No. 6, 1971, p. 29.
[121]Ibid., p. 29.
*See Glossary.

tionary, militant, and labour traditions of the Soviet people. The Pioneer organization is organically linked with the life of Soviet people and with its struggle for the building of communism. It introduces children to compulsory societal useful work. The Pioneer organization develops in Pioneers social involvement and collectivism. Here, the socially useful labour is regarded as being significant in the inculcation of moral, social, and political values.[122] The activities of the Pioneer organization incorporate the following principles:

1. Social and political guidelines.
2. Voluntary membership but active participation on the part of Pioneers in the organization.
3. Samodeyatelnost (the self-initiated activities) of Pioneers.
4. Consideration of age and individual differences.
5. Romanticism, interest, and the game in Pioneer life.[123]

However, the aims of moral education, which represent the true essence of communist youth movements as a whole, are expressed in the Pioneer motto always ready (vsegda gotov), the solemn promise, and the Pioneer rules, the latter being a code of conduct.

During an official ceremony at school, the 10-year-old pupil on admission to the Pioneer organization recites the following oath:

> I [full name], entering the ranks of the All-Union Lenin Pioneer organization, in the presence of my comrades, solemnly promise to love my Motherland passionately, and to live, learn, and struggle as the great Lenin bade us and as the Communist Party teaches us, and to always fulfil the Pioneer rules of the Soviet Union.[124]

As Grant correctly observes, it is, indeed, the ritual of the occasion which impresses on the pupil's mind the importance and responsibility of membership.[125]

The Pioneer rules help to pave the way for moral upbringing. These communist precepts state that the Pioneer loves his Motherland and the Communist Party of the Soviet Union; that he is preparing himself for membership in the Komsomol; that he reveres the memory of those who gave their lives for the freedom and prosperity of the Soviet homeland; that he is a friend of children of all nations of

---

[122]Kairov, op. cit., p. 295. See also Smiknov, V. F., *Vsegda Gotov*, Moscow, 1972.
[123]Ibid., pp. 295–6.
[124]Kairov, op. cit., p. 296.
[125]Grant, op. cit., p. 64.

the world; that he is diligent in his studies, disciplined, and polite; that he loves to work, and that he is thrifty with the nation's wealth; that he is a good comrade; that he cares for those younger than himself and helps his elders; that he will grow up brave and will not fear difficulty; that he tells the truth and cherishes the honour of his detachment; that he hardens himself and performs his physical culture exercises every day; that he loves nature and protects green plants, useful birds and animals; and that a Pioneer is an example to all children.[126] From the above, it is clear that the Pioneer can be an effective ally of the teacher, for he reinforces adult standards and socially acceptable behaviour which is being fostered by the school.

The Pioneer organization is a multi-purpose communist youth movement, for its functions are social, political, moral, educational, and recreational. The very structure and the function of the organization is closely bound up with the school and its curriculum.[127] Collective upbringing and political socialization are inculcated in the Pioneer organization but not without problems. Moral behaviour within the school and the Pioneer organization often results in a behaviour which is contrary to the individual's immediate egotistical needs and interests. That he must be prepared to sacrifice his own needs for the sake of the needs of his collective means that the process of collective upbringing, political socialization, and moral education is full of role conflicts. These conflicts, which are structurally determined, are built into the role. In simple terms, the school as a formal organization and the Pioneer organization give rise to a conflict between official pressure for conformity and the informal pressures to deviance.

First, let us examine collective upbringing and moral education promulgated by the Pioneer organization. The organization of the youth groups, conveniently, resembles that of the school. Each grade designates a Pioneer detachment, which is further subdivided into links (smaller units). The entire school represents a Pioneer regiment (druzhina).

The principles and methods employed in collective upbringing are essentially those suggested by Marx, Lenin, Krupskaya, Makarenko,

[126] *Soviet Education*, Vol. 25, No. 2, Dec., 1972, pp. 12–13.
[127] Grant, op. cit., p. 68.

Kalinin, and Sukhomlinsky. According to Marx, the collective alone provides the individual with the means that enable him to develop his personality.[128]

Hence, personal freedom can only be possible within the collective. Lenin stressed that the task of education was to obliterate the cursed rule 'Everyone for himself and one God for all' and replace it with 'All for one and one for all'. For Lenin, only those who were members of communist youth organizations dedicated themselves completely to the common cause. Krupskaya stressed the need for the Pioneer collective: 'It is necessary to teach children to act *collectively....*' Makarenko emphatically declared that it was inconceivable for the identity to exist without the collective in the Soviet Union. He believed that the school collective was a nucleus of child society and proceeded to define the collective in terms of the following attributes—unity, discipline, cohesion, and universality. Discipline, according to Makarenko, becomes not merely technical but a compulsory moral criterion.[129] Makarenko's children's collective is that of the close-knit totality based on the principle of unification. It is, above all, the nucleus of Soviet society, possessing all characteristics, privileges, and duties similar to any other collective in the Soviet Union. In Makarenko's collective the identity of the individual is subject to the rule of the collective. Although the individual has the right to belong to the collective voluntarily, once in the collective he must 'unconditionally subordinate his will to that of the collective'.[130]

Sukhomlinsky, the most influential Soviet educationalist during the 1960s and the 1970s, stated that the schoolchildren's collective and the pedagogical collective were organically linked with one another. For this reason, the schoolchildren's collective is the highest, the most complex form of the collectivist interaction. It is the 'school of citizenship, where the traits of the active builder of communist construction are being formed'.[131] In his chapter on the collective, Sukhomlinsky wrote that the collective was a means to an end and that man was the

[128]Quoted from *Khrestomatiya po pedagogike*, Moscow, 1967, p. 542.
[129]Makarenko, A. S., *Sobranie sochinenii*, Vol. 5, 2nd edition, Moscow, p. 133.
[130]Quoted in Sukhomlinsky, V. A. *Mudraya vlast kollektiva*, Moscow, 1975, p. 6.
[131]Ibid., p. 7.

aim of communist rearing. Among his numerous statements on the nature and the role of collective upbringing, the following asserts the importance of personal identity: 'The collective is not some kind of amorphous mass. It exists as a treasure of individual identities....' The rearing power of the collective commences by considering the individual's potential, his spiritual wealth, and his contribution to the collective. The collective acquires its rearing power only if the communal activity is such that it facilitates the development of the high ideal of spiritualized labour.[132] 'The spiritual world of the collective', wrote Sukhomlinsky, 'and the spiritual world of the individual are formed by a reciprocal interaction. Man derives much from the collective. But there is no collective if there is no many-faceted and spiritually enriched world of the people who form it.'[133]

Among the more specific rules of moral conduct within the collective are the following:

1. Respect general decisions of the collective, the rules adopted by all, and carry them out conscientiously.
2. Treat with respect the officers of the collective....
3. Learn to observe where your help is needed....
4. If you regard yourself as being right, prove it to others and defend truth.
5. Stop your comrade if he is doing something bad.
6. Complete the allotted task as best as you can, keeping in mind the work as a whole.
7. In all cases, help, instruct, and advise those who cannot cope with work, and learn to use advice given by your comrades.[134]

The Pioneers, apart from learning to observe values and norms governing the collective, also learn those roles which apply to the status they occupy. Thus the 13-year-old Pioneer, having learned the roles of a son, a pupil, an Octobrist, and a Pioneer, now has to learn the new role in respect to his position in the division of labour. Adult role-playing in the Pioneer collective is an important step in moral training of the schoolchildren. The Pioneer has to internalize a var-

---

[132]Ibid., p. 201.
[133]Ibid., p. 209.
[134]Based on Kairov, op. cit., pp. 248–9.

iety of societal roles. Typical social tasks (obshchestvennoe poruchenie) are: class captain, first-aid monitors, general monitors, gardeners,
librarians, sport organizers, teacher's aides, newspaper editors, and
school prefects.

Social tasks are divided into two categories—those that concern
the Pioneer alone and those that apply to the Pioneer collective.
These are the first tasks allocated to a newly conferred Pioneer in
grade 3:

1. Find out what has to be done at school or outside, within the
   area of Pioneer activities.
2. Cultivate flowers for the classroom. . . .
3. Find out who, among your comrades needs your help. . . .[135]

The Pioneer link, on the other hand, would be mainly engaged in
group activity, culminating with a meeting 'The Pioneer's task for the
summer' in order to allocate various tasks.

Collective discipline and the moral code of the Pioneer organization are, clearly, essential to communist socialization within the
school. The children's collective, within a clearly set up hierarchy of
positions and roles, suggests numerous role conflicts. This is obvious
from the fact that rules governing the collective demand justice when
allocating various tasks to different individuals. Children, obviously,
do get carried away with the feeling of power and, in some cases,
abuse their privileges in role-playing by becoming dictatorial, force-
ful, selfish, and élitist. One of the rules, in fact, is 'Don't place yourself
in a privileged position'.[136] There are many instances of self-
opinionated children's commissars being reprimanded by teachers or
children's collectives.

The Pioneer role conflicts are also structurally determined. The
conflicts, which are built into the role, are characterized by conformity versus deviance, the collective moral code versus individual
behaviour. The Pioneer link leader, for example, may fluctuate
between his role of a Pioneer and that of a friend. As a Pioneer it is
his duty to correct the behaviour of his friend and he may feel guilty
in reprimanding him. A tell-tale is the least popular among his peers,

[135]Based on Kairov, op. cit., p. 228.
[136]Ibid., p. 248.

and yet as a Pioneer leader his role may well require him to report on his friends if they are problem children in the class.

Group competitiveness is another prominent feature of communist upbringing. It reinforces the collective discipline and moral code of the Pioneer organization. It could be said that group competitiveness is virtually built into the role of a Soviet man. Known as socialist competition, group competitiveness pervades every facet of Soviet life. At school it involves all phases of activity and behaviour: moral conduct, sports, achievement, work training, personal grooming, and so on.

Behaviour, achievement, and moral conduct of each pupil is continuously evaluated by his peers, the latter having internalized the behavioural patterns of adults. As Bronfenbrenner puts it: 'Since each child's status depends in part on the standing of the collective of which he is a member, it is to each pupil's enlightened self-interest to watch over his neighbour, encourage the other's good performance and behaviour, and help him when he is in difficulty.'[137] In this way the children's collective reinforces adult standards as well as regulating behaviour by means of sanctions. However, the children's collective is more than just the major source of reward and punishment.[137] Sukhomlinsky played down the importance of sanctions within the collective. To him the strength of the collective was not so much in sanctions as (it was) in the fact that it takes on its own shoulders both good and bad and that it assumes responsibility for culpable action.[138]

Competition among links, detachments, and Pioneer regiments (druzhiny) require a careful consideration. Group competitiveness is used because children like to compete against each other—who can run faster, who can come first, who can do most, who can behave best, and so on. It is also used because in the children's collective it is by far the best method which produces quick and noticeable results.[139] However, incorrect usage of socialist competition may influence negatively moral instruction and upbringing of children. An obsession with winning at all costs may change children into selfish,

[137]Bronfenbrenner, op. cit., p. 50.
[138]Sukhomlinsky, V. A., *O vospitanii*, Moscow, 1975, p. 209.
[139]See Sukhomlinsky, V. A., *Mudraya vlast kollektiva*, Moscow, 1975, pp. 7–66.

calculating, and ruthless individuals who would stop at nothing. They may even discard their friends and raise themselves above the norms of the collective—all for the sake of victory and rewards. The dilemma of socialist competition is expressed in its conformity and deviance. The official interpretation of socialist competition denotes conformity or competitiveness for the sake of the collective rather than personal gains.[140] Unofficially, however, owing to role conflicts, which are built into the notion of the competitor, competitiveness may result in a behaviour which is contrary to the moral code of the collective. The individual is often unable to sacrifice his egotistical and hedonistic pursuits for the sake of altruistic goals that are shared by the collective. It is difficult to pinpoint whether the individual wishes to win for himself or for the sake of the collective.

The Soviet school curriculum is built around the notion of socialist competition. The author of this thesis well remembers the atmosphere of competition in the classroom in achievement, conduct, behaviour, punctuality, neatness, grooming, and sports. Competition was not only between rows in the classroom, or Pioneer links, but also between the individuals. Parents were drawn into this system. On parent–teacher nights, parents of the successful child were publicly praised, while parents of the not so gifted or badly behaved child were subjected to a sharp criticism by the class teacher. My own parents were among those fortunate enough to be awarded a certificate of merit which included praise for their successful rearing techniques directed towards the greater glory of the Motherland. The child concerned was also issued with a certificate of merit for academic excellence. By this method, children were clearly pitted against one another as competitors. This competition even reached the father's place of employment—where the boss, having been informed by the school principal, would comment on outstandingly high or low achievement among the children of his subordinates. My mother, because of my success at school, was elevated to a small committee of parents, whose task it was to visit the homes of under-achievers and offer advice and help. The mothers so elevated became very conscious of their status, and those visited were suitably humbled. The competitive pressures on the child and his family were simply enormous.

[140]See Sukhomlinsky, V. A., *Mudraya vlast kollektiva*, Moscow, 1975, p. 58.

School discipline, academic performance, and moral training depend very much on the effectiveness of the collective and its sanctions. The author remembers his own experience as a Pioneer link leader having to prepare the cartoon of his under-achieving friend for the class wall newspaper. The friend was depicted as untidy and dirty and carrying a school bag spilling over with 2's (an unsatisfactory mark). This involved him in a feeling of guilt and conflict over his role as a friend and a link leader. Children the teacher found difficult to discipline were also caricatured by their peers in the same manner. The teacher was able to use sanctions of the Pioneer collective against individuals rather than applying them himself directly. As Sukhomlinsky stated, the collective had also a positive role. Academically successful Pioneers in each link had to help the less successful members in order to improve the overall status and prestige of their own link in the eyes of the class and the school. In this sense, the collective had to assume full responsibility for its members. It was for the Pioneer link to hasten the unpunctual member, to enforce tidiness on the messy member, and to teach manners to the impolite. The teacher was able to criticize the whole link for the behaviour of the recalcitrant. While assuming their collective responsibilities for weaker and unproductive members, the academically successful and well-behaved children enjoyed a very satisfying sense of superiority. Thus the teacher left the collective to apply sanctions while he was free to administer the rewards.

3. The Educational and Ideological Functions of Komsomol Organizations

The All-Union Leninist Communist League of Youth (Vsesoyuzny Leninskii Kommunisticheskii Soyuz Molodiozhi–VLKSM) or Komsomol for short, is a massive communist youth organization. Although described as an independent social organization that unites broad masses of progressive Soviet youth, the Komsomol takes directives from the Party.[141] In fact the close relationship between the Komsomol and the Party is accentuated by the following statement taken from the rules and regulations of the Komsomol: 'The Komso-

[141] *Soviet Education*, Feb., 1975, p. 49.

mol learns from the Communist Party how to live, work, struggle, and triumph in the Leninist way.'[142] As an active helper of the Party, the Komsomol is responsible for the political socialization of youth.

More than 35 million individuals aged 14–28 belong to the Komsomol. Membership consists of secondary and tertiary students, members of the armed forces, workers, intelligentsia, and collective farmers. The school branch of the Komsomol included 8 million secondary students in grades 8–10, between the ages of 14–17.[143]

Being the third major socializing agency in the Soviet school, the Komsomol is entrusted with many duties—moral, political, social, vocational, cultural, recreational, and academic. Thus, Komsomol school-oriented activities include character education and moral upbringing, political indoctrination, labour socialization, the organization and leadership of pupils' collectives, clubs and societies, and, above all, serving as patrons of the Pioneers. More importantly, the Komsomol serves as an instrument for the selection and promotion of talented, industrious, ambitious, and ideologically convinced Soviet youth.[144] It is clear that the Komsomol plays a very crucial role in determining life chances of each new generation. In general, the Komsomol can affect social mobility.

The political role of the Komsomol cannot be emphasized enough. The Soviet regime, judging by its frequent appeals to the revolutionary era, hopes to institutionalize a revolution that grows in scope and in intensity. The purpose of such a revolution, as explained succinctly by Brzhezinsky, is to 'pulverize all existing social units in order to replace the old pluralism with a homogeneous unanimity patterned on the blueprints of the totalitarian ideology'.[145] Komsomol, with its singular communist morality, together with the Socialist dynamism of its members, hopes to stabilize and tranquilize the masses by appealing to a better future—communism and the new Soviet man.

The Komsomol was the main supplier of candidates for the Party in 1973, and 64% of new members came from the Komsomol (40% in 1966).

[142]*Soviet Education*, Mar., 1975, p. 3.
[143]*Bolshaya Sovetskaya entsiklopedia*, Vol. 24, Moscow, 1977, p. 507.
[144]*Soviet Education*, Mar., 1975, p. 4.
[145]Brzhezinsky, Z., *Power and Ideology in the USSR*, Praeger, 1962, p. 15.

TABLE 21. *Social and academic structure of the Komsomol*[146]

Social composition of the Komsomol in 1973		Educational structure of the Komsomol in 1973	
Workers	32.9%	Tertiary institutions	2241
Collective farmers	6.7%	Advanced colleges	2298
Employees	15.3%	Vocational–technical colleges (PTUs)	1473
Pupils and students	44.5%	Secondary schools	7000

The rules of communist morality for the Komsomol

The main aims of the Komsomol are to inculcate the youth in Marxist–Leninist values and norms, the heroic traditions of revolutionary struggle, the examples of selfless labour of workers, collective farmers, and the intelligentsia, and to prepare youth for the defence of their socialist Homeland. Every Komsomol member has to observe the moral code of the CPSU, namely:

1. Loyalty to the cause of communism and love of the socialist Motherland and of socialist countries.
2. Conscientious labour for the good of society.
3. Friendship and brotherhood among all peoples of the USSR and intolerance of ethnic and racial hatred.
4. Collectivism and comradely mutual aid (incorporating the principle: All for one and one for all).
5. High feeling of awareness of social duty and intolerance of violation of society's interests.
6. Honesty and truthfulness, moral purity, and simplicity and modesty in social and personal life.
7. Humane relations and mutual respect among people (incorporating the principle: Man is a friend, comrade, and a brother to man).
8. Intolerance of injustice, parasitism, dishonesty, careerism, and money grabbing.

[146]*Soviet Education*, Feb., 1975, p. 49.

166   *Education in the USSR*

9. Fraternal solidarity with the working people of all countries.
10. Everyone's concern for the preservation and multiplication of public property.
11. Mutual respect in the family, concern for the rearing of children.
12. Implacability toward the enemies of communism and the fostering of peace and friendship among nations.[147]

The above rules provide us with a summary statement of the broader aims of communist moral code. Apart from these, Komsomol members have to observe their own set of regulations, which encompass social, moral, and political values and norms. In short, a member of the Komsomol has the following duties:[148]

1. To be an active champion of the implementation of the enormous programme of communist construction and to prepare for life in a society that has affirmed peace, labour, freedom, equality, brotherhood, and the happiness of all people on earth.
2. To combine his or her labour, studies, rearing, and education with participation in the construction of communism.
3. To set model standards in labour and in studies by raising labour productivity continuously, by mastering technology, and by offering active support for all that is new and progressive.....
4. To master firmly knowledge, culture, science, and the principles of Marxism–Leninism.
5. To inculcate in the youth the policy of the Communist Party.
6. To be honest, truthful, sensitive, and attentive to people.
7. To oppose all manifestations of bourgeois ideology, parasitism, religious prejudice, various anti-social manifestations, and other vestiges of the past, and always to place social above personal interests.
8. To be a selfless patriot of the Soviet Motherland and to be prepared to give all his or her strength to it and, if necessary, his or her life.

[147]Rules and regulations of the All-Union Leninist Communist Youth League, in *Soviet Education*, Feb., 1975, pp. 93–94.
[148]In the original document these have been listed under nine broad categories (a)–(i), Part 1, *Members of the AULCYL, their Rights and Duties.*

9. To strengthen the might of the USSR armed forces, to study military sciences, to show vigilance, and to keep State secrets.
10. To promote the strengthening of the friendship of peoples of the USSR and friendship with the youth of socialist countries and the proletarian and labouring youth of the world.
11. To take an active part in the political life of the country.
12. To set an example for youth in the fulfilment of their social duty.
13. To strengthen the ranks of the Komsomol in every way, to increase its militance and the quality of its organization. . . .
14. To struggle boldly to develop criticism and self-criticism, and to fight against ostentation and conceit.
15. To reveal shortcomings in work and to strive to eliminate them, and to report them to Komsomol organs all the way up to the Central Committee of the AULCYL.
16. To strive for physical fitness and to engage in sport.

The Komsomol member's rights include being critical of his comrades: 'People guilty of suppressing criticism or of persecution for criticism must be called to account strictly before the Komsomol.' Although section 3(b) and (c) of the *Rules and Regulations of the All-Union Leninist Communist Youth League* (1971) makes provision for expressing opinions, making proposals, and criticizing any Komsomol as well as any Komsomol organ at Komsomol meetings, very few choose to exercise this option for fear of repercussions. During one recent survey, Komsomol members were shocked to learn that one of their senior students had written in the questionnaire that he did not gain anything from the Leninist assignment.[149]

Komsomol members are called to account for non-fulfilment of the demands of the rules and regulations and other petty offences. Those who fail to carry out their tasks and duties may be exposed to strong peer-group pressures in the form of 'comradely criticism, Komsomol censure, warning, or directives.'[149] The extreme measure of Komsomol punishment is a disgraceful expulsion from the organization.

The Komsomol as the primary socializing agency offers the first lessons in 'citizenship, collectivism, and comradeship'.[150] It cements

[149]*Soviet Education*, Feb., 1975, p. 98.
[150]*Komsomol v Vuze*, Moscow, 1976, p. 15.

the pupils' collective within the framework of socio-political indoctrination common to all schoolchildren.[151] It imbues the pupils' collective with a sense of political organization. Hence, preparing for the joining the Komsomol, and participation in social and communal tasks, suggest distinct stages in the moral development of youth. In schools, the Komsomol concentrates on socializing students in the values and norms of communist ideology, the Marxist–Leninist world view, and, more recently, in militant patriotism, humanism, and internationalism. Secondary students who belong to the Komsomol participate in educational and technological work affecting all branches of the economy. The Komsomol headed the 10 million pupil army in one massive expedition, 'My Homeland: The USSR', which was designed to familiarize schoolchildren with significant socio-political, historical, and economic achievements of the Soviet people in the last sixty years. The Komsomol organized all-union essay competitions on socio-political topics among senior secondary students and they have become a regular annual event. Established in 1967, the all-union essay competitions attract increasingly more secondary students. For instance, the competition 'My Soviet Motherland' attracted 3 million students, whereas the 1972 essay competition 'About the Motherland, friendship, and myself' had drawn 7 million students.[152]

Summer pupil terms under Komsomol leadership have become a form of vocational socialization of schoolchildren. In 1977 alone more than 10 million secondary students spent their summer holidays working for the State[153] (6 million in 1974).

The Komsomol always responded to the Party's call to provide workers for huge construction projects, and in the past they built Komsomolsk-on-the-Amur, Magnitogorsk (cities), the Turkestan–Siberian Railroad, the Dnepropetrovsk Hydroelectric Power Station, Bratsk, the Baikal-Amur Railroad (BAM), the Kama Truck Plant, and so on.

The Komsomol is actively involved in political socialization and patriotic upbringing of the schoolchildren. Between 1970 and 1974, 5

---

[151]*Soviet Education*, Mar., 1975, p. 15.
[152]Vypolnyaya Leninskie Zavety, *Vospitanie Shkolnikov*, No. 1, 1974, p. 9.
[153]*Narodnoe Obrazovanie*, No. 9, 1974, p. 10.

million students joined the All-Union Society for Voluntary Assistance to the Army, Air Force, and Navy (DOSAAF), 75% of those who joined were Komsomol members.[154]

Komsomol organizations participate in the All-Union physical fitness programme for youth, particularly in the 'Ready for Labour and Defence' of the USSR norms. By 1967 nearly 47 million young people passed the GTO norms.[154]

The Komsomol socialist competition reinforces political socialization. Schoolchildren gain a 'deep sense of the social character of their labour and of their responsibility for strengthening the might and prosperity of our great Homeland'.[155] The Komsomol-run socialist competition is regarded by many Soviet educationalists as an important means of involving youth in the construction of a new society. It is also regarded as an effective stimulus for raising academic achievement and vocational standards.[156]

Following the Seventeenth Congress of the VLKSM (the Komsomol) in 1974, Komsomol members are more actively involved in helping schools with work training, organization of industrial experience for pupils, and expanding the summer term work scheme—an early experience of manual, semi-skilled, and skilled labour for secondary students.

One of the most significant innovations of the Komsomol is the Leninist assignment (Leninskii zachet). This is yet another form of political socialization, and it involves the study of Lenin's works and documents of the Party Government, socially useful work, caring for the war veterans and invalids, helping Pioneers, passing the norms of GTO (Ready for Labour and Defence), and taking part in the paramilitary game—Eaglet (Orlyonok).[157] The Leninist assignment may last up to fourteen years assuming that the pupil joins the Komsomol when he turns 14. Each member has a special report book which includes academic achievement in all school disciplines from grade 8 to 10, competitions in school disciplines (predmetnye olimpiady), electives (fakultativy), public lectures, a programme of communist

---

[154]*Soviet Education*, Feb., 1975, p. 56.
[155]Ibid., p. 49.
[156]Ibid., p. 90.
[157]*Vospitanie Shkolnikov*, No. 1, 1974, p. 9.

ideology, labour commitments, the Komsomol task (Komsomolskoe poruchenie), a programme of the Komsomol members' cultural development, achievements in sport and evaluation (self-criticism), and so on. In short, the Leninist assignment represents a decade or more of the individual's contribution towards knowledge, culture, and ideology.

The Komsomol task (Ideology in practice), introduced recently, is a very important stage of collective and political socialization. Under the slogan of 'Social tasks for all', young Komsomol members participate in a new social experiment designed to socialize school youth aged 14–18 years in communist morality and to make them realize that the true value of man lies in his serving the Motherland and the Soviet people.

It would be wrong to assume that the Komsomol task solves all the problems of Soviet upbringing. Some teachers do regard it as an efficient means of moral training. Others fear correctly that over-zealous participation in communal tasks may lower the pupil's academic performance. One Soviet educationalist claims the opposite to be true. In grade 8B of the Moscow 842nd secondary school 77% of the top students are actively involved in the Komsomol task, whereas those who are not involved constitute the lower average group. It is further claimed that many Komsomol members perceive the power and the influence of the Komsomol task on their conduct, behaviour, and moral development. Out of a survey of 152 essays written by students in grades 7 and 9 on the topic 'My Komsomol task', 45% claimed that it aroused in them feelings of responsibility; 20% mentioned activity, initiative, creativity, and moral character-building traits; 12% included the feeling of comradeship and the collective; another 12% stressed high moral standards; and only 8% showed an interest towards communal work.[158] The majority, clearly, felt that the Komsomol task had a positive influence on the development of their personality. Larisa A., a student in grade 10, wrote:

> This year I will finish my studies. I already think, with sorrow in my heart, that soon I will have to part with my Komsomol task, which for me has become a personal task. The task by the Komsomol Committee—to work with a Pioneer detachment—helps me to experience my closeness to life, develop my character.... For the first time I experienced the feeling of responsibility for other destinies.[158]

[158]*Vospitanie Shkolnikov*, No. 4, 1974, p. 26.

In order to intensify ideological indoctrination of the pupils, the Central Committee of the Komsomol decreed that a Komsomol meeting entitled 'I am a citizen of the Soviet Union' be held throughout the USSR. The meeting was to be rich in Komsomol symbols and rituals—bringing out the Red flag of the school Komsomol branch, handing out membership cards to new members, congratulating the best workers of the summer labour term, and those who excelled in their school work were to be awarded with a Komsomol badge 'For academic excellence' (za otlichnuyu uchobu). The whole purpose of this meeting is to bring to the attention of every Komsomol member the importance of communist ideals, which include revolutionary, military, and labour traditions of the party and people and to prepare students for their patriotic tasks.[159]

The Komsomol plays an increasingly important role in social work and extra-curricular activities. Often, Komsomol members join the druzhiniki who help police to maintain law and order in the community. Lately, school Komsomol organizations are turning their attention to juvenile delinquency. Many 14- and 15-year-olds have joined various street gangs. Apart from committing minor offences they loiter in the parks or simply on the streets. They drink, sing songs well past midnight, and disturb the peace. Many letters have been written to the *Literaturnaya gazeta* about this anti-social phenomenon, particularly midnight singing in the entrance hall of multiple-storey flats to the annoyance of their occupants. The basic question that everybody seems to be asking is How do we keep our 'difficult' boys occupied and out of the streets?

The Komsomol is beginning to find itself more and more occupied with the previously mentioned social problem. Some school Komsomol organizations form special squads to combat delinquency. They organize many sporting clubs and cultural societies. They are assuming, not without reason, that everybody must have a hobby.

In Elektrostal the upbringing work with youth is done by Komsomol members, including ex-servicemen, from the local factories. One hundred and thirty-five such social workers are helping schools and the authorities with character training of youth outside school hours.

[159]*Uchitelskaya gazeta*, 8 Sept., 1977, p. 1.

Sport is used to draw young people in. The most popular sporting clubs include weightlifting, boxing, swimming, wrestling, and unarmed combat. The venture was so successful that now half of the boys in the city belong to these clubs. The next move was to clear the dark alleys of self-proclaimed guitar players. A contest for the best musicians was held and all joined a Komsomol-inspired ensemble. Some Komsomol members look after one or more difficult boys. Katya Gordeyeva took care of Andrew, who had problems at school and at home. She made a patient study of the boy's character and his interests. She discovered that among his forgotten hobbies was stamp collecting, and so she took the 15-year-old Andrew to Moscow to buy stamps. Katya, like many others performing similar shefstvo (adoption), often visited Andrew's school and home and had many discussions with his parents and teachers.[160]

In another case a group of Komsomol members from the teacher college at Elabuga decided to form the Makarenko detachment to deal with the town's fifty-odd juvenile delinquents. Most of them had a police record and had to report regularly to police stations. Within one year, following numerous home visits and discussions of the type 'You and the law', twenty-eight boys and girls were converted and taken off police custody.[161]

Being an active and dedicated Komsomol member carries certain socio-political privileges. It enhances social mobility and improves one's social prestige, be it through the Party or tertiary education. Since opportunities for entering tertiary institutions are becoming more and more competitive (three to five applicants for every place available) it becomes clear that during the past twenty years education has assumed a significant role in social mobility in the Soviet Union.[162] Assuming that the Soviet educational system is competitive and contest-oriented, in the sense that it is a centralized, massive system of educational competition in which 'élite status is the prize in an open contest and is taken by the aspirants' own efforts',[163]

[160]*Uchitelskaya gazeta*, 6 Aug., 1977, p. 2.
[161]Ibid., 29 Dec., 1977, p. 3.
[162]See Mobility in the USSR, *Soviet Studies*, July, 1966, pp. 57–66.
[163]O'Dell, F., *et al.*, Labour socialization and occupational placement in Soviet education, *Soviet Studies*, Mar., 1976, p. 420.

it would follow that élite status must be given on the 'basis of some criterion of supposed merit'.[163] Since academic excellence is taken for granted at entrance examinations to tertiary institutions it would seem that political involvement would be also taken into consideration. A glowing character reference (kharakteristika) from the Komsomol to a tertiary establishment would certainly carry some weight in determining the student's placement.

A Komsomol secretary keeps a cumulative record of each student, and if such a record is not satisfactory his career may be hampered. When job offers are allocated, the Komsomol record of the student is considered with his/her academic achievement. A weak student, who is also socially inactive, may not be recommended by the Komsomol and he/she may not get the more interesting jobs.[164] The Komsomol, of course, plays a leading role in filling manpower needs of the economy. Whenever large armies of workers are needed on strategic industrial and agricultural projects the Party always appeals to the Komsomol. Officially, students are supposed to volunteer for such work but, as one student remarked: 'You go if the Komsomol secretary tells you that you had better go.'[165]

Soviet sociological surveys have shown that it is more difficult for the son of a kolkhoznik or an unskilled worker to enter the prestigious tertiary institutions than it would be for a son of a white-collar worker. The only way to overcome the egalitarian paradox, whereby the élite recruits are chosen by the established élite, is by intensive socio-political participation of the working-class youth in the Komsomol. This does not mean that the weaker students may be automatically accepted in a tertiary institution. What is suggested is that, provided satisfactory marks have been obtained at the VUZ entrance examination, an active Komsomol member, with an excellent record of community involvement, industrial and work experience, and other forms of socially useful labour, could expect some help from his local Komsomol committee with his final placement at a tertiary institution. For the same reason, the Komsomol would not have the same

---

[164]From a conversation with a visiting Soviet scholar (Oct., 1975).
[165]From a conversation with a Soviet (Jewish) student who migrated with her family to Australia in 1975.

role for the children of the intelligentsia who, in general, tend to get better marks than those of manual workers.[166]

4. Conclusion

Of the three youth groups discussed, the Komsomol is by far socially and ideologically the most significant for the school-leaver's future prospects. The political role of the Komsomol has been stressed in the December 1977 decree 'On further improvements in education and upbringing of the secondary school pupils and their preparation for labour'. The Central Committee of the CPSU and the Council for Ministers called on the Komsomol to extend their ideological work in schools and to instruct the pupils in the spirit of communist ideas, revolutionary labour, and militant patriotism, and to imbue them with strict and absolute obedience to moral norms. The Komsomol was asked to show a far greater concern in their extra-curricular work. The decree reaffirmed the Komsomol moral code and urged every member to become a model citizen in 'diligence, industry, modesty, truthfulness, and immaculate conduct at school, at home, in the collective, and in public places'.[167] This latest emphasis on moral, political, and social upbringing at school indicates some of the shortcomings of the Soviet youth organization and the educational system. The document comments critically on the lack of effective ideological work and poor moral upbringing in schools. The potential of the pupil's collective in moral and socio-political education is not always realized and, consequently, the fundamental principle of the unity of education and upbringing has not always been achieved.[167]

The document is a major, public admission by the authorities that the Soviet educational system has fallen behind the Party's goals. The article, commenting on apathy and inertness of some Komsomol

---

[166]The sociologist N. Aitov claimed that the children of the white-collar workers got better results at the HSC than those of unskilled and semi-skilled workers (see *Sotsialnye issledovaniya*, Moscow, No. 2, 1968, p. 190). A close correlation betwen social status and educational attainment is discussed by V. D. Popov in Sociological problems of the transition to universal-secondary education, *Soviet Sociology*, No. 3, 1977, pp. 27–42.

[167]*Uchitelskaya gazeta*, 29 Dec., 1977, p. 1.

members, is particularly significant. A survey carried out by the Academy of Pedagogical Sciences in Latvian secondary schools to determine the relationship of Komsomol members to their societal tasks, has shown that a substantial number of senior students in the Komsomol, far from being ideologically convinced individuals, displayed egotistical and materialistic motives towards life.[168] When one Komsomol member was asked to work on a school magazine he replied: 'And who will be doing my lessons? Already I haven't switched my TV on for a whole week!'[168]

Here, obviously, school work and watching television were more important to the boy than active participation in the Komsomol. Personal motives have replaced utilitarian ideals. When asked about their participation in societal tasks or socially useful labour, out of 3554 senior students only 1846 (53%) felt that such participation was necessary, even if it had nothing to do with one's personal attitudes, interests, and desires. But 1662 (47%) indicated that societal work should be carried out only when it corresponds to one's personal interests.[168] What is even more significant is a discovery that many students involved in communal work do so without any special dedication or complete involvement. The majority felt that their social participation was dull and they were capable of performing more serious tasks. The study had revealed that, for the first time, the Komsomol is facing a serious challenge from the unofficial street gangs. 'We are still trying to ignore', writes the author, 'the interaction outside the school.'[168] Apparently, many Komsomol members were influenced by their unofficial peers and would refuse to perform their Komsomol tasks. Instead, their energy is dissipated and wasted on activities within the sub-culture. Soviet sociologists are now urging educators to take note of these sub-cultures and to try to counteract their negative influence on youth organizations. When 135 students were asked to list the agency of socialization that had the greatest influence on their vocational guidance, 122 (90%) named their sub-culture outside the school, not the school, the mass media, or the family.[168] The most important finding of the survey was that if the Komsomol organization is to become even more influential in shaping the communist personality of the future than the mass media,

[168]Ibid., 3 Sept., 1977, p. 3.

the home, and school combined as suggested by an American com-parativist, it must surpass the unofficial peer group influence.

Despite these problems, the Komsomol is, on the whole, the reserve and aid of the Communist Party. The educational, moral, and political role of the Komsomol is self-evident. If we take Khrush-chev's words seriously and accept that under communism the State will wither away and that society will function through the public organizations (including the Komsomol), we must, therefore, accept the ultimate importance of the Soviet youth organizations which not only train the youth in the virtues of a communist society but also maintain the 'new intelligentsia in tune with the regime'.[168]

Summing up then, Soviet youth organizations for children between the ages of 7 and 17 represent one of the best means for inculcating a Marxist–Leninist belief system. As Soviet children progress from the Octobrists to the Pioneers and the Komsomol, political socialization proceeds in a series of well-defined stages. From a mere character education in the primary school, socialization in Soviet youth organ-izations evolves into an increasingly sophisticated Marxist–Leninist doctrine which requires the pupil to be completely devoted to the communist regime.

Moral education and, more specifically, character education, is the most important ideological aim of the Soviet school today. At a recent meeting of the ideological aktiv in Moscow it was reaffirmed that the primary civic duty of educationalists was to instil in youth the values of a Marxist–Leninist outlook, dedication to the Party's work and Lenin's ideas, and a passionate love of the Motherland (Rodina).[169] The essence of ideological, political, and moral upbring-ing was described as a profound mastery of Marxist–Leninist doc-trine.[169]

Prokofiev, in his article manifesto 'The October, school, and peda-gogy' (1977), stated that the aim of communist education is a many-faceted and harmonious development of identity, which is ideologi-cally armed and is ready to participate in the creative labour of the people in the construction of communism.[170] He stressed the new image of the Soviet school. The school is no longer a mere edu-

[169]*Uchitelskaya gazeta*, 25 Oct., 1977, p. 1.
[170]Ibid., 11 Nov., 1977, p. 1.

cational establishment concerned solely with the acquisition of knowledge. Instead, the contemporary school in a developed socialist society is an important nucleus of the society in its strategy and tactics of communist upbringing.[170]

In retrospect, the emphasis on ideological education in the Soviet school has not changed. It is as pervasive now as it was during the Stalinist adjustments in the concept of ideology in communist education. Qualitatively, Soviet communist ideology has changed, and the new concept of Marxism–Leninism is developed socialism. It has been proclaimed explicitly in 1971 by the Brezhnev regime and (ever since) has been used by Soviet social scientists as a standard framework for analysis.[171]

A more salient change in the Soviet ideology is its appeal to man's inner, spiritual needs. This appeal to feelings, emotions, ideals, and, in general, to a non-cognitive imagery, suggests that the new ideology transcends the empirical realm and approaches a belief system. King was one of the first Western scholars to intimate a proximity of ideology to metaphysics. As a belief system he had found the concept of ideology very close to the apostolic fervour of St. Paul when he spoke of emptying himself out so that Christ might come in.[172] The passionate will to believe, which is so characteristic of the Soviet man/woman, can be compared with Tertullian's dictum: *Credo quia impossibile* (I believe because it is impossible). King, of course, was right in saying that ideology must not be considered only in the narrow sense of an external picture of life. The new, non-empirical (appealing to feelings, emotions, and ideals, in short the inner needs rather than reason) concept of Soviet communist ideology is, clearly, a belief system. What is required of the new man is his complete (almost blind) devotion and dedication to the communist cause. It is suggested that the seemingly contradictory concept of communist metaphysics is a more meaningful indicator of the shift from the empirical to the metaphysical domain in the Soviet ideology. As early as 1958, Markushevich, the then Deputy Minister of Education of the

---

[170]Ibid., 11 Nov., 1977, p. 1.
[171]On changes in the Soviet ideology, see Evans, A. B., Jr., Developed socialism in Soviet Ideology, *Soviet Studies*, July, 1977, pp. 409–28.
[172]King, E. J. (ed.), *Communist Education*, Methuen, London, 1963, p. 15.

RSFSR, when asked about the nature of Soviet morality, had this to say: 'It is not just verbal. First, it is the education of behaviour. Second, it is the education of the inner life.'[173] This statement captures the essence of Soviet moral education today.

Since its inception, Soviet education was based on the polytechnic principle, which proclaimed the unity of theory (the integration of science, the humanities, and technology) and practice (vocational training), thus bringing the school closer to life. The increased emphasis on labour socialization (to be discussed in the next chapter) in the Soviet ideology, confirms the view that Soviet schools attempt to offer a preparation for life. A group of American educationalists on their 1958 study tour of the USSR found the cultivation of the communist attitude towards labour alongside patriotism to be the most important feature of moral education.[174]

There is a distinct difference between the quantitative aspects of the ideology during the 1950s and the 1970s. Indoctrination has increased since the ascent of the Brezhnev regime. Political and ideological programs continue, but in greater quantities, to penetrate all areas of Soviet education. The introduction of new socio-political subjects (Obshchestvovedenie in grade 10 and Osnovy gosudarstva i prava in grade 8) in the Soviet secondary curriculum and numerous directives and decrees issued by the Ministry of Education concerning the study of the new 1977 constitution, the Party documents and congresses, in particular Brezhnev's speeches, the October Revolution, and Lenin's works, are a further proof of the increased magnitude of indoctrination during the 1970s.

The impact of ideology on moral education differs from school to school. In general, moral education in the Soviet school is effective despite obsolete methodology. Soviet educators painfully admit that Makarenko's warning that lecturing and exhortation are the least effective means of exerting influence still holds true today. Apart from using lectures, Soviet teachers continue to use dated slogans widely. Lenin's 'Study, study, study!' is a good example of a much-repeated but hardly inspiring piece of anachronism. The slogan was certainly relevant and meaningful in 1917, when more than two-thirds of the

[173]Bereday op. cit., p. 413.
[174]Ibid., pp. 410–12.

entire population was illiterate. Since 1970 total literacy has been claimed.

Not all Soviet teachers treat their political and moral roles seriously. Prokofiev notes that some schools are not aware of their new, ideological role in upbringing.[175] This issue was raised earlier in the *Uchitelskaya gazeta*, which criticized some teachers for failing to act as models of moral purity and who were guilty of serious breaches of pedagogical ethics.[176] Soviet sociologists claim that according to Marxism–Leninism, the principal task of socialization to communism is involvement of children and young people in the 'real system of societal relations on the basis of productive labour'.[177] However, it has been discovered that the Soviet secondary school (particularly in grade 8) has a very weak influence on the choice of an occupation and, thus, affecting negatively productive labour socialization.[178] One of the paradoxes of the Soviet ideology is the principle of the polytechnic labour school. In theory, labour socialization is inseparably linked with political and moral upbringing in the polytechnic labour school. In practice, however, there is a manifestation of a lordly scornful (to use Khrushchev's words) attitude towards unskilled labour.[179]

More and more Soviet students display anti-pushbutton, i.e. anti-cog-in-the-wheel philosophy (antiknopochnye nastroyeniya) as a protest against the dehumanizing effects of modern technology.[180] At the same time they also regard factory work as below their dignity. Instead, they pursue occupations that have higher social prestige. King's suggestion that the main objective of Soviet education during the 1960s was to prepare a docile majority and a disciplined labour force is still current.[181] It is, for the reasons above, that so much publicity has been given recently to the notion of labour as man's

[175]*Uchitelskaya gazeta*, 29 Oct., 1977, p. 1.
[176]Ibid., 25 Oct., 1977, p. 1.
[177]*Soviet Sociology*, No. 3, 1977, p. 38.
[178]Ibid., p. 29.
[179]*Uchitelskaya gazeta*, 29 Oct., 1977, p. 1. (Khrushchev, in *Pravda*, 21 *Sept.*, 1958, pp. 1–2, criticized school-leavers for their lordly scornful and wrong attitude towards physical labour.)
[180]Prokofiev's comments in *Uchitelskaya gazeta* (quoted above) are very similar to those of Khrushchev.
[181]King, op cit., p. 16.

honour, conscience, and duty in the Soviet ideology. Whatever the shortcomings of the polytechnic school, Lenin's famous maxim 'The whole of education and upbringing shall be directed to their training in communist morals' is more true today than it was fifty-odd years ago.

CHAPTER 4

Education for Labour, Patriotism, and Defence

I. EDUCATION FOR 'SOCIALLY USEFUL' LABOUR

When the US National Advisory Council on Vocational Training recommended that 'no one ought to leave the educational system without a saleable skill' (to be later reiterated at the Thirty-fourth International Conference on Education, organized by UNESCO in September 1973 in Geneva under the theme 'The Relationship Between Education, Training, and Employment'), it was merely echoing the Soviet educational ideology, which has always treated manpower training extremely seriously, regarding it as the most crucial task of character education and moral training of the school.[1]

The Soviet Union is one of the few countries in the world where education is geared to the needs of the State rather than to the wishes of the individual. The entire educational system could be envisaged as a vast network of manpower training and, more specifically, labour socialization.

Articles published in Soviet periodicals after 1970 indicate that vocational guidance, labour training at school, and occupational placement are treated extremely seriously by the authorities.

Political socialization in the Soviet Union is closely linked with labour socialization or the creation of positive attitudes to labour (trud), particularly blue-collar occupations. Soviet Marxism, unaccustomed as it was, had to solve the following dilemma of the Brezhnev regime—how to adapt the Marxian view which held that the contradictions in capitalist society were division of labour, undue specialization, and separation of intellectual from physical labour, to a socialist society beset by similar problems. What has alarmed Soviet educators is the way higher education is used by the youth to advance

---

[1] *Progress of Education in the United States of America: 1970–71* and *1971–72*, US Department of Health, Education, and Welfare, Washington DC, 1973, p. 38.

themselves on the social ladder. Since the thirties, education has assumed an increasing role in upward social mobility. The result was that significantly more Soviet students aspired to higher education than the system could have allowed for, and fewer and fewer wished to become workers. In the past, sociological surveys have shown that less than 10% of Soviet matriculants intended to become workers. As it turned out, unable to fulfil their dream of entering a VUZ, some had to settle for less (technical college). The majority, about 50% of all school-leavers, had to be content with much less—entering the labour force.

In a socialist society, all labour, according to Marx, should be of equal social prestige and merit. But to operate efficiently and effectively any industrially advanced nation must reward ambition and striving. Some kind of incentive has to be provided for individuals to be motivated to perform the more complex and intellectually demanding occupations. This, clearly, would contradict the Marxist doctrine of equality of labour, as it would result in the reemergence of differential roles and unequal material rewards closely linked to occupation, being the product of division of labour.[2] Because of an anomaly between the thirst for tertiary education and desire to serve the community through manual work, the authorities, aided by the mass media and schools, hoped to cool off unrealistic professional ambitions of children and teach them to respect and love the more humble jobs. In this sense, Marxist–Leninist ethics provide a useful service in giving equal prestige and social status to all kinds of unskilled and semi-skilled professions. Labour socialization in the Soviet school has become an important if not the chief means of guiding school-leavers to job opportunities. This, no doubt, has been necessitated by various sociological findings, all agreeing that there exists a gap between the idealistic career aspirations of the Soviet youth and the reality of present-day manpower requirements in the USSR.

1. Labour training in the school curriculum

Due to social, economic, and moral factors, the Soviet school curriculum during the 1970s was influenced by the mass media praising

[2]O'Dell, F., *et al.*, Labour socialization and occupational placement in Soviet education, *Soviet Studies*, 28, No. 3, 1976, pp. 419–27.

young people who had chosen to become labourers. A survey of articles published in Soviet educational journals between 1974 and 1977 has revealed a growing concern of Soviet educators about the unpopularity of blue-collar professions among school-leavers. To overcome this anti-Marxist and anti-communist trend, a series of curricula reforms were implemented and a new slogan, 'Communist attitude towards labour', was adopted in the Party's search for new secular ethic. Consequently, schoolchildren are taught to believe that only through work can one be happy, demonstrate one's love for one's country, and participate in the construction of a communist Utopia. The correct or a communist attitude to work, which is taught at school during labour-training sessions, is summed up thus:

> The most important task of the character education of the new man is to educate young people with the habit and the need to work conscientiously according to their abilities for the general good and to see in this the main purpose of life, its joy, and its happiness.
>
> A communist attitude to labour means, above all, an understanding of its vital necessity as the source of all material and spiritual benefits.... A love for work, a conscious habit of labouring for the general good to the full extent of one's abilities, seeing labour as one's primary duty, and a vital need, an honest attitude to work, unstinting struggle for high labour productivity—all these qualities characterize the communist attitude to labour.[3]

Today, labour training and vocational orientation plays a significant part in the school curriculum. Labour training at school could be divided into three distinct cycles catering for specific age groups:

1. Junior school (grades 1–3).
2. Middle school (grades 4–8).
3. Senior school (grades 9–10).

Until now, all grades used to have two-hour weekly sessions in work training (trudovoe vospitanie). Following the December decree 'On further improvements in education and upbringing of the secondary school pupils and their preparation for labour' (1977), all school labour-training programmes have to be revised and work sessions in grades 9–10 have been doubled from two to four hours weekly. In addition to this, students are encouraged to join work-and-rest summer camps and participate in socially useful labour during their sum-

---

[3]Ivanovich, K. A., *et al., Trudovoe politekhnicheskoe obuchenie v srednei shkole*, Moscow, 1973, pp. 33–34.

mer vacation. According to the 1971 school curriculum, the aims of labour training in the primary school were defined as follows:
  (a) broadening of children's labour experience and their knowledge about people's work and about techniques; education in the spirit of industriousness and a communist attitude to labour and to working people;
  (b) development of labour skills, of the fundamentals of work culture, and of the ability to plan and organize one's own and one's comrades' work;
  (c) development and character education of pupils during labour lessons ....[4]

A more serious labour training takes place in the secondary school, particularly in grades 7–10. Labour education takes place in school workshops, local study centres, and training areas run by patron enterprises.

Study of the labour-training curriculum shows that respect for labour, particularly manual work, has become today one of the most significant Soviet value judgements.

Despite all the efforts by the Soviet educational system and the mass media to put into practice a Marxist postulate of an equal respect and value for all types of occupations, career aspirations of school-leavers, based on substantially higher preferences for intellectual professions rather than manual ones, seem to contradict Marxist philosophy.

Educational reforms in labour training were long overdue. It appears that many schools in their preoccupation with academic results did not give adequate consideration towards improving work training. The school, writes Soviet sociologist Popov, must compensate for the shortcomings of the family in terms of labour socialization. He admits that the large size of urban schools (up to 2500 students) tends to restrict the potential of the school and significantly diminish the effectiveness of labour instruction. But he also adds that some schools have no facilities for socially productive labour. He states that this problem can only be solved by well-organized vocational guidance as early as possible and by involving all students in

[4]*Programma vosmiletnei shkoly* (nachalnye klassy), Moscow, 1971, p. 56.

productive work during summer vacations.[5] Poorly equipped school workshops, poorly qualified staff, and prevailing apathy of the school administrators, teachers, and pupils toward vocational orientation would have contributed towards reforms in work training at school. A certain teacher remarks that work training is too theoretical and not practical enough, and that the two electives—tractor and electronics—can hardly be sufficient in enriching the programme.[6]

Soviet educationalists appear to have been more successful with getting the students to participate in the so-called summer labour term. Students in grades 8–10 volunteer to work for the State during their summer school break. In 1977 10 million students took part in a patriotic movement called 'My work flows into the work of my Republic'.[7]

2. Work training in urban areas

An experimental study of work training took place in October, the suburb of Moscow in 1975. Twenty-one schools in the area were involved. An educational centre of computer technology was established and 2000 students in grades 9 and 10 were invited to study at the centre after school. The centre offered training in eleven professions. Students in grade 9 were expected to be available for six hours a week or 200 hours per year. They were taught programming, impulse technology, and the workings of the latest Soviet computers. At the end of the course 45% of students enrolled successfully completed the course and received certificates in different aspects of computer technology.[8] This centre is, of course, the only one of its kind in the USSR. Normally, students receive their vocational training in PTUs.

After 1975, following the introduction of universal secondary education, more and more students entering a PTU will be required to complete their secondary education as well as learn one or more occupations. Today's PTU is a secondary specialized polytechnic col-

[5] Popov, V. D., Sociological problems of the transition to universal secondary education. *Soviet Sociology*, Winter 1967/77, pp. 38–39.
[6] *Uchitelskaya gazeta*, 1, Jan., 1978, p. 3.
[7] Ibid., 6 Aug., 1977, p. 1.
[8] *Narodnoe Obrazovanie*, No. 9, 1975, p. 63.

lege which offers a broad range of occupations (semi-professional) covering heavy industry, health, education, arts, agriculture, food processing, forestry, book-keeping, and so on. Courses last from six months to three years, and, according to A. Bulgakov, there were 1100 different occupations to choose from in 1976.[9] In the past ten years there was a spectacular growth of vocational–technical schools in the USSR—from 4103 (1965) to 6356 (1975), and the student intake has doubled—from $1\frac{1}{2}$ million (1965) to 3 million (1975).[10] Five times as many new students (350,000) were admitted in the 1974–5 academic year than in 1971, and in 1975 40% of all students attended PTUs.

At a PTU the student who has completed at least eight years of general education may study from one to three years, depending on the trade involved. Students attending PTUs receive free food, uniform, and a stipend. For instance, at a rural PTU, students learning to be truck mechanics received in 1974 a stipend ranging from 86 to 104 roubles a month, being equivalent to the basic salary of a semi-skilled worker.[11] Upon completion of the course (which also includes aesthethetic training through literature, art, music, and the theatre), the student receives his diploma (pass or honours) and a classification on the vocational ladder of his particular profession. The Moscow PTU No. 11 (established in 1932) had 700 students in 1974. The school's administration has made an attempt to narrow the gap between technical and high school curriculum, thereby proving that a PTU could offer both vocational and academic training. 'When you enter the PTU No. 11', writes a correspondent, 'you can see an impressive array of departments, including history, literature, chemistry, physics, electrical and mechanical engineering, and metal science.' During the next three years the former eighth-graders will have to pass both academic and technical disciplines. The author also mentions that PTU-trained personnel receive good salaries ranging between 140 and 150 roubles a month.[12]

'Unfortunately,' writes A. Osipov, Deputy Chairman of the State

[9]Bulgakov, A., *Knizhnoe Obozrenie*, No. 17 (519), 1976, p. 6.
[10]The 1965 figures: *Pedagogicheskaya entsiklopediya*, Vol. 3, 1966, p. 553.
[11]The 1975 figures: *Knizhnoe Obozrenie*, No. 17 (519), 1976, p. 6.
[12]*Vospitanie Shkolnikov*, No. 4., 1974, p. 18.

Committee of the USSR Council of Ministry for Professional and Technical Education, 'experience has shown that students have incomplete and somewhat distorted ideas about vocational–technical schools. One would wish that the school and parents would help schoolchildren to learn more about PTUs, where it is possible to receive a profession and complete one's secondary education.'[13]

We get a further glimpse of work training from an article published in *Vospitanie Shkolnikov* in 1974. In Pervouralsk (Sverdlovsk region) there is a close co-operation between schools and the local industry in placing school-leavers in industry. The city has its own labour employment commission (komissiya po trudoustroistvu), which find jobs for students. The problem is, however, that often boys and girls seek employment after they have failed to gain an admission into the institute. Disillusioned, frustrated, and discontented, they ask just for any job, irrespective of what it is or where it is. Such an attitude is, clearly, undesirable. In Pervouralsk, in the last three years alone, 72% of school-leavers, or 3014 out of 4210, went to work in the local factories.[14]

In order to ascertain the needs of local industry and determine the potential workforce in the area, officials send out questionnaires at the beginning of the school year to all students in grade 10. In this way, school-leavers are booked, so to speak, for a particular job. While they are completing their secondary studies, students are introduced to various semi-professional skills, factory life, and norms. When they commence working we are told they are well adjusted, efficient, and, above all, valuable man-hours are saved that otherwise would be lost on training new workers. Often there is what is referred to as patronage (shefstvo) between the school and the local industry. For example, in Karaganda secondary school No. 17 closely co-operates with the main factory in the area. As a result, every fourth matriculant ends up working in that factory.[14] The Permsk bicycle factory works closely with secondary school No. 81. Under the patronage of the factory's administration the school organized a club of young technicians. There, experienced workers conduct instruction. The students in grades 9 and 10 regularly visit the factory and are

[13]Ibid., p. 21.
[14]Ibid., No. 3, 1974, p. 37.

introduced to various jobs. The factory administration organizes open days and profession days (dni professii). The senior students work for one month at the factory, presumably during their summer vacation, and every year half of them end up working there.[15]

3. Work training in rural areas

Work training in the village facilitates a union between man and nature. This is an aesthetic justification for the need to train boys and girls in rural areas for work on the land. Since 80% of all schools are found in rural districts, netting more than 50% of the total student population, it, indeed, makes sense to indoctrinate them with ethical and aesthetic maxims of man's intrinsic need to work for nature.

Every year educational journals publish hundreds of articles describing success stories of labour training in rural areas. One correspondent informs us that in their region (Tatyshlinsk, the Bashkirian ASSR) a council for communist upbringing and labour training was created. The council organizes inter-school competitions in labour training, and best students are awarded honour certificates. The author proudly informs us that 70% of candidates have taken the sacred profession of khleborob (corn-grower). In the region there are twenty-seven pupils' working brigades with 2300 students. The largest brigade has 520 members. In October of each year they prepare seeds for planting, and between January and February (winter), with the help of agricultural experts, they prepare various technological charts, programmes for summer work, and rosters. The corn-grower club is flourishing in the area, and its slogan is 'The village is your home and you are its master!' (Selo-troi dom, i ty ego khozyain!).[16]

In the Shcherbinovsk region (near Krasnodar) work training occupies 7% of the curriculum in order to enable the pupils to enter into life with their eyes opened.[17] Here, propaganda of significant labour achievements of the local collective farmers (kolkhozniki) plays an important role in professional orientation of the pupils. There are

[15]*Narodnoe Obrazovanie*, No. 9, 1975, p. 38.
[16]Ibid., No. 7, 1975, p. 64.
[17]Ibid., No. 8, 1975, p. 57.

public stands and display boards like 'Our heroes of labour', 'They studied in our school', and more. The slogan is 'Living in the village—know technology!', and, accordingly, out of 6000 pupils in the area over 1000 participated in mechanical–technical compulsory training (vseobuch). In 1974 hundreds of school-leavers were trained to become tractor drivers, technicians, builders, and so on. At Kalinin's kolkhoz over 700 students joined the brigade and some were awarded medals for excellence in labour. Others received diplomas of 'The enthusiast of harvesting' and the Komsomol badges 'Udarnik—1973' (shock-worker—1973).[18]

V. Lezova (Deputy Chairman of the Vladimirsk oblono), in her article 'Country students love labour', describes a successful work training in the Vladimirsk region, RSFSR. Between 35–40% of the students remain in the kolkhoz. She proceeds to describe an interesting experience of the secondary school of Andreevsk (the Alexandrovski district) which, for its exemplary work in labour training, was awarded an honorary certificate by the Presidium of the Russian Federation (RSFSR). It is a small school, with 536 students and 24 teachers. All students in grades 4–8 attend practical sessions in various workshops. The senior students (grades 9–10) study the tractor and other agricultural machinery.[19] In grades 5–7 the students learn the theory of agriculture, agricultural science, and technology, and gain experience working with different vegetable and crop cultures. They visit the local kolkhoz and are introduced to all aspects of agriculture. The senior students study the economics of industry and rural technology. The school's pupils' working brigade (ucheniicheskaya proizvodstvennaya brigada), created seventeen years ago, has 180 members. The brigade was allocated 35 hectares of cultivating land. The brigade cultivated 5 hectares of potatoes, 6 hectares of barley, 6 hectares of oats, and 15 hectares of grazing land. In 1975 the brigade helped the sovkhoz Andreyevsky and planted 5 hectares of cabbage and weeded 150 hectares of the winter wheat. With the help of the local agronomist, the brigade carried out many experiments, in this case to increase the potato yield. The brigade has its own traditions such as ceremonial acceptance of new members,

[18]Ibid., p. 58.
[19]Ibid., p. 60.

during which the uninitiated solemnly promise to work and study honestly and conscientiously. Every year in October the brigade celebrates harvest festival (prazdnik urozhaya). The brigade, remarks the author, has become a 'real school for preparation of the cadre for the sovkhoz Andreyevsky'.[20] As a result of excellent work-training programmes, every second worker at the sovkhoz is from the local school.

Another success story, this time in the Ukraine, is that of the Gayvoron district and its work-training centre—the leading one in the Republic. The author begins his article by quoting from Brezhnev's speech at the Seventeenth Congress of Komsomol: 'The upbringing of boys and girls in the spirit of respect and love towards labour always was and will be the most important task of the Communist Party....'[21] The work-training centre, established in 1961, occupies an area of 4000 square metres with many workshops serving thirteen local schools. Here, 2055 of the students in grades 9–10 undergo vocational training in twelve different professions ranging from truck-driver to cattle-breeder. It is interesting to note that the pupil's choice of a profession depends on the local needs. Surveys are carried out annually to determine the number of vacancies in industry and agriculture and, if necessary, the work-training programme is adjusted to a particular need that may arise from year to year. Fifty-four instructors co-ordinate work training for pupils in grades 4–8. Work training is taken very seriously by the local authorities. Every effort is made to achieve high standards in instruction and high quality in the pupil's mastery of a particular trade. Students are examined continuously throughout the year. More than 40% of the students, who had completed vocational training at the centre, end up working in jobs they were trained for.[22]

There are practical problems with school work-training. It ignores the problem that freedom of choice in vocational training depends on the availability of a variety of industrial and agricultural complexes within reach of the school. In practice, choice is limited to two or three specialities. This, clearly, could result in the training of numbers

[20]*Narodnoe Obrazovanie*, No. 8, 1975, p. 61.
[21]Ibid., No. 11, 1975, p. 57.
[22]Ibid., p. 58.

of young people in occupations that they will 'never fill, both because they don't want to, and because there are insufficient jobs available'.[23] The authorities are obviously aware of this particular problem, and since the majority of school-leavers will be directed to obtain vocational training in PTUs, which are designed to meet the needs of the national economy, the problem of redundancy should be solved.

Although 10 million secondary students (including 3 million rural students) participated in pupils' labour brigades and worked during their summer vacation in various branches of the Soviet economy, there are signs of non-conformism. One Soviet educator writes that community involvement tends to decrease with age, that two-thirds of youth leaders are girls, and that teenagers are bored with school-run activities, which are characterized by regimentation, authoritarianism, conformity, excessive guardianship, and so on—all of which deprive the pupil of his or her initiative and independence.[24]

Work training is even used to reform problem pupils. Ivan K. was the most difficult pupil in grade 5 and he was expelled from the school and sent to a labour colony (trudovaya koloniya). One teacher, however, noticed the boy's interest in plants so she let him work on the school's garden plot. The boy became so enthusiastic about working in the garden that his class-mates elected him as their group leader. The former delinquent is now a biology teacher.[25]

It seems that work training is fairly successful throughout the USSR. In certain non-Russian areas the pupils' labour brigades consist of many different nationalities and they are conducted in the spirit of internationalism. One such multi-national brigade exists in the Karachaevo–Cherkessii region (bordering Georgia). About fifty different minority groups live in this region. Five thousand students in grades 9–10 from fifty-eight country schools study tractor and other agricultural machinery, and in 1974 2238 received tractor licenses.

Nearly 80% of senior pupils were trained as mechanics. Students

[23]Price, R. F., Labour and education in Russia and China, *Comparative Education*, Mar., 1974, p. 20.
[24]*Narodnoe Obrazovanie*, No. 9, 1975, p. 6.
[25]Ibid., No. 8, 1974, p. 65.

help the collective farmers with planting, weeding, and harvesting. They service machinery and repair damaged units. The brigade helps to realize work training and moral and ideological upbringing. For instance, the Pervomayskaya brigade conducts active propaganda work with the local inhabitants. Senior students give talks and co-ordinated sessions of politinformatsiya, and they model themselves on the life of Lenin. Regular political and current affairs conferences are organized by senior students. They also discuss films they have seen and new books read. They visit places of revolutionary or military glory and periodically meet veterans of the Great Patriotic War.[26] Students also cultivate a substantial portion of the land and, to give one an idea of their efforts, it is sufficient to mention that they look after 1533 hectares of forest.

'Hand in Hand with the Kolkhoz' describes the pupils' labour brigades at Mekhonskaya (Kursk region). The brigade was created in the wake of the all-Union directive to attract more rural students towards socialist and productive labour. All students from grade 7 upwards work in the brigade, while those in grades 4–6 work at the school's experimental plot (opytny uchastok). The kolkhoz Rossiya has allocated 90 hectares of land for the brigade. The brigade, like most rural brigades, works the whole year around. In 1970 the brigade came first in the all-Republic labour brigades' competition and the school was awarded a bus—the first prize. The brigade produced high yields in the potato crop, beetroot, and cornflour, and the net yearly profit ranges between 12,000 to 15,000 roubles.[27] With the money earned, the school would normally provide free meals and free summer camps, and would purchase extra trucks and cars for training purposes.

The mass media have given a great deal of publicity to work training and labour socialization in rural areas. School-leavers, including matriculants who decide to stay in their villages and join the local collective farm as semi-skilled or skilled workers, are publicly praised. But there is a massive migration of young men from small, provincial towns and villages. In one year, migration from the village increased

[26]*Narodnoe Obrazovanie*, No. 9, 1975, p. 65.
[27]*Vospitanie Shkolnikov*, No. 4, 1974, p. 22.

threefold.[28] The territorial mobility and the so-called problem of small towns is, indeed, a serious socio-economic problem in the Soviet Union. Soviet rural industry is experiencing a chronic shortage of workers, which makes it difficult to fulfil targets in agriculture envisaged by the current five-year plan.

4. Work-training propaganda and the mass media

In the Soviet Union the very existence of the commonly used phrase black work (chornaya rabota) indicates the attitude that un-skilled and semi-skilled professions have the lowest esteem in the eyes of the Soviet youth.

Blue-collar professions were and still are the least popular in the Soviet-Union, and Khrushchev's educational reforms during 1958 were aimed at eliminating the wrong attitude towards physical labour and to diverting the majority of grade 8 students into factories, mills, and collective farms. Khrushchev wrote that a number of Soviet matriculants went unwillingly to work in factories, and some of them even considered this to be below their dignity.

> This lordly scornful, wrong attitude to physical labour is to be found also in some families, If a boy or girl does not study well, the parents and the people around them frighten the child by saying that if he does not study well, fails to get a gold or silver medal [for academic excellence—J.Z.], he will not be able to get into the university and will have to work in a factory as a labourer....[29]

A similar criticism, almost echoing Khrushchev, was voiced thir-teen years later by a Soviet educationalist:

> Unfortunately, there still occur instances of a remaining petty bourgeois, haughty attitude to the working man and workers' jobs. Also, for a long time, the training system was not based on preparing pupils for work, on developing in them a taste for manual jobs and a correct understanding of the role of productive labour in communist construction. Some pupils did not want to go into productive work, considering it to be almost an insult. Sometimes the young person finds himself in a false position because of the lordly, disdainful attitude to labour which still exists in some families. If he studies badly he is threatened by his parents with: 'If you don't get into a VUZ [vysshee uchebnoe zavedenie—higher educational institution], you'll end up in a factory as an ordinary worker.'[30]

[28]Shubkin, V. L., Nachalo puti..., *Novy Mir*, No. 2, 1976, p. 205.
[29]*Pravda*, 21 Sept., 1958, p. 1.
[30]Dyachenko, N., *Professionalnaya orientatsiya...*, Moscow, 1971, p. 117.

The dread of becoming an unskilled worker is particularly strong among city school-leavers. To overcome this, the two leading school journals, *Narodnoe Obrazovanie* and *Vospitanie Shkolnikov*, constantly refer to the importance of manual work. Articles deride and ridicule parents for pushing their little Mishas and Laras, without regard to their abilities, into medicine, engineering, and science, thus adding to the already apparent contradictions between the pyramid of desires and the pyramid of demands.[31] The school system, as correctly observed by Grant in 1964, wanted to reinforce Marxist ethics by breaking down the barriers between mental and manual work and by arresting the growth of a white-collar mentality and the emergence of a new upper class.

The schools have been urged by the authorities to fight the newly emerging work snobbery.[32] The reasons that can be offered for this new drive on labour socialization are ideological, social, and economic. Today's Soviet matriculants entered grade 1 in 1970, or 53 years since the Great October Revolution had taken place and nearly thirty years after the Great Patriotic War. For them the heroic era is nothing more than the distant past. It became even more necessary to maintain revolutionary zeal and purity through patriotic and communist labour. The social argument can be based on egalitarianism or simply humble jobs' prestige. Since 1958 the authorities have been trying to remove the social barriers between physical and intellectual work by publicizing in the mass media that all jobs are equally worthy of respect. One way of achieving it is to increase social prestige of blue-collar occupations and technical school training for these jobs. Various surveys in the Soviet Union have shown that the prestige of particular jobs among contemporary Soviet young people depends more or less directly on the amount of training required for a job.

The economic argument is similar to the one given by De Witt in 1961 who stated that polytechnic education reforms in 1958 were brought on by the prognosis of the manpower planners of Gosplan.

[31]Shubkin, op. cit., pp. 206–14. (See also Turchenko, V. N., *Nauchno-tekhnologicheskaya revolutsiya...*, Moscow, 1973, 1973, p. 145.
[32]Prokofiev, M., in *Uchitelskaya gazeta* (29 Nov., 1977, p. 1) comments on the dangers of a "scornful" attitude to "humble, physical labour".

We could say that a growing number of one-child families had contributed to low birth-rate years, not dissimilar to 1958. Hence there are labour shortages, particularly in blue-collar work.

Since 1958, despite the fact that there has been a lack of clarity in production training, schooling retained its polytechnic bias and there has been a fresh attempt to create a closer relationship between vocational training at school and future manpower needs. For the last twenty years the Soviet Union has experienced a remarkable growth of the university-trained intelligentsia coupled with a drastic shortage of blue-collar workers.

Since PTUs have assumed the role of major training establishments of individuals for sub-professional occupations, the mass media attempted to improve their overall public image which in 1976 had the lowest prestige of all educational institutions. Major newspapers like *Pravda* and *Isvestiya*, and educational periodicals like *Vospitanie Shkolnikov* and *Narodnoe Obrazovanie*, emphasized the growing prestige of PTUs in 1977, and spirited appraisals were given to the school-leavers who, despite counter influences (parents and teachers), stood firm in their decision to enrol in PTUs. The mass media spare no one in their criticism of wrong and, in many instances, inappropriate advice given by parents and teachers regarding vocational orientation. Individuals are strongly criticized for inflating the pupil's job expectations.

When a Moscow PTU asked the following question of its applicants Why did you enter a PTU?, hoping to discover which particular agencies of socialization were instrumental in the pupil's choice of a PTU, they received a number of revealing answers.

> For me [answered Sasha Levinsky] there was no real problem where to study next. I was firm in my decision to enter a PTU, especially the PTU No. 11, which trains the personnel for the ball-bearing factory where my parents work. At home my parents often talked about their factory and I decided to follow in their footsteps. . . .[33]

This is a straightforward case of like-father-like-son being, no doubt, the model answer sought. What is being implied is that children can be influenced by their parents in vocational guidance and that some parents are either too ambitious for their children or they

[33]*Vospitanie Shkolnikov*, No. 4, 1974, p. 18.

do not take the slightest interest. Non-working-class families, with their unrealistically high career expectations for their children, are made to feel just as guilty as some working-class families, who remain totally indifferent to their children's job aspirations. A middle-class mother confessed:

> When Kolya told me he wanted to go to PTU I did my best to change his mind. So did his teachers.... His school results were good and he, quite suddenly, decided to go to a PTU. I was so embarrassed in front of our neighbours for it seemed that our son was not as clever as theirs.... But now I am completely satisfied....[33]

This particular confession reveals that both the parents and teachers are promoting the wrong attitude towards manual labour and PTUs. It further suggests that PTUs are filled with school dropouts and individuals with low academic abilities. Another case of fulfilled dreams is quoted.

> A certain Nikolai N. at the age of 10 liked tractors and engines. [Don't they all at that age?—J.Z.] His father, a mechanic by training, looked upon this as providence, so he began to teach his boy about the engines.... As the boy grew his father took him to the local kolkhoz during the school vacation. From grade 7 (14 years of age) the boy began to drive tractors and conveyers during his long summer holidays. Naturally, after grade 10 he stayed in the village as a mechanic.[34]

In contrast, Valery as a boy liked calves and he found himself spending most of his free time looking after them. As the boy grew his parents became rather worried about their son's obsession and, to make matters worse, he happened to be academically gifted. 'They kept indoctrinating him', writes the author, 'with a "city" profession.' The boy was forbidden to visit the local State farm. 'Don't waste your time', they said. 'What can you learn from a calf?' The parents had won and the boy completed tertiary studies and became a dental technician. 'Now', continues the angry author, 'many have realized what a mediocre dental technician he is and what a wonderful calf-attendant he could have been.'[34] We are asked, clearly, to agree with the author that Valery's parents were irresponsible and wrong in changing his natural destiny. It is difficult to imagine that Soviet readers would be naive enough to judge Valery's parents as being irresponsible. Evidently many boys and girls had entered PTUs in direct defiance of their parents' wishes. Natasha Mitrofanova was one such case. She recalls:

> I got to know a girl from a PTU and she kept telling me about the college. When I

[34] *Narodnoe Obrazovanie*, No. 7, 1974, p. 63.

told my mother that I wanted to go to a PTU after grade 8, she became terribly upset and alarmed. 'Natasha', said my mother, 'have you gone mad? You have no other grades but 4's and 5's [very good—excellent—J.Z.]. You simply must complete the school and then go to the university! Why, your own girlfriends who get lower marks than you do don't even think of a PTU....'[35]

This particular case, apart from commenting on middle-class parental aspirations, argues very strongly for peer group influence on Komsomol members in vocational guidance and labour socialization.

There seems to be an upward social mobility in Soviet society during the 1970s. Parents, whenever possible, encourage their sons and daughters (who do not seem to need much encouragement) to complete secondary education at day-time polytechnic schools and enter a VUZ (a tertiary institution). Parents, clearly, are not convinced by lofty Marxist–Leninist ideals of egalitarianism, particularly the belief that all jobs are equal. An article in *Pravda* mentions a family crisis over a boy, Sergei, who out of the blue informs his well-to-do parents (his father lectures at a teacher college) that as soon as he matriculates he will seek employment at the local ball-bearing factory. The boy's mother is absolutely shocked but the father remains calm. 'Sergei did the right thing', said the father, 'if he does not feel especially attracted towards learning.' Sergei's mother, however, dreamed of her son studying at the university and becoming an historian. She even hired a tutor to improve the boy's grades. The article is critical of boys and girls of average abilities embarking on university careers. Parents are held responsible, and the article criticizes their unrealistic attitude towards vocations. Apparently there are parents who have only one ambition—to get their children, at all costs, into the university. For such parents and children the university diploma is not a carefully thought out perspective in life—but an end in itself. 'I don't believe', writes the author, 'that such students will make excellent specialists. Don't think that I am against higher education On the contrary, if one is attracted towards learning, and already at school showed a calling or wish to become an engineer, a doctor, or a teacher—good luck....'[36]

The moral of this article is that one should not be forced into a profession for which one has neither talent nor real desire and that

[35] *Vospitanie Shkolnikov*, No. 4, 1974, p. 18.
[36] Shvarts, A., Vernost profesii, *Pravda*, 15 May, 1976, p. 3.

any job is good as long as the worker earns the respect and recognition of his fellow-men. The author concludes, in romantic manner (paraphrasing Maxim Gorky) that 'the best profession is that of being a man'.[37]

Another writer informs us that secondary teachers are equally to blame by not guiding their students towards blue-collar professions. They take pride in enabling many of their gifted students to enter a tertiary establishment, but if the student is weak and undisciplined, he/she is destined for a PTU and only has him or her self to blame:

> Maybe I am exaggerating, but I think that the future of the working class is in your hands. As yet, the greatness of the Soviet worker and his role in the creation of the material and technical base of communism is insufficiently developed in the pupils. School-leavers don't know anything about the needs of worker cadres in different branches of the economy.

One often hears how proudly the teachers mention the percentage of school-leavers who entered tertiary institutions and yet they remain discreetly silent about those who went to a vocational school (proftekhuchilishche). Here, the following principle seems to operate. 'If a good student enters, let us say, MIFI (one of Moscow's tertiary institutes), it is due to our merits. But a weak and undisciplined student has himself to blame for his misfortunes, and the PTU is the only road left open to him....'[38]

This illustrates quite convincingly that some teachers attach a snob value to tertiary education and treat with contempt trade and industrial schools.

Clearly, the Soviet educational system has yet to eradicate the remaining petty bourgeois attitudes to blue-collar occupations. One way to solve it would be to increase the prestige of non-professional occupations and of the vocational colleges training the youth for these jobs. The mass media, as discussed earlier, attempts to obliterate the public's image of manual labour and vocational schools. The authorities are trying to up-grade trade and industrial schools, and the September 1977 decree 'On further improvements of the process of instruction and upbringing of the students within the network of professional and technical education' is one such measure. From six-month factory schools (FZO), which accepted individuals with

[37] *Pravda*, 15 May 1976, p. 3.
[38] *Uchitelskaya gazeta*, 15 Sept., 1977, p. 3.

primary education, vocational schools had evolved into three-year institutions, admitting 15-year-old secondary students, which offer both complete secondary education and vocational training.

5. The impact of work training on career aspirations of school-leavers

One of the major sociological studies of school-leavers' career aspirations in Siberia was carried out by Novosibirsk University between 1963 and 1973.[39] The survey, by means of questionnaires and interviews, was conducted among school-leavers completing the ten-year school (aged 17). The first survey, called Project 17–17, was to ascertain the students' future plans, hopes, and aspirations, and to test their attitude towards various occupations. The next study, Project 17–25, was a follow-up of the students' realization of their professional ambition. The aim was to discover a correlation (if any) between the students' vocational dreams and their actual employment several years later.

A noted Soviet sociologist Shubkin, in his monograph on career aspirations of the youth, introduces the concept of job pyramids illustrated in Fig. 5.

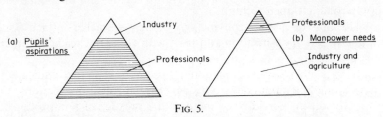

FIG. 5.

Figure 5 shows that there exists a vast gap between the career aspirations of youth and the actual needs of the Soviet economy.

If in the sixties the most coveted occupations were those of radio engineer, pilot, mathematician, and physicist, while at the bottom of the list were agricultural worker, book-keeper, shop assistant, waiter, cook, and house painter, then in the seventies medical research worker and writer were the two most esteemed professions. Physicist has lost its dominating position, and historian, journalist, teacher,

[39]Shubkin, op. cit., pp. 206–12.

TABLE   22. *Answers to Why did you choose your job given by 1157 PTU students in Dnepropetrovsk (1969)*

Answers	Percentage
Parents or peers	33
Own choice	44.9
By chance	15.5
Teachers' choice	6.6

and medical sister have improved their job prestige. But the social prestige of such common occupations like book-keeper, postman, welder, and milkmaid still remains low.[40]

In general, boys rated technology higher than science and the humanities, whereas girls preferred the humanities to science and technology. In terms of the overall prestige, technical occupations received the first choice, followed by science and the humanities. In practice, however, the pecking order was technology, the humanities science. There is a growing popularity of medicine and the humanities at the expense of science.

How successful then is labour socialization today? Studies have shown that between 1967 and 1977 schools had played a relatively minor role, almost insignificant, in influencing the pupils' choice of jobs (Table 22), let alone guiding them to accept such humble occupations as the metalworker, fitter and turner, and the milkmaid.

Every year the State requires 7 million workers (including 5 million blue-collar workers). Five million students had completed secondary education in 1977 and 2 million graduated from the trade and industrial schools[41] Of the 5 million who completed secondary school in 1977 nearly 50% wished to enter a tertiary institution and less than 10% wanted to enter PTUs.[41] It has been calculated by one study that 76.5% of grade 8 pupils, 60% of technical (specialized secondary

[40]Shubkin, op. cit., p. 210.
[41]*Sovetskaya Pedagogika*, No. 2, 1976, p. 42; *Uchitelskaya gazeta*, 9 Sept., 1977, p. 1; *Uchitelskaya gazeta*, 13 Dec., 1977, p. 1.

school) students, and 54% of PTU students intended to continue their education beyond grade 10. At the same time, 26% had no definite plans and 1 in 12 responded, 'I am not going to study'.[42] Nearly one-third of the total students in schools for working youth (shkola rabochei molodiozhi—ShRM) stated that they had to enrol as nowadays it is inconvenient to have very little schooling. Contemporary Soviet young people tend to orient themselves towards education in general, without concerning themselves with developing a particular occupational direction. There were 48% of such individuals in secondary schools.[42]

The above reveals many hidden problems in Soviet education and upbringing. A large percentage of schoolchildren have either a most confused impression of many jobs or no definite plans at all. Many more aspire to tertiary education than can ever actually receive it. In the 1960s, between 96% and 98% of all Soviet matriculants wished to enter tertiary institutions. In 1975 alone it was estimated that about 50% of all school-leavers had to enter the labour force, which requires a fresh intake of 5 million workers annually. However, in the 1968 study only 7% of grade 8 pupils intended to become labourers, and in another study 92% of matriculants hoped to continue their education at tertiary institutions. Some of the sociological studies between 1967 and 1977 show that, in general, four out of five students had wished to continue their education beyond grade 10 and less than 10% wanted to become blue-collar workers. According to Gosplan's estimates for 1975, the State Planning Commission, responsible among other things for the development of plans for future professional manpower needs and the allocation of quotas among the various educational institutions, only 15% of all matriculants were to enter tertiary institutions, another 21% were to enrol in technical colleges, and 64% had to join the labour force.[43] As illustrated earlier, career aspirations of school-leavers did not meet the needs of Soviet economy.

Soviet teachers exert a very weak influence on the choice of an occupation.[44] Recent Soviet sociological studies have shown that

[42]Popov, V. D., op. cit., p. 28.
[43]Shubkin, op. cit., p. 210.
[44]See *Sovetskaya Pedagogika*, No. 2, 1976a, p. 45; *Soviet Sociology*, No. 3, 1977, p. 29; and *Uchitelskaya gazeta*, 13 Sept., 1977, p. 1.

between 6% and 12% of school-leavers were directly influenced by their teachers in their choice of occupations. Since there exists a contradiction between the pupils' pyramid of desires and the State's pyramid of demands, the Marxist idea that all jobs are equally worthy of respect, and hence a Marxist–Leninist labor socialization, aiming at convincing the pupil of equal prestige in all kinds of physical labour, has failed to attract the majority of school-leavers towards blue-collar occupations. As the majority of Soviet youth are not prepared to accept the harsh reality, namely that they have to become workers, quotas have been maintained in most tertiary institutions and technical colleges. The only viable alternatives left for those who failed to be admitted into tertiary institutions were to join the workforce or to enter PTUs, which still have the lowest prestige of all educational establishments.

6. Work training and its socio-political implications

It should be emphasized that Soviet education is based on the polytechnic principle along the lines developed by Marx, Lenin, and Krupskaya. It is quite distinct from trade or technical training that takes place in PTUs. The aim of work training in secondary schools is to introduce children to blue-collar occupations, believed to be essential to their character and moral training or, as one Soviet sociologist puts it,

> What we are saying is that the 18-year-old citizen of the Soviet Union should not only write in his exit or entrance examinations that labour is good, and parasitism is evil. He must himself, with his own mind and hands, discover what is labour and what is an honestly earned rouble.[45]

The idea that each individual must experience a combination of productive labour and intellectual education is, clearly, Marxist. In his principle of education of the future, Marx stated that every child over a certain age will 'combine productive labour with instruction and physical culture, not only as a means for increasing social production, but as the only way of producing fully developed beings'.[46]

[45]Bestuzhev-Lada, I. V., Sotsialnye problemy sovetskogo obraza zhizni, *Novy Mir*, No. 7, 1976, p. 217.
[46]Quoted in Price, R. F., *Marx and Education in Russia and China*, London, 1977, p. 70.

Marx believed that in an intelligent social order each child from the age of 9 must, as an adult, submit to the general law of nature and become a productive worker. In order to eat, stressed Marx, he must work; and work not only with his mind, but also with his hands.[47]

Marx's radical principle of the manual-labour–education combination stipulated that intellectual education was to come first to be followed by physical training and polytechnic instruction. Such education would acquaint the child with the basic principles of all processes of production and at the same time give the child the habit of dealing with the most simple instruments of all production.

It would seem that the above-mentioned Marxist principle would be a self-fulfilling prophecy of the essentially egalitarian Soviet educational ideology. But Marxist polytechnic principle until now seemed to be an anachronism. The dread of becoming a drop-out and factory worker is still wide-spread among today's Soviet school-leavers.

A Marxist view requires an equal respect for all types of jobs (in order to eliminate the division of labour evil), and as such it cannot favour any specific profession. But the Soviet Union is only too anxious to maintain industrial growth, and technological occupations have received a privileged treatment which clearly, contradicts the Marxist principle.

While it is true to say that the Soviet educational system, being egalitarian, is not formally structured to select or to sponsor some for white-collar and others for blue-collar professions, the latest educational reforms indicate that allocation to jobs will become more pronounced. It seems that the authorities are forced to channel youth into non-professional occupations or, as one author puts it, the 'level of ambition of the manual worker strata will be "realistically", related to occupational possibilities'.[48] Allocating school-leavers to jobs suggests the 'tempering of ambition within the unstreamed and egalitarian Soviet general secondary school'.[49] Some teachers, as shown earlier, have taken upon themselves the task of deciding which pupils are suitable for academic (post-secondary) studies and which are destined for a vocational school.

[47]Ibid., p. 71.
[48]O'Dell, op. cit., p. 429.
[49]Ibid., p. 426.

As Soviet education is becoming more concerned with centralized recruitment of pupils, particularly during the 1980s, its ideology would tend to emphasize such moral traits as loyalty, communist attitude towards labour and people. Whether this may be ideologically conducive to the social integration of the professional and non-professional occupations is yet to be seen.[50]

It may well be that apart from fulfilling the needs of the Soviet economy, the Party is attempting to give equal status to all jobs. In doing so, white-collar occupations may become less élitist and more egalitarian. It could well be that since the war an élitist, ruling stratum has established so dominant a position in the Soviet Union that it became a potential threat to the Marxist–Leninist concept of a classless society. Although Soviet sociologists deny the existence of social stratification and upward social mobility in the Soviet Union for political reasons, they do, nevertheless, acknowledge the existence of social inequality. While commenting on the relationship between social differences and educational attainment, Popov wrote:

> We know that under socialism education has ceased to be the privilege of any particular classes or social strata since the first days of Soviet power. However, the social differences that continue to exist today make for inequality in the cultural and technical levels of workers, white-collar people, and professionals, and this in turn affects their attitudes toward education and their ability to help their children with their schoolwork. Analysis of empirical material has demonstrated a direct relationship between grade repeating and drop-out and the education and social status of parents.[51]

Differential socialization in the Soviet Union, if we are to take into account parental attitudes toward differential types of schooling and their obvious preference for white-collar occupations, is becoming more pronounced. For instance, the prestige with which vocational schools are regarded varies according to social class. In the predominantly working-class areas the prestige of PTUs has increased, and one study showed that 87.3% of boys and 95.8% of girls wishing to enter a PTU were from manual-working families, compared with only 5.9% and 1.4% from white-collar (professional) strata. Likewise, only 49% of boys and 68.4% of girls of working-class families wished to complete secondary education (being a stepping stone to a tertiary

[50]O'Dell, op. cit., p. 427.
[51]Popov, op. cit., p. 31.

institution) compared with 44.5% of boys and 24% of girls from white-collar families.[52]

Another problem that has arisen as a result of universal complete secondary education is the social attitude towards education. Society's interest in giving everyone a complete secondary education reduces interest in attaining it and, worse, does not always match individual attitudes.[53] This, no doubt, tends to undermine the Soviet educational ideology of the unstreamed and egalitarian schooling. The authorities have transformed PTUs into academic and vocational institutions. The PTUs are being promoted as an alternative route to tertiary education. Evening schools, providing complete secondary education, are available to the working youth. In one Sverdlovsk factory only 11% of the working youth attended such schools. This suggests that many of the young factory workers have decided to drop out of the contest system of their own choice. 'They come to accept', concludes one author perceptively, 'that they have been beaten by superior competitors or that the costs of staying in the race outweigh the still distant possible rewards.'[54]

The very notions of communist attitude towards work and socially productive labour suggest the existence in the Soviet society of the division of labour and, with it, differential roles and unequal material rewards closely linked to occupation.[55] Payment and reward by result could be regarded as a ubiquitous process in Soviet society. The ultimate inducement is the title of the Hero of Socialist Labour or a post in the Higher Council of the USSR, as in the case of one exemplary worker. A good, conscientious, and highly productive labourer, a shock worker (stakhanovets), is rewarded in many ways— extra monetary payments over and above award rates, medals, orders, titles, fame, publicity, free holidays at the Black Sea resorts, election to various local, regional, or national governing bodies, and an invitation to join the Communist Party. All these material benefits and rewards represent in terms of their status and prestige, a paradox within a supposedly classless society.

[52]O'Dell, op. cit., pp. 427–8.
[53]Popov, op. cit., p. 30.
[54]O'Dell, op. cit., p. 428.
[55]Ibid., p. 419.

Finally, early compulsory vocational guidance in Soviet schools tends to ignore the principle of freedom of choice and, at the same time, it works against the traditional contest and egalitarian Soviet educational ideology.

II. EDUCATION FOR PATRIOTISM AND DEFENCE

1. Militant patriotism in Soviet schools

'Class! Attention! Comrade Senior Lieutenant. The pupils of grade 9A, consisting of thirty men, are ready for instruction in military training. The commanding officer of the grade, Ivanov, reporting!'[56]

These words mark the beginning of a typical session throughout the USSR for introduction to military training, a compulsory school subject for 16- and 17-year-old boys in grades 9 and 10. The Great Patriotic War (as it is known in the Soviet Union) had a devastating effect on the entire nation. Twenty million Soviet soldiers and citizens were killed and a 12-million deficit in birth had accumulated between 1941 and 1945 (thus making the net loss in population 32 million, or 17% of the total). It took almost ten years after the war for the population growth to reach its pre-war figure of 194 million.

The war, clearly, had influenced the Soviet educational ideology. Not only the school had a duty to inculcate all young people with devotion and loyalty to the Soviet regime and the CPSU, but also develop a heightened responsibility to teach physical fitness and military training in preparation for any war.[57]

The new curricula, as decreed in the December 1977 document 'On further improvements in education and upbringing of the secondary school pupils and their preparation for labour', emphasizes Soviet patriotism and Socialist internationalism, civic and military duties. The pupils are to be brought up according to revolutionary, military, and labour traditions of the Communist Party, the Soviet people, and the armed forces.[58]

[56] *Vospitanie Shkolnikov*, No. 6, 1975, p. 13.
[57] *Soviet Education*, Jan., 1976, p. 3.
[58] *Uchitelskaya gazeta*, 29 Dec., 1977, p. 1.

General Epishev defines the overall purposes of Soviet military and patriotic education as follows:

Heroic and patriotic education constitutes an important element in the general system of a communist patriot and internationalist.... We are also concerned with instilling in every Soviet person a feeling of personal responsibility for the fate of socialism and the security of his Fatherland, and a striving to strengthen its economic and defensive might through his labour and, if necessary, to take up arms in its defence at a moment's notice. To him it is the sacred duty of every citizen of the USSR to be ever prepared to ward off an attack and to crush any aggressor.[59]

While in Australia there is an annual debate about the value of commemorating Anzac Day, which tends to be denigrated as a glorification of war, the youth of the Soviet Union is taught to venerate the deeds of the Great Patriotic War and to be in a constant state of preparedness to defend the Motherland.

1.1. MILITARY AND PATRIOTIC EDUCATION IN SOVIET SCHOOLS

Patriotism and militarism have always played an important part in Soviet education. However, since 1970 Soviet educational journals, including *Sovetskaya Pedagogika, Narodnoe Obrazovanie, Vospitanie Shkolnikov*, and *Nachalnaya Shkola* reflect the fact that Soviet education authorities have intensified their emphasis on the three fundamental socio-political 'Rs'—*Patriotism, Internationalism*, and *Militarism*. To perfect military and patriotic training has become a favourite theme of Soviet education journals during the 1970s—the era of detente with the West.

Military and patriotic education is conducted both within and outside the school by means of the school curriculum, clubs and societies of revolutionary and labour glory, museums of combat glory, paramilitary Summer Lightning and Eaglet games, excursions to the scenes of revolutionary combat, and labour glory of the Soviet people, the Red Scouts activities, the GTO norms, and paramilitary summer youth camps.

'The school', says the editorial in *Nachalnaya Shkola*, 'carries a great responsibility before society in the educating and training of brave and courageous citizens and patriots of our country.'[60]

[59]*Soviet Education*, Jan., 1976, p. 33.
[60]*Nachalnaya Shkola*, No. 2, 1974, p. 3.

As with work training, one can distinguish at least three stages of military and patriotic education in the USSR. Stage one, which begins in junior school (grades 1–3) consists mainly of character training and indoctrination in patriotism and internationalism. Children's literature is the main source of military and patriotic upbringing. The next stage, which embraces grades 4–8, continues political indoctrination through the curriculum, notably history, literature, geography, social studies, and art. Additional reinforcement of the ideology is provided by the Pioneer and Komsomol youth organizations. The third, and possibly the most concentrated stage of military and patriotic education, takes place in the last two years of secondary schooling (grades 9–10). The boys enrol for a compulsory subject, introduction to military training, in grade 9 and they are also expected to complete advanced norms of the ready for labour and defence programme.

The new school curriculum, introduced after 1970, made it also possible to intensify the cultivation of patriotism during history, literature, and geography lessons at all levels. A unique attitude towards Russian history and great achievements of the past, which, depict the virtues of the Russian people, pervades current Soviet education. This deification of the past includes the apotheosis of positive national heroes, ranging from Alexander Nevsky, who defeated the Teutonic knights on the frozen River Neva in 1240, to Mikhail Sholokov, the author of *Quiet Flows the Don*.

In 1974 the USSR Ministry of Education published a handbook, *Methodological Recommendations for Military and Patriotic Upbringing of Secondary School Pupils Outside School Time*. This, clearly, reflects the official attitude to military training in the Soviet Union today and the importance placed on it by the Government. The handbook's stated aim is to ensure that only well-educated, morally, and physically sound recruits enter the armed forces. Brezhnev has said; Today's army, navy and air force need educated individuals who are ideologically firm and physically fit, and who are able to combine the traditions of absolute bravery of their fathers with perfect knowledge of the latest military technology.

In June 1975 the Ministry of Education of the USSR and the Central Committee of the Komsomol organized the All-Union Congress in military and patriotic upbringing. The congress was attended by principals and military school instructors. The congress had raised new issues, not touched upon by the 1974 directive from the Ministry of Education of the USSR, concerning military and patriotic education of the pupils. The 1976 school curriculum was to assume a more decisive role (to be reiterated in the December 1977 educational decree) in military and patriotic upbringing of the pupils. The following aims were postulated:

1. To educate the pupils in the revolutionary, military, and labour traditions of the Soviet people.
2. To cultivate in the pupils a revolutionary vigilance.
3. To prepare the pupils for defence of their Motherland.
4. To ensure a supply of literate, moral, and physically fit new recruits.
5. To strengthen friendly relations between the school and the armed forces.[61]

As a result of the increased emphasis on political socialization, the primary school was directed to cultivate and develop in the children an interest towards heroic traditions and to help them in formulating and comprehending such concepts as the Motherland, heroism, patriotism, internationalism, and Soviet warrior (voin). Feelings of patriotism were to be developed further in grades 4–8, and military and patriotic education of senior students was to be based on the Leninist principle concerning defence of the socialist Motherland. It appears that defending the USSR is more apparent today than in the past.[62]

1.2. MILITARY AND PATRIOTIC EDUCATION IN THE PRIMARY SCHOOL

Most subjects in the primary school are readily used in political socialization. During literature lessons the pupils read and discuss stories depicting the Motherland (Rodina), Lenin, the Soviet Army, war heroes, and heroic deeds of children. Accordingly, the grades 1–3 readers are divided into themes such as: the Soviet Army, the

[61]*Vospitanie Shkolnikov*, No. 6, 1975, pp. 57–60.
[62]*Nachalnaya Shkola*, editorial, No. 2, 1974, p. 3.

October Revolution, famous Soviet people, and the past of our Motherland. The slogan 'I love you Russia, my Soviet land!' captures the essence of political socialization in the primary school.

'Let there always be the sun!' This innocent line belongs to a famous poem known to every young school child in the USSR. The poem expresses the hope that there will always be birds, trees, the sky, and of course, Mummy, and it is seen as a gentle symbol of peace.

Yet one of the constant themes of Soviet education journals is the military and patriotic upbringing of pupils. In one article in *Vospitanie Shkolnikov* (*Upbringing of Pupils*), the author writes: 'Military and patriotic upbringing of pupils is most fully realized during history, social studies, literature, and geography lessons. Pupils study the core of Marxist–Leninist theory, the history of the Communist Party and the Soviet Union.' The author goes on to say that the new curriculum for grades 1–3 renders great possibilities for cultivating patriotism. Special short stories, poems, and songs about the Motherland, Lenin, the Soviet Army, and the heroism of the Komsomol and Pioneers have been selected for that purpose in Russian elementary readers.[63] The Soviet ABC (bukvar) used in all first grades begins with a picture of Lenin as a boy, and it is not accidental that one of the articles in *Nachalnaya Shkola* (*Elementary school*) is concerned with patriotic training during lessons: 'It is necessary to reach that culminating point when love towards the workers of the Soviet Union will awaken in children; when they can feel proud of the great achievements in communist construction and begin to feel that they themselves represent a small section of that great army of workers which multiplies into the might of our Motherland.'

This is how little Vasya describes his love of the Motherland (Rodina) in an essay:

> My little Motherland is the village of Staromyshastovskaya. It is a very large village. Near our house is a field. There is a House of Culture (Dom Kultury) in the village and beside it a monument of our Lenin. On the large public square are two monuments—one for those who died for Soviet Rule in the Civil War and the other for the dead of the Great Patriotic War. I am so proud that grandfather is listed among the heroes whose names are carved in the stone....[64]

[63] *Nachalnaya Shkola*, editorial, No. 2, 1974, p. 2.
[64] Ibid., No. 11, 1975, p. 27.

One of the grade readers in the primary school, *Communist Moral-ity for Junior Pupils*, contains such sections as 'Communism—the shining future of the entire mankind', 'Follow the example of Communists', 'Work, learn and live for the people', and others. The story the *Word Rodina* begins thus: 'When we pronounce the word *Rodina* before us, as if we are opening up the infinite vastness—the forests, the fields, the mountains, the snow, the sand, the rivers, the oceans, and the islands.... But as the Volga takes its beginning from a small brook so does the Rodina begin at your home....'[65] The section that follows contains stories about the Revolution, the Civil War, and the Great Patriotic War.

Patriotic education in grade 1 is already present in the ABC, the prescribed text for all Soviet schoolchildren. Children are required to memorize a well-known communist song 'Oh my spacious native land' (Shiroka strana moya rodnaya), which commences with the following words:

Oh my wide native land,
With many forests, fields, and rivers.
I do not know such a land as yet
Where man breathes so freely.....

In grade 3, the schoolchildren are taught about the October Revolution and Lenin. As one teacher writes: 'Reading lessons provide us with colossal material for educating children on the model of Lenin.... During my lessons and extra-curricular work I try to explain to children the meaning of the Congress [of the Communist Party—J.Z.] and celebration of the sixtieth anniversary of the October [Revolution—J.Z.].'[66]

1.3. MILITARY AND PATRIOTIC EDUCATION IN
THE SECONDARY SCHOOL

One of the ideological aims of the Soviet school is perfecting military and patriotic training. Soviet patriotism in the secondary school

---

[65]Bogdanova, O. S., *et al.*, *Mladshim shkolnikam o kommunisticheskoi nravstennosti*, Voronezh, 1974, p. 11.
[66]*Nachalnaya Shkola*, No. 10, 1977, p. 55.

develops from 'a civic collectivist and communist attitude to labour'.[67] According to Balyasnaya, Deputy Minister of Education of the RSFSR, Soviet patriotism is inconceivable without proletarian internationalism'. She stresses the fact that military and political education is an integral part of the entire system of communist upbringing and that it is organically linked with mental, physical, and moral aspects of Soviet education.[67] Unlike Balyasnaya, we find it difficult to accept the necessary link between militant patriotism and proletarian internationalism.

The secondary school history course enables the pupil to master Marxist–Leninist doctrines on war as a socio-political phenomenon. The pupil studies Lenin's theory, 'any war is only a continuation of politics by other means'. The history assignments on the Great Patriotic War stress the role played by the Communist Party in directing the Soviet people's fight for their freedom, their land, and for other enslaved nations. In their essays pupils write about the massive character of Soviet heroism and the global significance of the Soviet victory over fascism. Reading the biographies of military heroes is seen as significant in the development of patriotism in the pupil.

1.4. WAR HEROES IN SOVIET TEXTBOOKS

During Russian literature lessons pupils read about the heroic feats of the partisan girl Zoya Kosmodemyanskaya, who was tortured and brutally murdered by the Gestapo in 1941; the pilot Nikolai Gastello, who deliberately crashed his burning plane into an enemy truck column; and Alexander Matrosov who, with his own body, covered the opening of an enemy bunker which was spraying his platoon with bullets. Every Soviet child knows the book by Boris Polevoy, *A Story about a Real Man*, which tells of Meresyev, a fighter pilot who lost both legs in a plane crash and who went through a personal hell learning to walk on artificial legs and how he danced to prove to his commanding officer that he was capable of resuming flying. Fadeyev's *The Young Guard*, depicting the heroism of a 1941 partisan band of

[67] *Vospitanie Shkolnikov*, No. 6, 1971, p. 2.

secondary school pupils, who sabotaged the enemy under the leadership of the schoolboy hero Oleg Koshevoy, is equally well known.

The 1975 officially prescribed textbook for Russian literature in grade 10, used by all Russian secondary schools, has a section of nearly 100 pages, 'Literature of the Great Patriotic War'. The next section of about 120 pages, called 'Literature during the fifties and sixties' contains, nevertheless, war literature written after the war ended. There we find Mikhail Sholokhov's famous work *Destiny of a Man* (*Sudba cheloveka*). Earlier sections of the textbook contain documents by Lenin and other party leaders related to the nature and purpose of literature.

The *Introduction to Military Training* (*Nachalnaya voennaya podgotovka*) is an applied discipline, which is taught to all boys in grades 9 and 10, two hours weekly. The boys are instructed by trained ex-servicemen or suitably qualified instructors in the rudiments of soldiering. At the end of the school year (in May), boys have to attend a five-day intensive army training, lasting more than thirty hours.[68] There they are taught to use all kinds of small-calibre weapons, and target shooting is the main event. The whole exercise is conducted on a competitive basis, and badges and merit certificates are awarded to the winners.

In some schools, military training is directed by the local council of returned soldiers and military personnel. For instance, in the town of Severomorsk (near Murmansk), the school year begins very auspiciously. Members of the armed forces stationed nearby visit every school. They give each child a picture of Lenin and address the assembled pupils on the value of bravery and the glory of fighting for the Motherland (Rodina). Over 300 sailors, cadets, and officers of the Northern Fleet participate in military training in Severomorsk alone, looking after eighty school-run voluntary army and navy clubs. The extent of pupil participation in these clubs can be gauged when we realize that Severomorsk has only 50,000 inhabitants.[69]

The authorities rely rather heavily on war heroes in character and moral education. Soviet schoolchildren are taught to model their lives on great heroes. One such hero is Shura Serebrovskaya, a nursing

[68] *Sbornik prikazov i instruktsii Ministerstva Prosveshcheniya*, No. 8, Mar., 1974, p. 29.
[69] *Vospitanie Shkolnikov*, No. 1, 1975, p. 10.

sister, who died in 1945 trying to save her wounded comrades-in-arms. 'We must remember those who have laid down their lives for our Motherland', write many Soviet schoolchildren in their essays every year. Shura, like many other war heroes, has become a living legend, a cult figure. 'Our Shura', one hears from the lips of boys and girls born in the 1960s. Every year, on Shura's birthday, schoolchildren come from far and near to visit her mother. They bring her flowers and listen to her reminiscences of Shura and they tell her about their studies and school activities. When they drink tea, especially from the faded flower-patterned cup that once belonged to Shura, they can hardly hide their feelings. Each child would discover Shura in his own way; one by reading her letters home from the front, and another by browsing through her favourite books. 'I was touched by the question of the stationmaster at Kaliningrad', writes one student, 'Have you come to see Shura? As if she was still alive.' Shura's devotion to duty, love of the Motherland, and her sacrifice are held up as ideal. 'Her noble and pure image even helps some problem children', writes another correspondent. 'When there comes a time for melancholy and one wishes to throw the books away, one immediately recalls a huge bookcase in Shura's room ...', writes one student. Another confesses: 'During difficult moments I think of Shura and I say "How would she have behaved in my place?"!'[70]

1.5. THE RED SCOUTS

The Red Scouts (Sledopyty) is a schoolchildren's club devoted to compiling information about the heroic past of the Soviet Union. Each school has its own branch of the Red Scouts, and in 1977 14 million schoolchildren belonged to them. To commemorate the sixtieth anniversary of the October Revolution, the Red Scouts launched more than 40,000 historical museums and rooms of military glory. They had erected and taken under their care almost 25,000 war memorials.

The Red Scouts perform a variety of communal tasks. They collect all the available material about the Revolution, the Civil War, and the Great Patriotic War. They gather information about history,

[70] *Vospitanie Shkolnikov*, No. 1, 1975, p. 7.

economy, current affairs, and culture. They arrange official meetings between the club members and war veterans. They work on the local farms or they turn into keen environmentalists and protect their green friends. They plant flowers and trees in public places. Their most exciting and challenging task is to search for lost veterans and those missing in action and presumed dead. A great many Soviet soldiers were reported missing in the Great Patriotic War and their graves were never found. A branch of the club is found at Pruzhany (near Brest, Hero City of the Soviet Union, and site of some of the bloodiest fighting of the war). The club receives many letters from relatives searching for missing servicemen and women. 'In 1940 my brother Khvorykh A. was called up. He was born in 1921 and served in Pruzhany. Help me to find his grave', is a typical letter. In another, an elderly woman is thanking the Red Scouts for caring for the grave of her daughter Anya. The club's motto is 'No one and nothing is forgotten'. The seventy boys and girls who belong to the Pruzhany club have also rediscovered the heroic feats of the 25th and 30th tank brigades, and the 205th and 208th rifle divisions. They have brought to light an act of heroism by Senior Lieutenant Gudinov who, in the early hours of 22 June 1942, rammed his plane into an enemy plane. Due to their efforts the pilot was posthumously awarded the Order of Patriotic War, 2nd class, in 1971. The school-children care for graves of soldiers, and they found the unmarked grave of 67 soldiers who were then ceremoniously reburied at a new location. The Red Scouts have traced more than 700 soldiers who died near Brest.[71]

The Red Scouts clubs of secondary school No. 148 in Gorky, 400 miles east of Moscow, make a special study of the famous 322nd rifle division with its thirty-four Heroes of the Soviet Union (the highest military award for bravery). They have collected hundreds of war documents and photographs relating to the division and have traced the names of its veterans with whom individual pupils correspond. With money these pupils earned during the summer holiday camps of labour and rest and the students' construction brigades, they have had a war memorial built in Gorky.[72]

[71]Ibid., No. 6, 1973, pp. 30–33.
[72]Ibid., No. 6, 1971, p. 3.

Thousands of war memorials are erected throughout the USSR with the holiday earnings of senior students. The young people of the Soviet Union are thrown into an active role in keeping alive the memory of the Great Patriotic War.

A detailed account of the Red Scouts in Minsk (the Byelorussian Republic) is presented by one of the local high school principals. He claims that when he confronted his senior students with the question Do you wish to participate in search and research activity into the unknown pages of history and heroic deeds of the Soviet soldiers during the years of the Great Patriotic War?, the majority answered 'yes'. One of the first projects was to locate the place of death of their local war hero, Boris Okrestin, the fighter pilot, who died near Minsk in 1944. The pupils became so involved with it that they decided to erect a monument to him. They began collecting funds by working as casual labourers at the local botanical gardens, collecting scrap iron and waste paper, and so on. When the monument was finally unveiled during a special school assembly, filled with official visitors, including Heroes of the Soviet Union, the Red Scouts delivered the following oath: 'We, the schoolchildren, promise ... to live like your son did, to love the Motherland (Rodina) as he did, and to fight against the enemies like Boris Okrestin did!'

To honour even further the hero, the Council of Ministers of the BSSR decreed that the 65th secondary school was to be named after Boris Okrestin, and one of the streets in Minsk was also named after him.[73]

In another incident the Red Scouts were asked to locate a missing Soviet tank, which was thought to be resting at the bottom of a tiny lake (sineye). The scouts searched the lake but failed to find the tank. Instead they found the remains of a Soviet plane. They continued their search for the rest of the plane, which was finally unearthed by the children near a small village. The two pilots were ceremoniously reburied and their personal belongings became the property of the school's museum of military glory. Following the press release, letters of thanks from relatives and friends began to pour in to the school. As the Red Scouts continued their search they discovered another

[73]Sivavikov, G. T., *Voenno-patrioticheskoe vospitanie shkolnikov*, Minsk, 1974, pp. 50–53.

fighter plane buried deep in the mud. The plane contained the remains of a pilot. From the documents it was established that the missing pilot's name was Gorbunov. Soon his relatives were traced, including Gorbunov's 85-year-old mother. In a moving speech, Gorbunov's mother said: 'After so many years you have found my little son!' One pupil recalls: 'I shall never forget that meeting. Thousands of people watched the burial of Gorbunov'. 'Thank you! I thank you my dear children,' said Ludmilla Gorbunova, the hero's daughter. 'I never saw my father, I had never heard his voice. I am grateful to you all for now I am able to visit his grave. I know that he died a heroic death and I am proud of him!' This particular school located nine aircraft crews thought to be missing. Such examples are many, and the Red Scouts throughout the Soviet Union continue their search for lost war veterans and missing soldiers.[74]

The Red Scouts, together with other schoolchildren belong to the All-Union expedition 'Motherland—USSR!' This expedition is designed to indoctrinate as many children as possible in the values of bravery, heroism, and militant patriotism. There is no doubt that this kind of activity may influence moral development of the individual. It could well awaken in some pupils deep patriotic feelings and love towards the Soviet people seen as defenders of the Motherland. As one Soviet teacher puts it: 'By studying war archives, documents, and literature, the students not only widen their knowledge but also acquire a communist consciousness!'[75] On the practical side, searching for lost soldiers is, clearly, the most effective form of military and patriotic upbringing.

1.6. PARAMILITARY SUMMER CAMPS

Military and patriotic upbringing of Soviet schoolchildren is specially organized; for this purpose youth camps represent a very important aspect of moral and socio-political education. It is clear that a great deal of indoctrination and socialization, particularly with respect to jobs in the armed forces, is taking place in those camps.

---

[74] Ibid., p. 53.
[75] From a conversation with a Soviet (Jewish) teacher who migrated to Australia in 1976.

These institutions seem to serve a dual function. They keep the youngsters busy during long summer vacations and, more importantly, they instruct them in the values of manhood, courage, and endurance. Although the very existence of these camps has eluded Western comparativists, their ultimate role in moral education and political socialization cannot be stressed enough.

During the summer, known as the Pioneer Summer (Pionerskoe leto), children receive physical and paramilitary training. Physical fitness is thought to be very important if one is to join the armed forces. Children learn various militant songs and they are taught to obey various military commands. A typical paramilitary summer camp is divided into a number of Pioneer detachments, each having its own special assignment. The official programme in the orienteer is used for this purpose. For instance, junior Pioneers (aged 10–11) plan their activities according to the section 'For the Pioneers about the defenders of the Motherland!' The section 'Pioneers are the friends of the Armed Forces' is for the 11- and 12-year-olds, and senior Pioneers (aged 13–15) organize their activities around the topic 'Pioneers—the future defenders of the Motherland!' Junior Pioneers are encouraged to gather information about the heroic past of the Motherland. Everyone has to give a talk to the group about a hero of his own choice.

Some camps are more specialized and they concentrate on a particular job in the army. In one, children may learn to drive the tank, in the other to fly the plane, and so on. The junior tankdriver (yuny-tankist) camp is described thus: 'On approaching it one sees a sign 'yuny tankist lager' with a young sentry standing beneath it. Children of 12 years upwards are eligible to attend and several hundred at a time spend fifty-two days in the camp. Upon arrival they are divided into squads of twenty-six, each led by a commander (kommandir) and a commissar (kommissar), chosen from among their ranks. The discipline is iron and imposed, to a large extent, by the children themselves. A typical day includes morning gymnastics, followed by military drills until lunch, followed by a study of military sciences, perhaps a visit to a neighbouring military camp or a film screening. 'Can you imagine,' writes one boy to another, 'I sit in the driver's seat of the tank and my hands master the multi-ton iron colossus—if only

I could sit in the tank for ever.' The boy goes on to list his achievements at the camp: 'I learned to drive a tank; fulfilled the 3rd grade in shooting; learned to use a Soviet machine gun (kalashnikov); completed the norms for the GTO (Ready for Labour and Defence course) for a silver badge and I was issued a certificate "junior tank driver".'[76] 'Junior airman' camps are just as popular. The camp located near Vladimir and run by a lieutenant-colonel in the reserve caters for nearly 150 boys. Every boy who fulfils the norms and tests of the camp's programme is rewarded by a ten-minute flight in an AN-2 plane. The camp's register shows that twenty-six former members are now fully fledged pilots and another twenty-seven have entered air force academies.[77]

1.7. PARAMILITARY SUMMER LIGHTNING AND EAGLET
GAMES FOR SCHOOLCHILDREN

Both the Komsomol and Pioneer organizations are actively involved in organizing union-wide military sport games called Eaglet (Orlyonok) and Summer Lightning (Zarnitsa).

The Summer Lightning game is for the Pioneer members aged 12–14. The main objectives of the game are:

1. To develop the feeling of collectivism, comradeship, and friendship.
2. To cultivate ideological convictions—love towards the Motherland (Rodina), the Soviet people, and the armed forces.
3. To partake in the All-Union march to places of the revolutionary, military, and labour glory.
4. To complete the GTO norms.

By participating in the game, the Pioneer is able to fulfil the following Pioneer law: 'The Pioneer honours the memory of the fallen fighters and he prepares himself to become a defender of the motherland.'[78] The ultimate aim is, clearly, to prepare the Pioneers in grades 5–7 for their compulsory unit introduction to military training in grades 9 and 10.

[76] *Vospitanie Shkolnikov*, No. 3, 1975, pp. 28–30.
[77] Ibid., p. 30.
[78] Ibid., No. 1, 1974, p. 56.

EIU – H*

The Summer Lightning game is rich in symbolism and rituals. At a general meeting of the school's battalion, young soldiers (yunarmeitsy) elect their leaders and commanding officers. Each battalion is then divided into companies and platoons. Each company, in imitation of the Soviet army, has a commanding officer, a political officer, scouts, soldiers, medical post, firemen, signalmen, and transport officers with all positions filled by the pupils. The pupil soldiers, in an excess of military zeal, try to model themselves on adult soldiers by saluting and wearing military epaulets, even though officially this is forbidden, one article notes with reluctant pride. Twelve–thirteen-year-olds use air rifles while the 14–15 age group use small calibre rifles. This age group also learns to assemble a machine gun (kalashnikov). First-aid training is extensive and heavily stressed in the Zarnitsa. Children from 10 to 15 learn to wear gas-masks and to render first aid to people suffering from gas poisoning, biological or chemical infections, and radiation exposure. They learn to perform a partial de-contamination of a radiation victim. All young soldiers must wear the Pioneers' red tie or Komsomol badges. Officers carry insignias on the left sleeves, denoting their rank. The insignia consists of a green patch (size 1.5 × 4 cm) and the Zarnitsa symbol. In addition to this, officers wear pips on their shirts, which range from three small pips (red stars) for a platoon leader to three large pips for a battalion commander.[79]

The new directive concerning the Zarnitsa states that the entire military and patriotic education of youth should be directed towards fulfilment of the Pioneer promise and rules of the Pioneers of the Soviet Union.[80] The young soldiers are encouraged to study Lenin's work and life, the history of the Communist Party, revolutionary and heroic traditions of Soviet people, and so on. The game Zarnitsa is an obvious example of political socialization in the Soviet Union. It is designed to imbue the pupil with feelings of patriotism, militarism, and collectivism. The pupil is meant to develop a better understanding of such political concepts as communism, patriotism, the Red Flag, the Motherland (Rodina) and so on.[80] In addition to its political role, the Zarnitsa has also an important moral and social

[79]*Vospitanie Shkolnikov*, No. 3, 1975, pp. 56–57.
[80]Ibid., p. 56.

role. The Zarnitsa tests specifically such attributes as bravery, collectivism, discipline, and comradeship. 'One for all and all for one' is the main slogan here, and it could be regarded as a moral imperative.[81]

The game was based on the theme My Motherland—the USSR) (Moya Rodina SSSR), and the seventh grand final was held in the summer of 1977. Since the date coincided with the sixtieth anniversary of the October Revolution, the All-Union march was called 'Following the footsteps of Lenin and the October' (Idiom dorogoi Lenina, dorogoi Oktiabria).

It should be stressed that the Zarnitsa provides both military and vocational training for secondary students. During their war games, students are socialized into blue-collar professions prior to their compulsory military service.

The Zarnitsa could be seen as one of the most effective methods in character education. Children are being prepared for their service in the armed forces. The entire organizational structure of the Zarnitsa resembles very closely the army. From the very beginning, children are taught to obey orders from their officers. They are then very thoroughly drilled in all aspects of soldiering. Shooting practice commences in grade 5, and the 12- and 13-year-olds compete for the 'Junior Rifleman' certificate. They use only air rifles, but the rest is real. However, the next age group (14–15) use a small-calibre weapon during their target-shooting practice and they are awarded the 'Marksman' certificate.

In the course of the game, children are taught to identify topological data on maps (reading distances from maps), measure levels of radiation fall-out, locate radiation-free areas, and render general assistance to the public during crisis. Senior students are given more responsible tasks—repairing damaged telephone wires, using a field telephone, operating a radio transmitter, and even directing the movement of a military column.

The Eaglet (Olyonok) game, being the next logical progression from the Zarnitsa, represents the final phase of political and military socialization of Soviet youth. The Eaglet game caters for the 16–17

[81] Ibid., No. 5, 1977, p. 47.

age group. The game takes two or more years to complete and its main aims are:

1. To strengthen the feeling of Soviet patriotism in moral education of youth, particularly readiness to defend the Socialist Motherland.
2. To provide a practical reinforcement of knowledge and skills associated with military training.
3. To maintain active participation of boys and girls in the All-Union examination of physical education and military and patriotic training, all leading towards a successful completion of the 'Ready for Labour and Defence' norms.
4. To ensure that every Komsomol member is actively involved in the All-Union march through the places of military glory.
5. To direct the Komsomol members to construct room museums of military glory, war memorials, shooting galleries, and sports grounds.[82]

Student staff officers directing the game have the following tasks:

1. To select the best young soldiers at school.
2. To organize a series of tasks and discussions dedicated to wars.
3. To organize a school competition for the top expert of guns.[83]

At the end of the school year the semi-finals and finals are held. Competitions between schools help to determine the winners of the game, who are sent as official delegates to the All-Union parade of the Eaglet.

It is of interest to note that during the finals the participants are required to run 100 metres wearing a gas-mask, assemble a machine gun (kalashnikov), erect a tent, get through an infected area of 50 metres, drive an army truck, operate a portable transmitter, gain points in target shooting and hand-grenade throwing, and offering the victim paramedical assistance.[84]

It is possible that many young Soviet pupils remain unresponsive

---

[82]*Vospitanie Shkolnikov*, No. 4, 1972, p. 52.
[83]Ibid., No. 4, 1975, p. 28.
[84]Ibid., p. 29.

to the patriotism and militarism which pervades their classroom lessons and their leisure time, and perhaps the reporters in educational journals are over optimistic about the effectiveness of the programme. However, the large membership and number of the paramilitary clubs suggest that interest in them is widespread. Pupils lacking sufficient patriotic fervour would still be unable to avoid the memories of past heroism, which permeate the officially prescribed textbooks used in all schools, the militarily oriented class projects, and the compulsory military training subject in grades 9 and 10. Such deviants would be subjected to pressure from their peers, teachers, the school curriculum, and the communist youth organizations. They would not find social acceptance. If there is a rebellious, pacifist youth sub-culture in the USSR, such as we have in the West, its views are never heard. Success in the USSR is achieved through conformity. The government-directed military and patriotic education of Soviet youth is designed to train a whole generation of teenagers who are physically fit, emotionally ready, and technically trained to assist the armed forces in the defence of their Motherland.

Education for labour and defence represents an important phase of communist education. Inculcating in the pupils a deep feeling of Soviet patriotism is consistent with the school's Marxist–Leninist ideology.

The majority of Soviet schoolchildren are taught to believe that it is their sacred duty to defend their country.[85]

The mass media, the school, and the Party promote militant patriotism among the Pioneers and Komsomol members. Participating in paramilitary youth games like the Summer Lightning and the Eaglet, visiting historical places noted for their military glory during the Great Patriotic War, searching for the lost war veterans, constructing war memorials, and, in short, being actively involved in the preservation of the great heroic past (1917–45), could be regarded as visible signs of the communist ideology being successfully put into practice.

It is, however, difficult to judge the ultimate internalization of the ideology by the Soviet youth. It could well be that some (and it is difficult to estimate their number) individuals may not readily accept

[85] *Vospitatelnaya rabota v shkole*, Moscow, 1976, p. 41.

the official interpretation of the ideology. The mass media reports instances of apathy, indifference, cynicism, and parasitism within the ranks of the Komsomol, yet one of the surveys designed to discover the most characteristic moral and social values of the Soviet youth showed that the majority ranked patriotism first in order of preference.[86]

[86]Harasimiw, B. (ed.), *Education and the Mass Media in the Soviet Union and Eastern Europe*, Praeger, New York, 1976, p. 120.

CHAPTER 5

Education of Teachers

1. Introduction

The need for teachers in the Soviet educational system is determined ten years in advance. Between 1968 and the 1978 All-Union Congresses of Teachers 2.3 million teachers were trained.[1] According to Prokofiev, 4.5 million pedagogues were employed in education.[2] This suggests that nearly 50% of Soviet pedagogues are young men and women in their early thirties. Every year, on the average, 150,000 new teachers graduate from 63 universities, 201 pedagogical institutes, and 408 teacher colleges.[3] Of the 160,000 teachers who graduated in 1978, most (up to 80%) were sent to rural areas. The 1960s and the 1970s in the USSR, as in other developed countries, signified a rapid expansion in the education sector. The 1970/1 academic year was a record year for enrolments in secondary schools due to a high birth rate (5,341,000) in 1960. This, no doubt, had influenced the growth of teacher-training institutions. If in 1970 164,000 students were enrolled in pedagogical institutes, by 1978 their numbers rose to 180,000, representing a 10% increase on the 1970 figure. In 1980, 105,000 first-year students (92,000 in 1975) have been enrolled in teacher colleges and 175,000 (163,000 in 1975) have entered pedagogical institutes. A high proportion of students (over 40%) were enrolled on a part-time basis, attending evening lectures or studying externally. Universities have increased their commitments in teacher

[1] Rozov, V., Novye tendenstii v razvitii pedagogicheskogo obrazovaniya, *Sovestskaya Pedagogika*, No. 2, 1979.
[2] Prokofiev, M. A., Vsesoyuzny syezd uchitelei, *Uchitelskaya gazeta*, 29 June 1978, p. 3.
[3] Editorial, *Sovetskaya Pedagogika*, No. 7, 1979, p. 3.

training. If in 1968 only 4500 university graduates were trained as teachers, then by 1977 the numbers rose sharply to 20,000, representing an increase of 440%. The social class composition of the student body at the VUZ has changed significantly. If during the 1960s the majority of university and college applicants came from the intelligentsia stratum (white-collar professionals), by 1978 up to 60% of the first-year students in pedagogical institutions (up to 80% in pedagogical colleges) came from the workers and kolkhozniki families. In order to offset the intelligentsia bias in the social class structure of the student body, special arrangements have been made (since 1973) to accept rural candidates without the entrance examinations (vne konkursa). Between 1973 and 1978 63,000 rural students were enrolled without entrance examinations, an average of 12,000 students per year of 8% of the total first-year intake. The total first-year intake in education in the 1979/80 academic year was 280,000 according to Prokofiev. In the 1979/80 academic year 17,000 applicants from remote rural areas were admitted into higher institutions without entrance examinations.[4] According to Rozov, in 1978 the vast majority of education students (65%) came from the workers and kolkhoz workers' families. Thus the social composition of the student body in teacher education was influenced by the 1973 vne konkursa admission policy, preference for applicants from the workers and the kolkhozniki families, and the introduction of preparatory faculties, which were to prepare young workers and kolkhozniki candidates for university and college entrance examinations. In 1978 16,000 of such candidates were being coached by college lecturers in 163 preparatory faculties. Ten per cent of the first-year intake in education came via preparatory faculties.

Russian has three closely related words for teaching: pedagóg (pedagogue), uchítel (teacher), and vospitátel (instructor). All three are semantically significant to the definition of the professional teacher and the teacher's role and status. The roles of everyone within the educational structure, so perceptively observed by Adams, are equally clearly defined, from the pre-school child to the Minister of Education.[5] Soviet teachers play a vital part in the intellectual, moral,

[4] *Uchitelskaya gazeta*, 20 Nov., 1979, p. 2.
[5] King, E. J. (ed.), *Communist Education*, Methuen, London, 1963.

social, political, aesthetic, physical, and vocational training, and guidance of the future Soviet citizens. Through a very complex but centralized network of political and educational bureaucracy, Soviet teachers are always kept clearly informed of what their roles and duties are. All major agencies of socialization—the mass media, the peers, the school, the community, and parents reinforce the desired Marxist–Leninist adult values. This, no doubt, means that professional function of teachers is virtually sanctioned and institutionalized by the system.

The present status of Soviet teachers owes much to the educational revolution, initiated by Lenin, Krupskaya, Lunacharsky, Makarenko, Shatsky, and many others. The Soviet authorities were quick to grasp the strategic importance of educational reforms. High academic standards were seen as the necessary prerequisites in the process of restructuring a nation. To fulfil the national aims of peace, prosperity, and stability, high quality education had to be achieved in most schools. Since teachers are thought to be generally successful in fulfilling their special responsibility in the upbringing process, their ideological role in the community is substantially higher than is the case for their counterparts in the United States. This is so, even though Soviet teachers have no power to select books or teaching methods, design curriculum or introduce new units, options, and assessment. Everything, ranging from the set textbook to examination (in other words the total process of curriculum design, development, and implementation) is determined by the State. However, the teacher is not necessarily confined to a work-to-rule model, as there are opportunities for upward social mobility via educational research and higher administration. Teachers are encouraged to contribute research reports, articles, short notes, and letters to numerous educational periodicals, and they are paid most generously for the published work. Attending regional seminars and conferences, presenting papers at pedagogical symposia, writing books, and, perhaps, being appointed as district inspectors, provide the opportunities for upward mobility. The status of teachers is further secured by the strict quota on admissions to teacher-training institutions, the uniform salary scale, conditions of teacher employment, and the security of tenure (guaranteed employment for life for all newly trained teachers). All the decisions affecting the role–status of the Soviet teachers are made centrally.

Unlike the American and the British teacher, the Soviet pedagogue is completely subservient to the ideals and needs of the Communist Party of the Soviet Union. Thus the CPSU exerts a very powerful influence on curricula, teaching methods, textbook content, and the official interpretation of knowledge, attitudes, and beliefs. Soviet culture transmitted in schools is, clearly, based on Marxist–Leninism. Hence, indoctrination or, to use a more neutral term, political socialization, is the most important goal of upbringing in the school. In this sense, the Soviet teacher–instructor (vospitátel) has a vital task—that of interpreting, transmitting, and sharing the Marxist–Leninist ideology. The basic difference between Soviet teachers and their Western counterparts is the degree of their necessary involvement in the political and moral functions of schooling, which is aimed at producing citizens who will become conformist, convinced, and dedicated to the regime. Apart from mastering their teaching disciplines, Soviet teachers are also required to be aware of CPSU policy on education and be equally involved in cultural, social, and political life of the nation. Soviet teachers occupy an important place in the community. They enjoy, in most instances, the degree of status, prestige, and power that is so conspicuously absent in the teaching profession in the United States and England. Soviet teachers as professionals command admiration and respect from all levels of the society. They belong, of course, to the ranks of the intelligentsia or the élite upper stratum of the Soviet society.

2. Training of Soviet Teachers

Soviet teachers, by virtue of their higher education and training, belong to the intelligentsia stratum, and they enjoy, according to Soviet educators, the 'greatest respect of society'.[6] The CPSU and ministries of education award gifted and outstanding teachers with public honours in the form of medals, orders, honorary titles, honorary certificates, badges, and monetary premiums. Since 1930 nearly 300,000 dedicated and outstanding teachers have been awarded

[6]*Sovetskaya Pedagogika*, No. 7, 1979, p. 3.

medals and orders of the Soviet Union. The most significant public recognition of teachers was the introduction of a public holiday in 1965 to commemorate Teacher's Day (Den Uchítelia), which is celebrated each year on the first Sunday of October. All-Union Republics award the title 'Honoured School Teacher' (Zasluzheny Uchítel Shkóly). This honoured title, which carries a salary increment, was first introduced in 1940 by the RSFSR. Since then, 14,000 such awards have been made in the RSFSR, but only 1400 in the Ukrainian SSR and a mere 340 in the Latvian SSR. The Ministry of Education of the USSR and other Union ministries award the honorary title 'Exemplary Educator of the USSR'. Only 8000 such awards have been made. Honorary certificates and medals (named after prominent Russian and non-Russian educators) are awarded to teachers for excellent educational achievements: the N. K. Krupskaya (Ministry of Education of the USSR), K. D. Ushinsky (Ministry of Education of the RSFSR), A. D. Makarenko (Ministry of Education of the Armenian SSR), and S. Gogebashvili (Ministry of Education of the Georgian SSR) medals. Up until 1977 only 285 individuals were awarded the Krupskaya medal. The highest honorary title 'Hero of Socialist Labour' has been bestowed on 143 educators for their outstanding contribution in the field of education and communist upbringing. The Soviet Government has also introduced (since 1973) the badges of 'Winner of Socialist Competition' (Pobedítel' Sotsialistícheskogo Sorevnonániya), 'Shock-worker of the Ninth Five-year Plan' (Udárnik Deviátoi Piatilétki), and the 'Shock-worker of the Tenth Five-year Plan' (Udárnik Desiátoi Piatilétki). Since 1973 453,000 awards have been made. These are obviously not as important as the highest honorary title of the USSR, 'Hero of Socialist Labour', and other more prestigious titles and medals. The above hierarchy of awards for excellence in all spheres of education and upbringing suggests that the Soviet Government wishes to further improve the already high status of teachers and to provide incentives for them. Whether such measures are Marxist or not is not relevant as far as the authorities are concerned.

3. Teachers' income and status

Although, officially, the Soviet Government states that inflation is unknown in the USSR, teachers' salaries have been increased three times between 1972 and 1979. In accordance with the Directives of the Twenty-fourth Congress of the CPSU, teachers' salaries were raised by an average of 20% in 1972. An elementary school teacher, with sixteen years of teaching experience, earned 110 roubles, whereas a skilled factory worker earned 150 roubles. Obviously, the teachers' salaries did not accord with their status and prestige. Further increases in teachers' salaries were decreed in 1976 and 1979.

Rural areas experience such a chronic shortage of teachers, that between 60 and 80% of new graduates are posted to rural schools. Some teachers never arrive at the schools to which they have been appointed. They manage to find employment elsewhere, often close to home.[7] In order to encourage teachers to stay in rural areas they are allocated rent-free accommodation (not always on time) and free electricity and heating. They are also provided with a garden plot to grow vegetables and supplied with fruit and vegetables by a local kolkhoz. The extent of the above services and goods would vary from one place to another, depending, at times, on the local authorities—in this case the kolkhoz manager or the regional education director. Numerous complaints have been made in the *Uchitelskaya gazeta* by newly settled teachers concerning poorly built or promised but non-existent flats, the lack of heating facilities, and other services.

On the status of teachers, Lenin wrote: 'Our schoolteacher should be raised to a standard he has never achieved and cannot achieve in bourgeois society.' It could be said that measures adopted by the Soviet Government and the CPSU towards increasing the social status and moral weight of teachers represent, to a certain extent, a realization of Lenin's much-quoted historic aphorism.[8] The Soviet teacher's status is, clearly, determined by his ascribed rather than

[7] In 1977, out of 150,000 newly trained teachers, 15,000 (10%) did not report to their schools (*Uchitelskaya gazeta*, No. 72, 1978, p. 1).

[8] *Sovetskaya Shkola*, p. 220.

achieved role. The content of his ascribed role is very vividly described by Soviet educators in the following defining statement:

> The Soviet teacher should be a master of sophisticated ideological, theoretical, and
> political training; he should be erudite, educated, and he should exhibit profound
> knowledge of his subject. His knowledge should correspond to the latest achieve-
> ment in the areas of societal and pedagogical research, adolescent physiology, child
> and educational psychology, and relevant teaching methods. He should have the
> necessary organizational skills. He should be an individual who is dedicated to the
> construction of communism, a patriot, and an internationalist who is aware of his
> duties to this country and its people.[9]

Soviet teachers are readily praised by the Government, Party officials, and educationalists. At the 1960 All-Union Congress of
Teachers, Khrushchev said: 'Each [Communist] Party and Soviet
worker, despite his position, has to remember that he owes much to
school and to teachers.' Brezhnev, on the occasion of the fiftieth
anniversary of *Teachers Newspaper* (1976) highly praised the Soviet
teacher:

> The people's teacher [naródny uchítel] is the pride of Soviet society. He has
> earned unanimous respect for his selfless service to the cause of public education, for
> his generosity of heart, noble spiritual qualities, and love of children. The Party
> highly commends his ideological conviction, self-sacrificing work, and major contri-
> bution to the formation of a new man.[10]

At the June 1978 All-Union Congress of Teachers, Prokofiev in his
address defined the new tasks of teachers as follows: 'Today's teacher
is a skilful instructor, a political fighter, a brilliant expert of his discipline, who has mastered the skill to teach improvisingly scientific
truths and who, by his own life and work, asserts moral principles of
communism among youth.' The editorial of *Teachers Newspaper*
emphasizes the teacher's role in communist upbringing: 'The Soviet
teacher is an active, creative force. To children and youth he is a
model of lofty communist ideals and morality.'[11] The editorial ends
with the following words:

> The Central Committee of the Communist Party of the Soviet Union, Presidium
> of the Supreme Soviet, and the Council of Ministers of the USSR would like to wish
> Soviet teachers new creative achievements and they express a firm belief that

[9] *Uchitelskaya gazeta*, 1 July, 1978, p. 1.
[10] *Sovetskaya Shkola*, p. 220.
[11] *Uchitelskaya gazeta*, 29 June, 1978, p. 1.

workers in education will conscientiously fulfil their lofty duty towards the Party and people, that they will give their inspired work to the great task of upbringing of the new man, the active builder of communist society.

These are, clearly, familiar clichés of the past. Prokofiev attempts to define the new, characteristic feature of the Soviet teacher as a harmonious fusion of his cognitive, moral, and communal activity.

Thus the new emphasis seems to be on the teacher's political role. Moscow teachers have started a campaign: 'Higher political educa- tion for every pedagogue', reflecting the official concern for the teacher's better and deeper understanding of Marxism–Leninism. The role of teachers' collectives is also emphasized. The editorial 'The moral climate of the collective' states: 'The teacher is essentially a collectivist.... This is why the Party demands that major efforts in ideological and upbringing work should be concentrated in labour collectives.' The same editorial reports that not all pedagogical collec- tives have fulfilled the tasks they were asked to do.[12] Apart from the moral and political roles of the teacher (to introduce the pupil sys- tematically to current affairs and the political life of the Party and the Soviet Government, to develop in the pupil a dedication to the Motherland, the Communist Party, as well as to contribute to his political maturity, class awareness, rejection of the capitalist ideology and morality and to prepare the builders of communism), the teacher is also asked to improve vocational orientation and work training in the Soviet school. Preparing 17-year-olds for work is regarded as the most important task of the Soviet teacher. At the same time the most important goal of the Soviet school is the realization of the aims of the Twenty-fifth Congress of the CPSU and the new constitution of the USSR and the continuing perfection of the teaching and upbring- ing process.[13]

Prokofiev, in his speech at the 1978 All-Union Congress of Teachers (delivered on 28 June), had this to say about the role of the Soviet teacher:

The Soviet teacher is a fighter on the ideological front. He is an active guide of the Party's politics. He constantly follows Lenin's behest—to strengthen the link between the school, life, and the practice of the building of communism. The Soviet

[12] *Uchitelskaya gazeta*, 22 Nov., 1979, p. 1.
[13] Ibid. (editorial), 1 July, 1978, p. 1.

teacher shapes [formiruyet] the future generation.... He stands on the threshold of future achievements in science, technology, and culture.[14]

4. Ideology and the training of Soviet teachers

The relationship between ideology and education has always been a grey area. Instructing all children in socially desirable moral values, attitudes, and beliefs is an emotional issue, raising political, social, and ethical considerations. The major assumption behind the relationship between ideology and education is the belief that schools can build a new social order. Fundamentally, educators are hopelessly divided on the question Can education be a catalyst of social change? Educational leaders in the Socialist block, as well as in developing countries (especially Tanzania), are compelled to accept the reconstructionist ideology in curriculum, namely that education, under certain conditions, can change the very fabric of our society.

In the United States, sociological surveys have supposedly demonstrated that there is no significant correlation between formal political instruction in the school (e.g. civics) and the student's political attitudes. These findings have prompted some to conclude, somewhat hastily, that the school cannot build a new society. Coleman (1965) was one of the few scholars who, having established the necessary link between ideology and teaching, attempted to correct the popular myth that schools as political systems were ineffective.

The topic 'The role of ideology in the training of Soviet teachers' seems to beg the question. However, the relationship between ideology and Soviet education is more than apparent to those who have been educated under the system. Ideology, in this case a prescribed set of a Marxist–Leninist belief system, is the backbone of the entire educational network and upbringing process in the USSR. Such an arrangement ensures, at its best, a gradual social, cultural, and ideological shift, but at its worst it merely reinforces the *status quo.*

The entire philosophy of Soviet education, with its peculiarly dual function of education (obrazovanie) and upbringing (vospitanie) can be expressed by the well-known quote from Marx: 'Philosophers have only interpreted the world in various ways, but the real task is

[14]Ibid., 29th June, 1978, p. 2.

to change it.' As noted by King (1963), the most distinctive single feature of communist education is that it does ideologically encompass all educational aims and concerns. In other words, the whole system works towards a common purpose, which is always defined and ratified by the CPSU and the USSR Ministry of Education. In the USSR, education and upbringing are directed, to use Lenin's words, towards the realization of communist morality. King has suggested, in my opinion correctly, that there is more to the concept of communist ideology than a mere cognitive imagery. He believes that communist ideology should be treated as a distinct belief system that comes, paradoxically, very close to Christianity. According to King, Marxism–Leninism comes very close to the 'apostolic fervour of St. Paul, when he spoke of emptying himself out so that Christ might come in'.[15] At all times, the concept of communist ideology in education seems to be almost synonymous with the dictum 'I believe because it is impossible.' This, no doubt, explains the Soviet quest for perfection in technology, science, and the humanities, which resulted in outstanding achievements.

Perhaps their ardent belief in the new communist society of the future is not so far fetched after all. The Soviet dream of the new Utopia is, according to Price, 'open and developmental' (1977, 220). It is the kind of dream that Pinkevich (1930) deemed fit to describe as follows:

> We dream of a man fully equipped with all the knowledge of the present day and to whom all that is truly beautiful is dear; we dream of an active, strong man, struggling through the revolutionary classes of contemporary society for a realization of ideals, which throughout the world will bring peace and happiness to all mankind.

The key role of communist education is to prepare educated and ideologically convinced individuals who have mastered the communist world view. The Soviet student is described as someone who pursues the meaning of life in creative labour for the common good.

Soviet teachers learn, share, and transmit some of the following Marxist–Leninist traits, which are supposed to be characteristic of

[15]King, op. cit., p. 15.

Soviet man: Soviet humanism and patriotism, new communist attitude towards labour, collectivism and internationalism, comradeship, truthfulness, honesty, courage, and discipline.

5. Soviet Educators on the Teacher's Role

During the last ten years the Party directives stressed the need to raise the quality of training teachers and to improve their political image. 'Under present conditions', writes Panachin, 'only a teacher who is equipped with a profound knowledge of Marxist–Leninist theory, who has completely mastered the knowledge he is teaching, and who has mastered the skill of teaching can work successfully in the school.'[16] This is an official statement made by a high-ranking administrator on today's role of Soviet teachers. Complete mastery of Marxism–Leninism is as important as the command of knowledge, attitudes, and skills of teaching. The CPSU is well aware of the growing need for the teacher's moral and political stabilizing influence in a society that is rapidly changing under the impact of the West. The CPSU depends on the teacher for the resolution of many ideological, social, and cultural issues, which are likely to arise in the not so distant future. The propagandist role of the teacher is clearly spelled out by the decree 'On the 50th anniversary of the Komsomol and the tasks relating to the communist indoctrination of youth', which stated that the main function of teacher colleges is the training of the young teacher who is ready to fulfil a propagandist mission in the school and society. Teacher colleges are specifically asked to train teacher–propagandists, teacher–activists, and teacher–indoctrinators. Units in education are necessarily linked with Marxist–Leninist theory, for the world—according to a lecturer from the Moscow State Pedagogical Institute—has become the arena of the ever-mounting ideological struggle between the two systems—capitalism versus communism. At the 1971 All-Union Congress 'On organization and content of work on ideological indoctrination in pedagogical colleges' paramount attention was drawn to improving political socialization

[16]*Sovetskaya Pedagogika*, No. 7, 1973, p. 5.

of the future teachers. The indoctrination of education students is designed to prepare them for the 'fulfilment of their lofty patriotic duty to their Motherland, to the Party, and to the people, representing the political role of the Soviet teacher—the instructor of young generations of builders of communism. Of course, these words are very reminiscent of the hollow slogans and clichés of the 1930s. One could hardly anticipate enthusiastic response to the Party's rhetoric. What then has changed? There is a greater emphasis on the teacher's involvement in the community and a constant pressure on the teacher to upgrade his qualifications, knowledge, teaching methods, and other skills. Education students, apart from celebrating important political events—the birth of Lenin, Victory Day, the Great October Revolution anniversary, and so on, participate in seminars on Lenin. They research the revolutionary, military, and labour traditions of the Party and they are actively involved in many useful extra-curricular activities designed to help the community and the Party. For instance, many college and university students assume the sponsorship (shefstvo) of a small group of schoolchildren. Such Komsomol sponsors organize clubs and societies for children, and their work ranges from tutoring the less able pupils in academic subjects to conducting Octobrist and Pioneer meetings. Very often college students take under their wings the town's juvenile delinquents. This is done on a one-to-one basis. The student is allocated one case—a problem child, normally a 15- or a 13-year-old. This is what a grade 3 teacher has to say about the upbringing work of education students on their routine teaching round:

> This year the sponsors [shefy] conducted seven excursions and nine Pioneer rallies with my children. They have conducted regular activities in the physical culture and popular mathematics clubs. They have held fifteen talks. They have taken the children to the movies each week. They have conducted paramilitary drill games as well as counting, reading, and drawing competitions. They have staged amateur talent shows and they have organized exhibits and displays for all parents' meetings and holidays.[17]

Soviet teachers today are not merely subject specialists and skilled practitioners of their art. They are expected to have mastered the principles of Marxism–Leninism and to clearly perceive the political

---

[17] *Uchitelskaya gazeta*, No. 40, 1978, p. 2.

aims of the Party and the nation. They are required to be actively involved in the social and political affairs of the nation.

Ideological training of education students is not without problems. Many teacher colleges are criticized in the *Teachers Newspaper* for not providing a very effective programme in Marxism–Leninism. Even the prestigious Leningrad Pedagogical Institute has been recently criticized by the USSR Ministry of Education for falling behind in its propagandist tasks. Soviet education lecturers openly confess that many of the graduates have been inadequately prepared for their would-be socio-political upbringing work in the school. Often, the teachers' college academic curriculum is blamed for these shortcomings. There is a need for more up-to-date units and courses in communist upbringing, particularly those concerned with the rationale and methodology of communist morality and education. Sometimes lecturers are criticized for their apathy and apoliticism. They are rebuked for not taking their propagandist role and duties seriously enough, for escaping from their upbringing tasks into academic research. Prokofiev, the USSR Minister of Education, observes that not all schools are aware of their new role, that of facilitating the many-faceted development of the pupil's identity, who is always ready to participate in the collective work of his people. Since not all teachers are actively involved in political indoctrination, and this has become apparent in the rising anti-Soviet manifestations among youth, Prokofiev recommends that a more effective selection procedure should be introduced in teacher colleges. At the 1977 meeting of the ideological seminar in Moscow it was reaffirmed that the primary role of teachers was to imbue the pupil in the spirit of a Marxist–Leninist world view. It was also pointed out that many school-leavers demonstrated a mere average, and often very superficial understanding of social sciences, particularly politics. Clearly, not all Soviet teachers were the models of dedicated and convinced practitioners of a Marxist–Leninist belief system. Ineffective training of teachers in Marxism–Leninism was discussed at the All-Union Conference 'Problems of raising social and political activity of the future teacher during the educational process in VUZ' (January 1978). The Conference stressed that societal and political activity was, indeed, a 'social and professional prerequisite in the formation of the

238   *Education in the USSR*

teacher's ideological orientation'.[17] The dilemma of trained pedagogue professionals and trained Marxist–Leninist disciples will continue to exist as long as the contradictions between rhetoric and
reality remain unresolved.

6. The training of elementary schoolteachers

Are Soviet teachers better trained for the job than our teachers? A
difficult question to answer as there are some poorly trained teachers
in any country. On paper the Soviet teacher appears to be better
trained. On the average, Soviet diploma courses for primary teachers
are one year longer, as colleges offer four-year and five-year diploma
courses.

All teacher colleges and institutes are directly administered by the
USSR Ministry of Higher and Specialized Secondary Education. The
Ministry, helped by the Ministry of Education of the Republic, controls, authorizes, and implements all educational curricula, prescribes
textbooks, and approves examinations. The Ministry also determines
the annual admission quota according to the needs of the Soviet
economy. Unlike in the West, all qualified teachers are guaranteed
employment.

The most remarkable feature of Soviet teacher education is its high
degree of uniformity of curricula and teaching methods, standard
textbooks, and externally prescribed final examinations. It is, with
minor variations, almost identical throughout the Soviet Union. Such
uniformity makes it possible to maintain comparatively similar educational standards in all fifteen republics. Thus the USSR has established a single centralized system of teacher education.

Teacher training in the USSR is carried out by primary teacher
colleges (pedagogicheskie uchilishcha), pedagogical institutes (pedagogicheskie instituty), and universities, with the main bulk of primary
teachers coming from the 600-odd teacher colleges.

Prior to the 1960s reforms in education, primary teacher colleges
offered mainly three-year diploma courses. Since then most of them
have been upgraded and converted into four-year courses. Shorter
courses are available for better-qualified candidates. Admission, as to
any tertiary institution (VUZ), is by competitive entrance examin-

[17] *Uchitelskaya gazeta*, No. 17, 1978, p. 2.

ation, which normally includes Russian language and literature and other core units, depending on the faculty requirements. The candidate's school record and character reference are also considered. Rural applicants are encouraged to apply and some are accepted (especially those from remote regions, who may be, in one or another, educationally disadvantaged) without konkursnye ekzaminy.

Today, primary teacher colleges offer two types of diploma: Diploma of Pre-school Education and Diploma of Primary Education. Both are four-year teaching qualifications.

The current curriculum for profession No. 2121 (primary teacher) contains up to ten core disciplines and a multitude of related units and modules.

The primary teacher college curriculum can be, for convenience sake, divided into three major areas of study—social sciences (politics), education and core disciplines, and minor units.

The 1975 curriculum included the history of the CPSU (the Communist Party), Marxism–Leninism, scientific communism (social sciences), a modern language (English, French, or German), history and philosophy of education, child and educational psychology, curriculum studies, educational administration, comparative education, teaching methods, botany, zoology, geology, environmental sciences, child care and the core disciplines, Russian language and literature, mathematics, and science.

Since the primary school curriculum consists essentially of mathematics, science, and Russian language, the main emphasis at the primary teacher college is on the three Rs and teaching methods. Physical education, music and singing, and art teachers are trained at specialized pedagogical colleges of physical education, music colleges, and art colleges. A certain proportion of graduates of the art and music colleges of the Ministry of Culture of the USSR and the physical education colleges administered by the Committee of Physical Culture and Sport of the Council of Ministers of the USSR may become teachers.

Most subjects at the college are obligatory. Mathematics and Russian are allotted 900 contact hours (approximately 20% of the total curriculum). Education units take up another 500 hours and the remainder is divided between science, physical education, art and craft, educational technology, and other minor studies. At the end of the fourth year the student has to submit a diploma thesis (on education) and pass the three State examinations in Russian language and literature, education (pedagogika), and political science.

7. Teaching practice

Teaching experience commences in the first year as a three-week field study in science. In the second year, teaching practice is based on a four-week experience of the collective life at a Pioneers' summer camp. School experience lasts for twenty-four working days in the third year and forty-eight days in the fourth year.

The overall quality of teaching practice has improved following the 1972 decree issued by the Ministry of Education of the USSR. The following three guiding principles were to emerge from it:

(a) Familiarity.
(b) Continuity.
(c) Summer camp.

Familiarity, as the name suggests, ensures that the student-teacher gets a sufficient amount of school experience, sitting-in at lessons, teaching under supervision, assisting the grade teacher with marking homework, setting assignments, organizing weekly programmes, and conducting excursions. In fact an assistant to the grade teacher. This type of necessary teaching experience is acquired by the student-teacher during the first two years at college.

Continuity of teaching experience is one of the highlights of educational reform in teacher education during the seventies. A more serious teaching practice takes place during the third, fourth, and fifth years. It lasts between 17–19 six-day weeks or approximately 120 days. During the five-year teaching practice the student-teacher is meant to acquire:

(a) the ability to understand and work with the pupils' collective;
(b) the ability to master skills for active social and communal involvement;

(c) the ability to relate educational philosophy to parents and the community at large;
(d) the ability to plan, direct, and evaluate the curriculum process;
(e) the ability to conduct extra-curricular activities for the grade;
(f) the ability to master educational administration.

Thus during teaching practice the student-teacher becomes aware of the multi-functional role of a Soviet pedagogue. The student-teacher must satisfy the requirements of the school by mastering teaching subjects, administrative process, and curriculum, be able to become a fine psychologist and direct the pupils' collective in the grade, and take an active part in rearing pupils in the spirit of communism and according to economic, social, and cultural needs of the society.

Educating children for life, work, and citizenship is the main task of the Soviet school. The school year is divided into four school terms. Term one begins on 1 September and term four ends in May. The fifth, unofficial term, is organized for children during their three-month summer vacation. Children who wish may participate in the fifth labour term. It incorporates the principle of work and play. It resembles our summer camp with one difference—the children work for three or four hours a day at a Soviet summer camp. If the camp is near a local village then the local collective farm (kolkhoz) provides plenty of work for Soviet schoolchildren. The city camp would be concerned with maintenance work at the school. Children paint the walls, repair desks, etc. A strict daily regime is observed in all summer camps. The children get up, eat, work, play, and rest according to a time-table set by the teacher and his assistants. Student-teachers are encouraged to run these camps in the process of which they gain valuable experiences of life within the collective. They become Pioneer leaders, instructors, and co-ordinators. Many children attend these camps, which are obviously designed to keep them busy, healthy, and happy. Clearly, an attempt is being made to exercise a greater social control of teenagers during their free time. These work-learn-and-play camps form the basis of socio-political indoctrination of teenagers during their long summer break.

8. Reforms in teacher training

The rising academic standards in schools require that teachers are more highly trained. The 1980 level of school work has advanced far beyond the level of teacher training in the USSR in 1970. Since 1975 Soviet teachers have been coerced by the authorities to upgrade their qualifications through attending in-service courses.

The teacher's knowledge, particularly in the sciences, needs to be updated almost every five years in order to keep up with the explosive growth of human knowledge. Teaching methods, educational theories, and the social, intellectual, and psychological needs of the pupil will require, according to Soviet educationalists, different approaches in decades to come.

Apart from being concerned with improving the quality of general education, Soviet educationalists are equally concerned with political indoctrination and moral education. At the teacher college the student is exposed to over 500 hours of politics, which are designed to prepare him for the important upbringing work at school. During training at the college, the 17-year-old student has to be moulded into a psychologist, philosopher, social worker, community leader, educationalist, and teacher.

Soviet educationalists maintain that in view of the complexity of upbringing and instruction in the primary school in the 1980s it is essential that all primary teachers should be tertiary (five-year) trained.

Reforms in the curriculum suggest that teacher training was excessively academic and not school oriented. There is now more emphasis on upbringing and vocational training.

The insufficiency of the historical, social, and economic approach in teacher education has been strongly criticized. Teaching for citizenship, labour, and life is to be intensified.

Teacher education courses have been restructured. Sociology, which has been banned, is coming in again. Educational psychology has been largely rewritten. Social psychology is now taken in the first and second years. Educational psychology has been shifted from the second into the final (fourth) year. History of education (istoriya pedagogiki) is now taught earlier, namely in the first two years. All these changes indicate that little thought was given to the curriculum planning and that some basic faults of curriculum design have been made inadvertently.

Teacher education in the USSR has both positive and negative features. On the negative side it is plagued by sterility, conformity, and indoctrination. Teaching methods are unimaginative and monotonous. Textbooks, especially in the humanities, are of inferior quality, especially with regards to content. The emphasis in learning is still on facts and comprehension rather than application and evaluation. Experimental education is only beginning to be recognized in the USSR, and educational research in educational sociology, philosophy, and curriculum studies is developing rather slowly. The authorities are very suspicious of innovations in learning, and open classroom teaching is yet to be seen. De-schooling, of the type advocated by Ivan Illich, is denounced as decadent and bourgeois. Examinations have not been abolished.

A significant and radical change in the teaching profession was the introduction of the All-Union certification of teachers in January 1975. The April 1974 decree of the Council of Ministers of the USSR 'On the attestation of teachers of general schools' (Ob attestatsii uchitelei obshcheobrazovatelnykh shkol) stated that teachers, in addition to their normal promotions, could, if they wished, be examined by a local Educational Attestation Commission (Attestatsionnaya Kommisiya) competing for the newly introduced status titles of teacher-methodist (uchitel-metodist) and senior teacher (starshy uchitel). The massive attestation or registration of teachers in the USSR was designed to improve the overall quality of teaching and learning, and to hold teachers personally responsible for the quality of learning and upbringing of the pupils. Of course, many irregularities with the examination procedures, unethical practices and tactics, and pure vindictiveness of certain attestation commissions have been reported in the *Teachers Newspaper* between 1975 and 1980. Power lends itself to abuse, and Soviet educational administrators are no exception. However, the more serious issue at stake is the need for such educational titles in the already highly hierarchical and bureaucratic educational structure in the USSR. The very notion of egalitarianism, as understood by Marx, has clearly changed under the influence of such traditional social class criteria—education, occupation, income, power, prestige, and status. To award the teacher with better incentives for work (something that Marx did not tolerate), to give them more power, prestige, and status seems to work against the Marxist concept of egalitarianism.

Another remarkable feature of the Soviet educational system is the existence of many central educational institutes concerned with the advanced and in-service training of teachers. Approximately one-fifth of Soviet teachers receive advanced training at these centres. Each year these establishments organize a series of special lectures, seminars, and courses. Nearly 4500 regional, urban, and local curriculum and methodology centres and 187 special advanced training institutes for teachers (instituty usovershenstvovaniya uchitelei) are responsible for in-service education. Here teachers update their knowledge, teaching methods and skills, receive help with curriculum design and implementation, and analyse fundamental problems of schooling, particularly upbringing (vospitanie). Instituty Usovershenstvovaniya Uchitelei and Metodicheskie Kabinety, as autonomous curriculum centres of various educational administration bodies, are designed to upgrade teachers' qualifications, prepare them for work with new curricula and programmes, and introduce them to the latest developments in educational theory and practice. Between 1968 and 1975 more than 5 million individuals completed in-service teacher education courses. However, in-service teacher education has to resolve many problems. Some units and courses are poorly designed with barely adequate content and reading involved. Some faculties use an inadequate and ineffective one-way lecturing technique, ignoring the teacher's academic qualifications, teaching experience, interests, and needs. Dry academic language, meaningless clichés, abundance of technical concepts (not clearly explained), abstractiveness, sterility, and excessive verbalism tend to confuse rather than educate the experienced pedagogue who wishes to upgrade his knowledge and teaching skills.

9. Innovations in teacher education

The innovative features of teacher education and teacher employment can be summarized under the following headings: (a) the introduction of attestatsiya (consisting of a stiff accreditation procedure) involving written and oral examinations resulting in reclassification of practising teachers. If successful, a teacher may be awarded the title of senior teacher (starshy uchitel) or teacher-methodist (uchitel-metodist), the latter carrying more influence and prestige; (b) the introduction of a new honorary title the people's teacher of the USSR (narodny uchitel SSSR); (c) preparation of elementary schoolteachers with higher educational qualifications (since 1972, fifty-six new faculties of pedagogy and methods of elementary education were opened, with 20,000 students); (d) preparation of pre-school teachers with higher education (involving 34 pedagogical institutes and 213 pedagogical junior colleges); (e) the introduction of the five-year educational programme for students wishing to major in Russian language and literature; (f) the introduction of a new major in education—introductory military training and physical education; and (g) substantially revised programmes and curricula affecting all teacher-training institutions.

10. Future problems

First, there are administrative problems in higher education. The Soviet-created dual distinction between the VUZ pedagogue who has completed higher education (via university or institute) and teacher training and the elementary school teacher, who has been trained at an uchilishche (similar to a German Pädagogische Hochschule), suggests an élitist hierarchy and a division between elementary and secondary teaching profession. The career prospects for many elementary schoolteachers are not as good as for secondary teachers. Elementary schoolteachers receive lower incomes and they are under pressure to upgrade their academic qualifications by completing five-year teaching diplomas.

On the positive side the remarkable growth of in-service training for teachers wishing to update their knowledge and training skills is likely to influence the quality of teaching force.

Second, the problem of supply and demand. School enrolments show a downward trend in the USSR. Births have declined from 5,341,000 in 1960 to 4,087,000 in 1969 (a loss of more than 20%). This will affect enrolments in grade 8 in 1984 and grade 10 in 1986.

In the 1965/6 and 1971/2 school years, 15.2 million pupils attended the elementary school (grades 1–3) compared with 12.5 million in 1978—a loss of 2.7 million or nearly 18%. In the 1971/2 academic year, 5.3 million pupils attended grade 4 compared with 4.1 million in the 1977/8 academic year—a loss of nearly 20%. Enrolments in grade 8 (1977/8), just under 5 million, represented the lowest figure since 1965. The 1970/1 academic year was the year of explosion in secondary education which, unless the birth rate is to increase, is over. By 1978 enrolment in secondary schools had decreased dramatically by 4.8 million.

Unless there is a corresponding reduction in teacher intake, the USSR may, for the first time in its history, experience a surplus of teachers. There already exists a surplus of engineers.

Finally, the Soviet teacher, notwithstanding his present high status and prestige in the society, is likely to experience ideological, moral, intellectual, and social problems in the future. As the USSR moves closer and closer to communism, the resultant shift in the ideology and socio-economic changes may contribute to role conflicts being experienced by teachers. Accepting one's ascribed teaching role would be the most difficult ideological and moral issue. To be an intellectual, moral, and social conformist, and to accept the contradictions that are inherent in the prescribed interpretation of Marxism–Leninism, would become progressively more difficult for the more enlightened and aware individuals. Higher educational standards in teacher colleges and universities may result in better-trained practitioners of art, and this may be dysfunctional, for the more perceptive individuals may not accept (if this is not occurring already) the official ideology. Educating individuals too much is just as perilous to the State as not educating enough. There are already obvious signs that not all members of the intelligentsia strata, as mentioned in the

December 1977 educational reform, where some teachers were criticized for obvious failures in upbringing (vospitanie), are dedicated and ideologically convinced builders of the new society.

Conclusion

The main aim of this book was to examine the current and official Soviet educational philosophy. It has dealt with social, moral, and political aspects of Soviet education.

In the past, Soviet education, particularly its curricula, was viewed by Western educators at a descriptive level. Such studies invariably concentrated on the educational structure rather than principles of Soviet education.

This book dwells upon certain Communist principles incorporated in the Soviet educational system. It has been established, on the basis of current Soviet educational criticism and my own upbringing in the USSR, that one of the foremost educational principles today is training the young generation in a spirit of Marxist–Leninist ethics which, among other things, necessitates the formation of a belief system based on love of the Socialist Motherland, comradeship, love of Socialist labour, and so on. These and other related moral values, which formulate character education, are also inculcated through extra-curricular activities of many kinds—sporting, artistic, dramatic, and scientific, organized through the young Pioneers and the Komsomol.[1]

It has been also shown that most major curricula reforms, apart from purely administrative ones, in the USSR between 1964 and 1977 have been political in nature. Recent curricula changes could be regarded as primarily ideological rather than pedagogical.

It is conceivable that the socio-political and moral aspects of curricula reforms in the 1970s are designed to weaken social stratification in the USSR, to improve the status and prestige of the blue-collar worker, to strengthen the place of ideology in education, and to create the new socialist man.

The Soviet educational system is far from perfect. This fact has

[1]Mohr, C. B., Science education in the USSR, *Slavophile*, 1966, pp. 28–29.

248

eluded certain Western educators who commented in the 1960s on the virtues of the Soviet curriculum. They seemed to be unduly impressed by the bias of Soviet education towards technical sciences and, oddly enough, glossed over the nature of political socialization in Soviet schools.

Soviet education was and still is riddled with administrative and socio-political problems. This becomes quite apparent, judging by an impressive number of educational reforms introduced between 1970 and 1978. The key concept of Soviet education, the polytechnic school, established to train the youth for socially useful labour, has proved to be more difficult to achieve than originally anticipated. In 1978, or sixty years after the October Revolution, the authorities were still obliterating the seemingly growing contempt for manual work among Soviet youth who at the same time (which I find somewhat paradoxical) supposedly value highly such moral attributes as love of truth, fidelity to the Party, and love of work. Social stratification and upward social mobility, as discussed in Chapters 2 and 4, indicate the presence of a rather deviant and certainly anti-Marxist belief system. Soviet youth is becoming more and more consumer oriented and less and less communist convinced. The seventies are characterized by a growing wave of conspicuous consumption affecting all strata of Soviet society.

Despite the ceaseless and all-pervasive ideological indoctrination of Soviet youth, there are visible signs, as revealed by numerous Soviet sociological studies, of parasitism, apathy, and indifference towards the Party, the State, and society. However, it would be difficult, if not impossible, to substantiate the claim that for the majority of Soviet youth political socialization is a mere 'ritual rhetoric'.[2] All we can say is that a certain percentage of Soviet students pay lip-service to the official ideology.

Arguing from a Marxist philosophy, the most fundamental goal of Marxism, namely the creation of a free, classless society, has not been, strictly speaking, achieved. On the contrary, what has been shown is that the very structure of specialized and tertiary education with competitive examinations and restricted entry into the more popular

[2]Price, R. F., *Marxism and Education in Russia and China*, Croom Helm, London, 1977, p. 268.

tertiary courses like engineering and medicine has clearly worsened, as noted by Price, the prospect for the realization of a truly classless society by means of effective communist education and upbringing.[3] Price argues, in my opinion correctly, that the monopoly of power and the mass media by the CPSU and State bureaucracy constitutes the real barrier towards the attainment of a classless society. This book suggests that the very nature of recruitment of students by different post-secondary educational institutions, success within such institutions, and the ultimate placement of graduates and other successful individuals into the hierarchical posts, make it very difficult to implement a genuine Marxist educational philosophy.[3]

The continuous stream of articles delineating and discussing problems dealing with labour socialization, moral education, political indoctrination, participation in socially useful labour, patriotism, and collective upbringing in official periodicals ranging from *Literaturnaya gazeta* to *Sovetskaya Pedagogika*, indicate that the authorities admit and recognize these problems and are seeking to eliminate them.

This is the only guide the Western observer has when confronted with a task of evaluating the results of recent curricula reforms in the Soviet Union. In this one should be guided by the Party's concern for improving the overall effectiveness of upbringing (vospitanie) of the Soviet youth. Apart from some improvements in child-rearing methods, both the Party and the educators have conceded that the problem of upbringing does exist and that its satisfactory solution is one of the most urgent tasks of Soviet education.

[3]Price, op cit., p. 345.

Bibliography

ADAMS, A. E., The status of teachers in the USSR, *New Era*, April 1962, pp. 69–76.
ADASKIN, I. A., *et al.*, *Oplata truda rabotnikov narodnogo prosveshcheniya*, Moscow, Profizdat, 1974.
AGAFONOV, V. (ed.), *Problemy nravstvennogo vospitaniya studentov*, Moscow, 1975.
ALEKSEYEV, A. N., *Ateisticheskoe vospitanie uchashchikhsia pri izuchenii istorii SSSR v srednei shkole*, Moscow, Proveshchenie, 1976.
ALEKSEYEV, M. N. (ed), *Problemy formirovaniya kommunisticheskogo mirovozzreniya*, Minsk, 1975.
ANISOV, M., *Khrestomatiya po istorii sovetskoi shkoly i pedagogiki*, Moscow, Prosveshchenie, 1972.
ARET, A. YA., *Samovospitanie shkolnikov*, Moscow, 1975.
ARUTOV, P. R., *Politekhnicheskii printsyp v obuchenii shkolnikov*, Moscow, Pedagogika, 1976.
ASATUROV, K., *Narodnoe obrazovanie i pedagogika v SSSR*, Moscow, Nllobshchei pedagogiki APN SSSR, 1971.
ASHBY, G. F., *Pre-school Theories and Strategies*, MUP, 1972.
AVERIN, A., Vospityvat patriotov–internatsionalistov, *Narodnoe Obrazovanie*, No. 12, 1974, pp. 53–58.
BADMAYEV, V., *Elementy pedagogiki i psikhologii v partiinoi propagande*, Moscow, 1973.
BALIASHNAYA, L. K., *et al.*, Shkolnyi kollektiv i pionerskaya organizatsiya, *Sovietskaya Pedagogika*, No. 5, 1974, pp. 19–27.
BAUER, R. R., *The New Man in Soviet Psychology*, Harvard UP, 1959.
BEEMAN, A. E., The American image of Soviet education, 1917–1935, PhD thesis, Wisconsin, 1965.
BELENKOV, G. I. (ed.), *Obuchaya vospityvat–iz opyta prepodavaniya literatury*, Moscow, 1974.
BEREDAY, G., *et al.*, *The Changing Soviet School*, Boston, 1960.
BEREDAY, G., *et al.*, *The Politics of Soviet Education*, London, 1960.
BESTUZHEV-LADA, I. V., Sotsialnye problemy sovetskogo obraza zhizni, *Novy Mir*, No. 7, 1976, pp. 208–21.
BILLINGTON, J., *The Icon and the Axe*, New York, 1970.
BLAKE, W. N., Education in Karl Marx's concept of labour, PhEd thesis, Alberta, 1967.
BOGDANOVA, O. V., *Mladshim shkolnikam o kommunisticheskoi nravstvennosti*, Voronezh, 1974.
BOLDYRIOV, N. I., *Metodika vospitatelnoi raboty v shkole*, Moscow, Prosveshchenie, 1974.
BOLDYRIOV, N. I., Marksistsko–Leninskoe uchenie of morali..., *Sovetskaya Pedagogika*, No. 9, 1974, pp. 92–106.
BOWEN, J., Anton Makarenko and the development of Soviet education, PhD thesis, Illinois, 1960.

BOWEN, J., *Soviet Education: Anton Makarenko and the Years of Experiment*, Wisconsin, 1962.
BRICKMAN, W., Selected bibliography of the history of education in Russia to 1917, *Paedagogica Historica*, 14, 1974, pp. 164–9.
BRONFENBRENNER, U., *Two Worlds of Childhood: US and USSR*, Penguin Education, 1974.
CALKINS, J., Two worlds of early childhood: government sponsored child centres in the Soviet Union and California, PhD thesis, Claremont, 1976.
CARY, C. D., Peer groups in the political socialization of Soviet school children, *Social Science Quarterly*, Sept. 1974, pp. 451–61.
CARY, C. D., Patterns of emphasis upon Marxist–Leninist ideology: a computer content analysis of Soviet school history, geography, and social science textbooks, *Comparative Education Review*, Feb. 1976, pp. 11–29.
CHABE, A. M., Soviet education: its implications for United States education, *Educational Forum*, Nov. 1976, pp. 15–19.
CHAUNCEY, H., *Soviet Preschool Education*, Vol. 1, New York, 1969.
CHERNOKOZOVA, I. N. et al., *Etika uchitelia*, Kiev, 1973.
CHERNYSHENKO, I. D., *Sistema obshchestvenno–poleznogo truda v sovremennoi sovetskoi shkole*, Minsk, 1974.
CHINN, J., The socio-demographic consequences of urbanization in the Soviet Union, PhD thesis, Wisconsin, 1975.
Class structure of Soviet Society, *Soviet Sociology*, No. 3, 1967, pp. 3–6.
COLEMAN, J. S. (ed.), *Education and Political Development*, Princeton UP, 1968.
COMMEAU, I., Competitive examinations in the Soviet Union, *Comparative Review*, July 1974, pp. 45–48.
COUNTS, G. S., *The Challenge of Soviet Education*, New York, 1957.
COUNTS, G. S., A word about the Soviet teacher, *Comparative Education Review*, June 1961.
DANILOV, A., Postoyanno deistvuyushchii faktor kommunisticheskogo vospitaniya, *Narodnoe Obrazovanie*, No. 4, 1974.
DANILOV, A., *Shkoly RSFSR*, Moscow, 1975.
DE GEORGE, R. T., *Soviet Ethics and Morality*, Ann Arbor, 1969.
DE WITT, N., Polytechnical education and the Soviet school reform, *Harvard Educational Review*, Vol. 30, 1960.
DE WITT, N., *Education and Professional Employment in the USSR*, Washington DC, 1961.
DE WITT, N., Costs and returns in education in the USSR, PhD thesis, Harvard, 1962.
DEMIDOV, N., Vospityvat obshestvenno–politicheskie interesy, *Narodnoe Obrazovanie*, No. 8, 1974.
DOROTICH, D., History in the Soviet school (1917–37): changing policy and practice, PhD thesis, McGill, 1964.
DOWSE, R., et al., The family, the school, and the political socialization process, *Sociology*, No. 1, 1971, pp. 21–45.
DULOV, A. I. (ed.), *Ideino–politicheskoe i nravstvennoe vospitanie shkolnikov*, Irkutsk, 1974.
DUNSTAN, J., An educational experiment: Soviet mathematics and physics boarding schools, *Soviet Studies*, Oct. 1975, pp. 543–73.
Education and social mobility in the USSR, *Soviet Studies*, July 1966, pp. 57–65.
ELIAS, E., Family and school in the USSR, *Where*, May 1967, pp. 8–9.

FITZPATRICK, S., *The Commissariat of Enlightenment*, London, 1970.

FRENKEL, YU., *et al.*, *Trudovoe obuchenie i proforientatsiya*, Moscow, Pedagogika, 1974.

GAPOCHKA, M. P., Formirovanie osnov dialektiko–materialisticheskogo mirovozzreniya uchashchikhsya v protsesse obucheniya, *Sovetskaya Pedagogika*, No. 2, 1973, pp. 83–95.

GONCHAROV, N. K., Vsestotonnee razvitie lichnosti i shkola, *Sovetskaya Pedagogika*, No. 1, 1970, pp. 70–86.

GORDIN, A. YU., *Problemy detskogo kollektiva v russkoi i sovetskoi pedagogike*, Moscow, Pedagogika, 1973.

GORDIN. A. Yu., *Formirovanie otnoshenii pedagogov i uchashchikhsia v sovetskoi shkole*, Moscow, Pedagogika, 1977.

GRANT, N., Recent changes in Soviet secondary education, *International Review of Education*, No. 11, 1965, pp. 129–42.

GRANT, N., Fifty years of Soviet education, *Irish Journal of Education*, Winter 1967, pp. 89–106.

GREEN, B., University autonomy and Soviet totalitarian control, PhD thesis, Radcliffe, 1960.

GUIDRY, L. J., Soviet methods of teaching morality in primary textbooks and children's literature, PhD thesis, Kansas, 1972.

GUROVA, R. G., *Sotsiologicheskie problemy obrazovaniya i vospitaniya*, Moscow, Pedagogika, 1973.

H. H., Education and social mobility in the USSR, *Soviet Studies*, July 1966, pp. 57–66.

HANS, N., *The Russian Tradition in Education*, London, RKP, 1963.

HARASIMIW, B. (ed.), *Education and the Mass Media in the Soviet Union and Eastern Europe*, New York, Praeger, 1976.

HECHINGER, F. M., *The big red schoolhouse*, New York, Doubleday, 1959.

HIGGINS, J., Problems of the selection and professional orientation of Soviet pedagogical students, *Comparative Education*, June 1976, pp. 157–73.

HINNERS, J., *et al.*, Soviet corrective measures for juvenile delinquency, *Criminology*, July 1973, pp. 218–26.

HOLMES, L. E., Western perceptions of Soviet education: 1918–31, *Educational Forum*, Nov. 1974, pp. 27–32.

HOPKINS, E., Literature in the schools of the Soviet Union, *Comparative Education*, Mar. 1974, pp. 25–34.

HOPKINS, M. W., *Mass Media in the Soviet Union*, New York, 1970.

HUNT, H. N., *The Theory and Practice of Communism*, Pelican, 1963.

IGOSHKIN, V., Pionerskie ritualy, simvolika, *Vospitanie Shkolnikov*, No. 6, 1971, pp. 28–33.

IVANKOV, V. T. (ed.), *Voprosy kommunisticheskogo vospitaniya*, Moscow, 1973.

IVANOVICH, K. A. *et al.*, *Trudovoe politekhnicheskoe vospitanie v srednei shkole*, Moscow, Pedagogika, 1972.

JACOBY, S., *Inside Soviet Schools*, Hill & Wang, New York, 1974.

JAHN, H. R., USSA/USSR: two worlds apart, *Comparative Education Review*, Oct. 1975.

JENNINGS, M., *et al.*, *The Political Character of Adolescence*, Princeton UP, 1974.

JUDGE, J., Education in the USSR: Russian or Soviet, *Comparative Education Review*, June 1975, pp. 127–45.

KALININ, A. D., *Pre-school Education in the USSR*, Moscow, 1969.

KALININ, A. D., *Narodnoe obrazovanie v SSSR*, Moscow, Pedagogika, 1972.

254   Education in the USSR

KASHIN, M. P., *Narodnoe obrazovanie v RSFSR*, Moscow, 1970.

KASHIN, M. P., *Ob itogakh perekhoda sovetskoi shkoly na novoe soderzhanie obrazovaniya*, Moscow, 1975.

KASHIN, M. P., *Ob itogakh perekhoda sovetskoi shkoly na novoe soderzhanie obshchego abrazovaniya*, *Sovetskaya Pedagogika*, No. 3, 1976, pp. 24–32.

KASHIN, M. P., Zadanie na zavtra: o novykh programmakh obucheniya, *Izvestiya*, 22 April 1976, p. 5.

KASSOV, A., *The Soviet Youth Program*, Cambridge, 1965.

KHALIAPINA, M. A., Sistema voenno–patrioticheskogo vospitaniya uchashchikhsia srednei shkoly, in *Voprosy vospitaniya i obucheniya*, Omsk, 1973, pp. 56–67.

KING, E. J. (ed.), *Communist Education*, London, Methuen, 1963.

KLINE, G., *Soviet Education*, London, RKP, 1957.

KOLOMINSKII, YA. P., Sotsialno–psikhologicheskie kharakteristiki detskikh kollektivov, *Voprosy Psikhologii*, No. 3, 1974, pp. 31–40.

KOMALDINOVA, E., *Voprosy teorii kommunisticheskogo vospitaniya, 1960–70*, Bibliografichesky ukazatel, Moscow, 1972.

Kommunisticheskoe vospitanie shkolnikov, Moscow, 1971.

Komsomol v shkole (sbornik), Moscow, 1972.

Komsomol v vuze, 2nd edn., Moscow, 1976.

KONNIKOVA, T. F. (ed.), *O nravstvennom vospitanii shkolnika*, Leningrad, LGPU im. Gertsena, 1968.

KONSTANTINOV, N., *et al.*, *Istoriya pedagogiki*, Moscow, 1974.

KOROL, A. G., *Soviet Education for Science and Technology*, London, 1957.

KOROLIOV, F. F., *Ocherki po istorii sovetskoi shkoly i pedagogiki*, Moscow, 1958.

KOROLIOV, F. F., Vsestoronnee razvitie chelovecheskoi lichnosti ..., *Sovetskaya Pedagogika*, No. 7, 1961, pp. 12–36.

KOROTOV, V., Metodika ubezhdeniya, *Vospitanie Shkolnikov*, No. 4, 1973, pp. 9–15.

KOROTOV, V. M., *Samoupravlenie shkolnikov*, 2nd edn., Moscow, Prosveshchenie, 1976.

KOROTOV, V. M., *Vospitatelnaya rabota v shkole (Sbornik dokumetov)*, Moscow, Prosveshchenie, 1976.

KOTELNIKOVA, L. A. (ed.), *Formirovanie novogo cheloveka* (bibliography), Moscow, 1973.

KOUTAISSOFF, E., Soviet education and the new man, *Soviet Studies*, Vol. 5, 1953.

KOVALIOV, S. M., *Marksism–Leninism i formirovanie novogo cheloveka*, Pedagogika, Moscow, 1973.

KOVALEVSKII, K., Teachers and Parents, *New Era*, Sept. 1973, pp. 175–8.

KOZHEVNIKOV, E. M., Osnovnye printsipy formirovaniya lichnosti ..., *Sovetskaya Pedagogika*, No. 11, 1974, pp. 10–20.

KREUSLER, A. A., Contemporary education and moral upbringing in the Soviet Union, PhD thesis, Ann Arbor, Uni. Microfilms International, 1976.

KRUPSKAYA, N. K., *Izbrannye pedagogicheskie proizvedeniya*, Moscow, APN RSFSR, 1955.

KUDRIAVTSEV, F. S., *Voenno–patrioticheskoe vospitanie studentov pedagogicheskikh institutov*, Leningrad, 1975.

KURILENKO, T. M., *Vospitanie kommunisticheskoi nravstvennosti*, Moscow, 1975.

KUZIN, N. P., *et al.*, *Education in the USSR*, Moscow, Progress, 1972.

KUZIN, N. P., *et al.*, *Sovetskaya shkola na sovremennom etape*, Pedagogika, Moscow, 1977.

KUZMINA, N. V., *et al.*, *Problemy obucheniya i vospitaniya studentov v vuze*, Leningrad, 1976.

KUZNETSOVA, E. S., *et al.*, *Metodika vospitatelnoi raboty v shkole*, Prosveshchenie, 1967.
LANE, D., *Politics and Society in the USSR*, London, 1969.
LARMIN, O. V., *Obshchestvennaya psikhologiya i kommunisticheskoe vospitanie*, Leningrad, 1971.
LAW, D. A., A contemporary study of the concepts of truth, freedom and documentary in the American and Soviet educational systems, PhD thesis, Utah, 1966.
LAWRENCE, F., Makarenko: pioneer of communist education, *Modern Quarterly*, Autumn 1953, pp. 234–40.
LEBEDINSKII, V. V., *Osnovnye etapy pionerskogo dvizheniya*, Moscow, 1974.
LEBEDINSKII, V. V., Rol komsomolskoi i pionerskoi organizatsii v vospitanii, *Sovetskaya Pedagogika*, No. 1, 1974, pp. 83–96.
LEBEDINSKII, V. V., *Teoriya i metodika pionerskoi i komsomolskoi raboty v shkole*, Moscow, Prosveshchenie, 1976.
LEHRMAN, S. M., The pedagogical ideas of A. S. Makarenko, PhD thesis, Pittsburg, 1972.
LENIN, V. I., *O vospitanii i obrazovanii*, Moscow, Prosveshchenie, 1973.
LERNER, I. YA., *Problemy formirovaniya kommunisticheskogo mirovozzreniya uchashchikhsya vii–x klassov*, Moscow, 1974.
LEVIN, D., *Soviet Education Today*, 2nd edn., London, 1963.
LEVIN, D., *Leisure and Pleasure of Soviet Children*, London, 1966.
LEVIN-SHIRINA, F. S., *et al.*, *Vospitanie i obuchenie detei 3–7 let (ucheb. posob.)* Moscow, 1975.
LIKHACHIOV, V., Edinstvo metodov esteticheskogo i nravstvennogo vospitaniya, *Vospitanie Shkolnikov*, No. 4, 1971, pp. 12–15.
LIKHACHIOV, V., *Teoriya kommunisticheskogo vospitaniya*, Moscow, Pedagogika, 1974.
LIKHACHIOV, V., Literatura i iskusstvo, *Sovietskaya Pedagogika*, No. 12, 1974, pp. 84–96.
LILGE, G., Lenin and the politics of education, *Slavic Review*, Vol. 27, 1968.
LITTLE, D. R., JR., The policy-making process in the Soviet education, PhD thesis, California, LA, 1965.
LITTLE, D. R., JR., The Academy of Pedagogical Sciences and its political role, *Soviet Studies*, Jan. 1968, pp. 387–77.
LOUIS, J., All work and no play, *Times Educational Supplement*, 19 June, 1970, p. 12.
LOBANTSEV, G. I. (ed.), *Sovetskii uchitel*, Moscow, Pedagogika, 1975.
LUNACHARSKII, A. V., *O vospitanii i obrazovanii*, Moscow, Pedagogika, 1975.
LYNDA, A. S., *Metodika trudovogo obucheniya*, Moscow, Pedagogika, 1975.
MAKARENKO, A. S., *O kommunisticheskom vospitanii*, Moscow, 1956.
MALKOVSKAYA, T. N., *Vospitanie sotsialnoi aktivnosti starshykh shkolnikov (ucheb. posobie)*. Leningrad, 1973.
Marks i Engels o vospitanii i obrazovanii, Moscow, 1956.
MARKUSHEVICH, A. I., The educational system of the USSR, *International Review of Education*, Vol. 16, 1970, pp. 381–4.
MARYENKO, I. S. (ed.), *Nravstvennoe vospitanie shkolnikov*, Moscow, Prosveshchenie, 1969.
MARYENKO, I. S. (ed.), *Organizatsiya i rukovodstvo vospitatelnoi rabotoi v shkole*, Moscow, Prosveshchenie, 1974.
MARYENKO, I. S. (ed.), *Primernoe soderzhanie vospitaniya shkolnikov*, Moscow, 1974.
MARYENKO, I. S. Primernoe soderzhanie vospitaniya shkolnikov, *Narodnoe Obrazovanie*, No. 12, 1974, pp. 40–46.

MARYENKO, I. S. (ed.), *Nravstvennoe vospitanie Sovetskikh shkolnikov*, Moscow, Pedagogika, 1975.
MATIATIN, O., Education of the future in the USSR, *Contemporary Review*, Sept. 1973, pp. 119–23.
MATTHEWS, M., Class bias in Soviet education, *New Society*, 16 Dec. 1966, pp. 911–13.
MATTHEWS, M., *Class and Society in Soviet Russia*, London, Allen Lane, 1972.
MATTHEWS, M., Soviet Students, *Soviet Studies*, Jan. 1975.
MEDVEDEV, V. M., *Formirovanie u shkolnikov kommunisticheskogo mirovozzreniya*, Kuibyshev, 1977.
MEEK, D. L., *Soviet Youth, Some Achievements and Problems*, London, RKP, 1957.
MENCHINSKAYA, N. A., et al., *Problemy formirovaniya kommunisticheskogo mirovozzreniya*, Minsk, 1975.
MILKOVA, V., *Vyshshee obrazovanie v SSSR i za rubezhom (1959–69)*, Moscow, 1972.
MILN, H., Soviet education today, *Journal of Russian Studies*, Vol. 19, 1970, pp. 24–26.
Ministry of Education of the USSR, *On the Main Trends in the Field of Education in the USSR in 1968–70*, Moscow, 1970.
MITTER, W., On the efficiency of the Soviet school system, *Comparative Education*, Mar. 1973, pp. 34–47.
MONAKHOV, N. I. (ed.), *Nravstvennoe vospitanie uchashchikhsya obshcheobrazovatelnoi shkoly*, Moscow, 1974.
MONOSZON, E. (ed.), *Formirovanie mirovozzreniya starsheklassnikov*, Moscow, Pedagogika, 1972.
MONOSZON, E. (ed.), *Formirovanie mirovozzreniya uchashchikhsya vosmiletnei shkoly*, Moscow, 1974.
MONOSZON, E. (ed.), Pedagogicheskie osnovy formirovaniya kommunisticheskogo mirovozzreniya shkolnikov, *Narodnoe Obrazovanie*, No. 9, 1974.
MONOSZON, E., Sostoyanie i zadachi issledovaniya protsessa formirovaniya mirovozzreniya shkolnikov, *Sovetskaya Pedagogika*, No. 4, 1976, pp. 9–19.
Moral i eticheskaya teoriya, Moscow, Nauka, 1974.
MURATOV, YU., XVII syezd VLKSM i zadachi shkolnykh komsomolskikh organizatsii, *Narodnoe Obrazovanie*, No. 9, 1974, pp. 9–13.
MURATOV, YU. I., Soyuz shkoly i komsomola v vospitanii molodykh stroitelei kommunizma, *Sovetskaya Pedagogika*, No. 4, 1974, pp. 3–11.
MCCRACKEN, J. W., Living in an urban world: Moscow—a history unit for tenth grade slow learners, PhD thesis, Carnegie-Mellon, 1973.
MCKINLY, S. K., Comparative analysis of the character education process in the United States and the Soviet Union, PhD thesis, Ohio, 1973.
Narodnoe khozyaistvo SSSR v 1973 g., Moscow, 1974.
Narodnoe khozyaistvo SSSR v 1974 g., Moscow, 1975.
Narodnoe obrazovanie v RSFSR (1917–1967), Moscow, 1967.
NBAKUMOV, A. A., et al., *Narodnoe obrazovanie v SSSR Obshcheobrazovatelnaya shkola, 1917–1973 g.*, Moscow, Pedagogika, 1974.
NECHAYEVA, V. G. (ed.), *Nravstvennoe vospitanie doshkolnikov*, Moscow, Pedagogika, 1972.
NECHAYEVA, V. G. (ed.), *Nravstvennoe vospitanie v detskom sadu*, Moscow, Prosveshchenie, 1975.
NEZHINSKII, N. P., *A. S. Makarenko i pedagogika shkoly*, Moscow, Pedagogika, 1975.
NOAH, H., Financing schools in the USSR, PhD thesis, Columbia, 1964.
NOVE, A., *Stalinism and After*, London, 1975.

NOVE, A., Is there a ruling class in the USSR? *Soviet Studies*, Oct. 1975.
NOVIKOV, YU. V. (ed.), *Opyt pedagogicheskoi deyatelnosti S. T. Shatskogo*, Moscow, Pedagogika, 1976.
NOVIKOVA, L. I. (ed.), *Kollecktiv, lichnost rebyonka...*, Moscow, 1970.
NOVIKOVA, L. I. (ed.), The collective and the personality of the child, *International Review of Education*, Vol. 16, 1970, pp. 323–39.
Novye issledovaniya v pedagogicheskikh naukakh, vyp 9, Moscow, Pedagogika, 1974.
NOZHKO, K., *et al.*, *Educational Planning in the USSR*, Paris, 1968.
O sostoyanii i merakh po dalneishemu sovershenstvovaniyu narodnogo obrazovaniya v SSSR, Moscow, Politizdat, 1973.
O vvedenii novogo kursa Osnovy Sovetskogo gosudarstva i prava, *Vospitanie Shkolnikov*, No. 2, 1975, p. 68.
Obuchenie i vospitanie shkolnika, Leningrad, 1972.
OGORODNIKOV, I. T., *et al.*, *Lenin o vospitanii i obrazovanii*, Moscow, Prosveshchenie, 1973.
OGORODNIKOV, I. T. *et al.*, *Pedagogika shkoly*, Moscow, Prosveshchenie, 1977.
OGURTSOV, N. G., *et al.*, Vospitanie obshchestvennoi aktivnosti shkolnikov, Minsk, 1972.
OSIPOV, G. V., Basic characteristics and distinguishing features of Marxist Sociology, *Soviet Sociology*, No. 1, 1966, pp. 7–12.
Osnovy kommunisticheskoi morali, Moscow, 1975.
Osnovy marksistsko–leninskoi filosofii, Politizdat, 1977.
Osnovy marksistsko–leninskoi estetiki, Moscow, MYSL, 1975.
Osnovy zakonodatelstva soyuza SSR i soyuznykh respublik o narodnom obrazovanii, *Narodnoe Obrazovanie*, No. 10, 1973, pp. 11–13.
OUNSTED, J., Moral education in Russia, *Learning for Living*, 1 May 1962, pp. 17–18.
OWEN, J., Mid-term in Moscow, *Education*, 13 Sept. 1968, p. 258.
OWEN, J., Curriculum innovation in the USSR, *Journal of Curriculum Studies*, Nov. 1969, pp. 219–29.
PANACHIN, F. G., *Nekotorye voprosy razvitiya Sovetskoi shkoly*, Moscow, Znanie, 1973.
PANACHIN, F. G., *Pedagogicheskoe obrazovanie v SSSR (1917–1973)*, Moscow, Pedagogika, 1976.
PANACHIN, F., Obshcheobrazovatelnaya shkola v 1975/6 uchebnom godu, *Vospitanie Shkolnikov*, No. 5, 1975, pp. 2–6.
PANCHESHNIKOVA, L., *Obrazovatelnaya i sotsialno–professionalnaya struktura naseleniya v SSSR*, Moscow, Statistika, 1977.
Pedagogicheskaya entsiklopedia, Moscow, Sov. Entsiklopedia, Vol. 1, Moscow, 1964; Vol. 2, 1965; Vol. 3, 1966; Vol. 4, 1967.
PENNAR, J. *et al.*, *Modernization and Diversity in Soviet Education*, New York, 1971.
Pionerskaya rabota v shkole, Moscow, Prosveshchenie, 1972.
PALTEROVICH, I. L., *Formirovanie nauchno–ateisticheskogo mirovozzreniya shkolnikov*, Moscow, Pedagogika, 1975.
Pedagogika i shkola za rubezhom, Moscow, Pedagogika, 1974.
PETROVA, V. I., Planirovanie vospitatelnoi raboty v nachalnykh klassakh, *Nachalnaya Shkola*, No. 9, 1974, pp. 4–13.
PISARENKO, V. I., *et al.*, *Pedagogicheskaya etika*, Minsk, 1973.
POLIANSKII, S. N., *Khrestomatiya po pedagogike*, 2nd edn., Moscow, Prosveshchenie, 1972.
PRICE, R. F., Labour and education in Russia and China, *Comparative Education*, Mar. 1974, pp. 13–23.

Primernoe soderzhanie vospitaniya shkolnikov, Moscow, Pedagogika, 1976.
Problemy formirovaniya nauchnogo mirovozzreniya studentov v protsesse izucheniya obshchestvennykh nauk, Moscow, MGU, 1974.
Problemy formirovaniya kommunisticheskogo mirovozzreniya uchashchikhsia vii–x klassov, Moscow, 1974.
Problemy sotsialisticheskoi pedagogiki, Moscow, Pedagogika, 1973.
Professionalnaya orientatsiya selskoi molodyozhi, Moscow, Ekonomika, 1973.
Professionalnaya orientatsiya uchashchikhsya v sovetskoi shkole (ucheb. posobie), Cheliabinsk, 1974.
Prognozirovanie razvitiya shkoly i pedagogicheskoi nauki, Vol. 1, Moscow, Akademiya Pedagogicheskikh Nauk, 1974.
Programma kursa istorii KPSS, Moscow, 1975.
Programma kursa marksistsko–leninskoi filosofii, Moscow, 1975.
Programma vosmiletnei shkoly na 1974/5 uchebny god (nachalnye klassy i–iii), Moscow, Prosveshchenie, 1974.
Programma vospitaniya v detskom sadu, Moscow, 1975.
Programma vospitaniya v detskom sadu, Moscow, 1976.
PROKOFIEV, A. G., *Voenno-patrioticheskoe vospitanie v vysshei shkole,* Moscow, Vysshaya Shkola, 1973.
PROKOFIEV, M., *Higher Education in the USSR,* Unesco Educational Studies, Paris, 1961.
PROKOFIEV, M., *Narodnoe Obrazovanie v SSSR,* Moscow, 1967.
PROKOFIEV, M., Present and future of Russian schools, *Times Educational Supplement,* 20 Jan. 1967, p. 101.
PROKOFIEV, M., Aktualnye problemy kommunisticheskogo vospitaniya uchashchikhsya, *Narodnoe Obrazovanie,* No. 8, 1973, pp. 2–8.
PROKOFIEV, M., Towards universal secondary education in the USSR, *Prospects,* No. 3, Autumn 1974, pp. 297–300.
RADINA, K. D., *Emotsionalno-nravstvennoe vospitanie pionerov,* Leningrad, 1975.
RAVKIN, S. I. (ed.), *Khrestomatiya po pedagogike,* Moscow, Prosveshchenie, 1976.
REDL, H. B., *Soviet Educators on Soviet Education,* New York, 1964.
Rekomendatsii po organizatsii sistemy vospitatelnoi raboty obshcheobrazovatelnoi shkoly, Moscow, Prosveshchenie, 1976.
REMEIKIS, T., Theory and practice of communist education, MEd thesis, University of Illinois, Urbana, 1958.
ROSEN, S. M., *Higher Education in the USSR,* Moscow, 1963.
ROSEN, S. M., *Education and Modernization in the USSR,* Addison-Wesley, London, 1971.
RUDMAN, H. C., *The School and the State in the USSR,* New York, 1967.
SARSENBAYEV, T., *Problemy internatsionalnogo vospitaniya lichnosti,* Alma-Ata, Nauka, 1973.
Sbornik materialov po nachalnoi voennoi podgotovke, Moscow, Prosveshchenie, 1973.
SCHAPKER, P. E., A study of the role of significance of the Soviet school-internat within the framework of the post-Stalin educational scheme, PhD thesis, Marguette, 1972.
SENKEVICH, G. T. (ed.), *Ideino-patrioticheskoe vospitanie shkolnikov,* Minsk, NII PED BSSR, 1974.
SHATSKAYA, V. N., *et al., Iskusstvo i voenno-patrioticheskoe vospitanie,* Moscow, Progress, 1975.

SHCHUKINA, G. I., *Teoriya i metodika kommunisticheskogo vospitaniya v shkole*, Moscow, 1974.
SHCHUKINA, G. I., Soderzhanie i osnovnye napravleniya vospitaniya kommunisticheskoi morali, *Sovetskaya Pedagogika*, No. 11, 1974, pp. 91–103.
SHCHUKINA, G. I., *Pedagogika shkoly*, Moscow, Progress, 1977.
SHEPTULINA, A. P. (ed.), *Dialekticheskii materialism*, Moscow, Vysshaya Shkola, 1974.
Shkola i selskoe khozyaistvo, Moscow, Pedagogika, 1974.
SHLAGINA, N., Rabota po pravilam Oktiabriat, *Nachalnaya Shkola*, No. 10, 1975, p. 36.
SHNEKENDORF, Z. K., *Vospitanie yunykh internatsionalistov...*, Moscow, Prosveshchenie, 1974.
SHORE, M., *Soviet Education. Its Psychology and Philosophy*, New York, Philosophical Library, 1947.
SHUBKIN, V. L., Nachalo puti: razmyshleniya o problemakh vybora professii, *Novy Mir*, No. 2, 1976, pp. 188–219.
SHULGIN, V. N., *Marks i Engels v ikh pedagogicheskikh vyskazyvaniyakh*, 4th edn., Moscow, 1925.
SHULGIN, V. N., *Obshchestvennaya rabota i programma GUS*[a], 3rd edn., Moscow, 1926.
SHURNIK, L. S., Education and examination in the USSR, *Educational Research*, Feb. 1968, pp. 99–108.
SHUSTOVA, A. I. (ed.), *Metodicheskie ukazaniya k programme vospitaniya v detskom sadu*, 3rd edn., Moscow, Prosveshchenie, 1975.
SIMON, B. *et al.*, *Educational Psychology in the USSR*, London, 1963.
SIVAVIKOV, G. T., *Voenno–patrioticheskoe vospitanie shkolnikov*, Minsk, 1974.
SKATKIN, L. N. (ed.), *O pedagogicheskom nasledii S. T. Shatskogo*, Moscow, 1975.
SKATKIN, M. N., Marxist–Leninist ideas on polytechnical education, in Shapovalenko, S. G. (ed.), *Polytechnical Education in the USSR*, UNESCO, 1963.
SOLDATENKOV, A. D., Opyt izucheniya rezultativnosti patrioticheskogo vospitaniya shkoly, *Sovetskaya Pedagogika*, No. 10, 1974, pp. 46–53.
Sotsialisticheskie problemy obrazovaniya i vospitaniya, Moscow, Pedagogika, 1973.
SMITH, R. E., Guidance in Soviet schools, PhD thesis, Ohio State University, 1966.
SPIRIN, L. F., *Obshchestvenno–politicheskoe vospitanie uchashchikhsia*, Moscow, Prosveschenie, 1974.
Spravochnik rabotnika narodnogo obrazovaniya (Panachin, F. G.), Moscow, 1973.
Sputnik pionerskogo vozhatogo, Moscow, Molodaya Gvardiya, 1976.
STREZIKOZIN, V. P., *Aktualnye problemy nachalnogo obucheniya*, Moscow, Prosveshchenie, 1976.
SUDHALTER, D. L., The political and psychological indoctrination of schoolchildren in the USSR, PhD thesis, Boston University, 1962.
SUNTSOV, N. S. (ed.), *Trudovoe obuchenie*, Moscow, Prosveshchenie, 1974.
SYSOYENKO, I. V., *Formirovanie kommunisticheskogo mirovozzreniya u uchashchikhsya starshykh klassov*, Moscow, Pedagogika, 1973.
Teoriya i metodika pionerskoi i komsomolskoi raboty v schkole, Moscow, Prosveshchenie, 1976.
TOMIAK, J. J., *The Soviet Union*, London, 1972.
TOMIAK, J. J., Fifty-five years of Soviet education, in *The History of Education in Europe* (ed. T. G. Cook), London, 1974.
TREFIMOVA, N. N., *Nravstvennoe vospitanie i razvitie mladshykh shkolnikov v protsese obucheniya*, Voronezh, 1975.

TRETHEWEY, A., The changing Soviet school system, 1952–72, *The Forum of Education*, Sydney, Mar. 1973, pp. 83–96.

Trudovoe obuchenie i vospitanie uchashchikhsya, Moscow, Pedagogika, 1975.

TSELIKOVA, O. P., Kommunisticheskii nravstenny ideal, *Sovetskaya Pedagogika*, No. 10, 1974, pp. 96–106.

Uchebny plan nachalnykh, vosmiletnikh i srednikh shkol na 1975/76 uchebny god, Sbornik prikazov i instruktsii, No. 5, 1975, p. 30.

Uchenye zapiski MGPI im. Lenina, Vol. 442, 1972 (see 'Iz istorii marksistsko-leninskoi pedagogiki').

UILDRIKS, G., Educational psychology in the Soviet Union, *Paedagogica Europaea*, 1965, pp. 138–49.

UNGOED-THOMAS, J. R., The Soviet school as a formal organization, *Moral Education*, 1/2 Sept. 1969, pp. 33–40.

UNGOED-THOMAS, J. R., Moral education in the Soviet Union, *Moral Education*, 2/1 Mar. 1970, pp. 3–10.

Urok v nachalnoi shkole, Moscow, Prosveshchenie, 1975.

Ustav srednei obshcheobrazovatelnoi skholy, Moscow, Pedagogika, 1970.

VILCHKO, YU. A., Kharakter deyatelnosti starsheklassnikov i formirovanie ikh mirovozzreniya, *Sovetskaya Pedagogika*, No. 4, 1976, pp. 52–57.

ZAJDA, J. I., Curriculum reforms in the Soviet Union, in Bessant, B. and Price, R. F. (eds.), *Problems and Prospects for Comparative and International Studies in Australia*), La Trobe Uni., Melbourne, Nov. 1977, pp. 125–39.

ZAJDA, J. I., Primary schools in the USSR, *Primary Education*, May 1977, pp. 9–13.

ZAJDA, J. I., The role of ideology in the training of Soviet teachers, a paper presented at the SPATE Congress, Melbourne, 19 May, 1978.

ZAJDA, J. I., Teacher Education in the USSR, *Primary Education*, July 1978.

ZAJDA, J. I., Moral Education in the Primary School, *Primary Education*, August 1979.

ZAJDA, J. I., Soviet Education Today, *Core*, (Univ. of Birmingham), June 1979.

ZAJDA, J. I., Education for Labour in the USSR, *Comparative Education*, No. 3, 1979.

ZAJDA, J. I., Education and Social Stratification in the Soviet Union, *Comparative Education*, No. 1, 1980.

ZAJDA, J. I., Educational reforms in the USSR and their socio-political implications, *Forum of Education*, No. 3, 1979.

ZAJDA, J. I., *Teacher Training in the Soviet Union*.

Glossary

Akadémiya pedagogícheskikh naúk SSSR: Academy of Pedagogic Sciences of the USSR. It is the most prestigious and the most influential institution for educational research, curriculum innovations and educational planning.

Attestát zrélosti: 'Certificate of Maturity'. A high school diploma awarded to students.

Aktív: Activists.

Aspivánt: Graduate students (plural: **aspiranty**) in higher education, studying for the Kandidat degree (masters).

Aspirantúra: Graduate (Kandidat nauk only) program.

Attestatsiónnaya kommísiya, 293: Educational Certification Commission, concerned with the teacher in-service and upgrading programs.

Bábushka: Grandmother (plural: **bábushki**). In the past grandmothers taught children to read and write, while parents went to work.

Bilét: 'ticket'. Here it refers to examination questions. The candidate completing the final year at school has to pass external examinations, consisting of written and oral tests. During an oral examination, the candidate enters an examination room and draws his own set of questions from a box, containing thirty sets of papers. Although the candidate is expected to know the entire syllabus, only three questions are asked, dealing with any topic covered by the school curriculum.

Bódraya zhízn: An experimental summer school set up by S. Shatsky.

Chórnaya rabóta: Black work. The term is used in a derogatory manner and it refers to unskilled labour. Soviet parents and students are very sensitive about chórnaya rabóta.

Den uchítelya: The Teachers Day, a national celebration on the first Sunday in October.

Desyatilétnyaya shkóla: Ten-year school, providing complete elementary and secondary schooling.

Détskii sad: Kindergarten for children aged 3–7. The Soviet Kindergarten operates on a full-time basis and most children spend between 8 and 12 hours daily.

Détskii trud i ótdykh: Shatsky's famous alternative school.

Dnevník: The pupil's weekly progress book used in the ten-year school.

Dni proféssii: Profession days. Used in schools for labour socialization and vocational orientation. .

Diplóm: Diploma or the equivalent of a first degree in the USSR. All Soviet university graduates receive Diplóm as their first award.

Dóktor naúk: Doctor of Sciences. It is the highest academic degree in the USSR. It is awarded by major dissertation only. It represents between five to ten years of graduate research, and the youngest Dóktor naúk graduates are in their thirties.

Doktoránt: Doctor of Science candidate. The official title of an American Ph.D. candidate visiting the USSR.

DOSAAF: The All-Union Society for Voluntary Assistance to the Army, Air Force and Navy.

Doshkólnoe vospitánie: Pre-school education (training).

Druzhína: Regiment, e.g. of Pioneers. The School Pioneer unit.

Druzhíniki: Auxiliary police-vigilantes (normally Komsomol members).

Fakultatívy: Electives/Options/Units offered to senior high school students, in addition to their core curriculum in humanities and science.

Gosplan: The State Planning Commission.

GTO: Ready for Labour and Defence norms, being a school program in physical fitness and military training.

GUS: Gosudarstvenny Uchyony Soviet—The State Academic Council.

Institút: Institute. A higher educational institution.

Institúty usoveshénstvovaniya uchítelei: In-service teacher institutes.

Istóriya pedagógiki: History of pedagogy.

Kandidát naúk: Candidate of Sciences. The first graduate degree in the USSR, which is equivalent to a good M.A. (by research only) from a British university.

Kandidát pedagogícheskikh naúk: Candidate of Pedagogic Sciences, being the first graduate degree for teachers.

Kandidátsky mínimum: A two-year graduate program, consisting of a series of units, which an aspirant must pass before he is allowed to commence work on his dissertation. Once a dissertation is completed it must be defended orally before an examination committee, consisting of senior professors, various experts in the field and others. Defending one's dissertation is a major hurdle and some candidates, having completed their two-year program of units may drop out.

Kandidát v chlény: Probationary member in the CPSU.

Kharakterístika: Character reference from the school, or Komsomól, which is required of all college and university applicants. An excellent reference from the Komsomól may help an average candidate to get it.

Kolkhóz: Collective farm.

Kolkhóznik (plural, **Kolkhozniki**): Collective farm workers.

Kolkhóznoe krestyánstvo: Kolkhóz peasantry.

Kommunistícheskoe povedénie; vospitánie: Communist etiquette and upbringing. An article written by A. Makarenki.

Kompléksnye prográmmy (GUS): Topic oriented and interdisciplinary curriculum introduced by the State Academic Council between 1923–1925.
Komsomól: Communist League of Youth. Also known as VLKSM. The third stage of the youth movement, for young people aged between 14 and 27.
Komsomólskoe poruchénie: Komsomol social task or assignment.
Kónkursnye ekzáminy: Competition entrance examinations. All colleges and universities in the USSR have Kónkursnye ekzáminy. They are very difficult to pass and many high school graduates sit for them more than once. No time limit is imposed and candidates may attempt these examinations as often as they like. Strict quotas in most universities influence the competitive nature, and the degree of difficulty of Kónkursnye ekzáminy.
Krásnye sledopýty: Red scouts, a recent invention of patriotic training. Red scouts search for lost war veterans, and although they perform many useful community tasks, the nature of their activities is essentially patriotic and paramilitary.

Léninskii zachét: The Leninist assignment for Komsomól members (see pp. 167–170).

Mirovozzrénie: A word-view, an outlook on life. It corresponds to *Weltanschauung* in German.

Nachálnaya skhóla: The three-year elementary stage of schooling for children.
Nachálnaya voénnaya podgotóvka: Introduction to Military Training, a compulsory course for boys in grade 9.
Naródnoe khozyáistvo SSSR v 1978 godú: National Economy in the USSR in 1978. An annual publication by the Soviet Bureau of Census and Statistics.
NEP: The New Economic Policy, a radical departure from socialism, which allowed capitalism to prosper in the USSR between 1920–1927.

Oblono: The Regional Educational Authority in a large city, controlling all schools in the area.
Obrazovánie: Education or schooling.
Obshchestvovédenie: Social sciences/studies. A course of study in Marxist-Leninist theory, politics and current affairs taught to students in grade 10.
Obitógakh perekhóda sovétskoi shkóly na nóvoe soderzhánie óbshchego obrazovániya: On transition of the Soviet school and the new content of general education (Kashin's article).
Obshchéstvennoe poruchénie: Social/communal task or assignment, normally given to Komsomól members.
Okommunistícheskoi étike: On communist ethics. An article written by A. Makarenko.
Oktyabrýata: The Octobrists.
Orlyónok: Eaglet, an annual national paramilitary olympics for the 16–17 age group (Komsomól members).
Osnóvy zakonozdátelstva o naródnom obrazovánii: The Basic Law on Education, a major educational decree brought into effect in 1974.
Ot razrushéniya vekovógo ukláda k tvórchestvu nóvogo: Lenin's article (April 1920) discussing communist labour.

Partíinost: Party mindedness, complete devotion to the Party.
Patriotízm: Patriotism.
Pedagogícheskie institúty: Pedagogic institutes (Teachers Colleges) offering graduate diplomas.
Pedagogícheskie uchílishcha: Pedagogic schools (Teachers Colleges) preparing elementary teachers.
Pionér: Pioneer.
Politekhnícheskoe obrazovánie: Polytechnic education.
Politekhnízm: Polytechnical approach to education.
Politinformátsiya: School-based political sessions and seminars.
Pólnoe srédnee obrazovánie: Complete secondary education.
Povedénie: School conduct, which is assessed, like any other subject on a five point scale (5—excellent and 2—unsatisfactory). Students who are failed in povedénie may be expelled by the Principal.
Predmétnye olimpiády: Subject olympics or competitions in academic subjects (usually mathematics and science) within and between schools. The aim is to discover gifted students so that they could be given an opportunity to study in special schools.
Professionálno-tekhnícheskoe uchílishche (PTU): Professional-technical school/college, training high school graduates for various semi-skilled and skilled occupations.

Rayono: The District Educational Authority in a small, provincial town, which receives directives from the nearest city-based Oblono.
Ródina: Motherland.

Salyút: Salute.
Shéfstvo: Adoption, patronage.
Shkóla i rabóchii klass (School and the Working Class) and **Shkola i obshchestvennyi stroi** (School and the Social Structure)—two important articles written by Pavel Blonsky in 1917.
Shkólainternát: Boarding school.
Shkóla rabóchei molodiózhi: Evening (part-time) school for working youth.
Sovkhóz: state farm.
Srédnie spetsiálnye uchébnye zavedéniya: Secondary specialized educational establishments, providing general education and vocational training for semi-professional occupations.
Stakhanovets: Shock worker, a person who works above his norm. Named after Stakhanov, a coal miner who exceeded his daily production norm by 1,000%
Subbótnik: Unpaid work in spring.
Svobódnoe vospitánie: The Russian version of alternative schools during the 1920s.

Tékhnikum: Technicum, a secondary specialised school.
Trudováya kolóniya: Corrective labour colony for juvenile delinquents.
Trudovóe vospitánie: Working training in schools.

Uchébnye kabinéty/kabinétnaya sistéma: School departments and faculties. The Soviet secondary school is divided into various faculties.
Uchílishche: Secondary specialised school.
Uchenícheskaya prozvódstvennaya brigáda: Pupil's working brigade.
Utrennik: A morning talk, dedicated to various important socio-political events.

Vólya, múzhestvo i tseleustremlyónost: (The will, manhood and purpose), one of Makarenko's articles.
Vospitánie: upbringing or character training in schools, embracing moral, social, cultural and political aspects of schooling.
Vseóbuch: Universal drive on literacy during the 1920s.
VUZ: Vyshee Uchebnoe Zavedenie—Institution of Higher Education.

Yásli-Detskii sád: Nursery, crèche, representing the first phase of pre-school education for children up to the age of 3.

Zakálka: Seasoned, tough, fully physically fit.
Zarnítsa: Summer Lighting, being the name of an annual national paramilitary olympics for the Pioneers (aged 12–14).
Zaslúzhenyi uchítel' shkóly: Honored School Teacher, a title awarded for excellence in teaching.
Závuch: Deputy principal (school).
Zvyózdochka: A little star, a unit (6–7) in the Octobrist movement.

A list of Soviet periodicals useful in this study

Doshkolnoe vospitanie (Pre-school Education) a monthly journal.
Izvestiya (News) a daily.
Komsomolskaya pravda (Komsomol Truth).
Literaturnaya gazeta (Literary Newspaper).
Nachalnaya shkola (Elementary School).
Narodnoe obrazovanie (People's Education).
Novoe vremya (New Time).
Novye issledovaniya v pedagogicheskikh naukakh (New research in pedadogic sciences).
Novye issledovaniya v pedagogike (New research in pedagogy).
Pionerskaya pravda (Pioneer Truth).
Pravda (Truth).
Russkii yazyk za rubezhom (Russian Language abroad).
Sbornik privazov i instruktsii Ministerstva prosveshcheniya RSFSR (Manual of Rules and Regulations of the RSFSR Ministry of Education).
Semya i shkola (Family and School).
Sotsiologicheskie issledovaniya (Sociological Research).
Sovetskaya pedagogika (Soviet Pedagogy).
Uchitelskaya gazeta (Teachers Newspaper).
Voprosy psikhologii (Problems in Psychology).
Vospitanie shkolnikov (Upbringing of the Pupil).

Name Index

Subject Index

269